"Charles Campbell has produced an informative and stimulating analysis of Canadian policy and practice in the field of immigration. Based on his own work in the field and years of research, his provocative criticisms and constructive proposals deserve careful study by all Canadians. This book will stimulate and engage participation in the long overdue immigration debate."

—*William Bauer, former Canadian Ambassador, recipient of the Raoul Wallenberg Foundation Award for his work on behalf of Soviet Jewry and human rights, and former member of the Immigration and Refugee Board.*

"It if ain't broke, don't fix it. But if it *is* broke and it's important, fix it you must. Canada's immigration/refugee system is 'Exhibit A'. Charlie Campbell's important book tells us the dreadful story of how we got into this mess and how we can get out, while maintaining the best of Canadian compassion and values. *Betrayal and Deceit* is an unsettling read until you get to the answers. They are there for the taking. Governments need a great big push in that direction. Campbell points the way."

—*Gordon Gibson, public affairs commentator and author.*

"Charles Campbell has written a strong, detailed and careful analytical study of the politics of Canadian immigration, persuasive because it's no rant; it's calmly devastating. Mr. Campbell, for ten years a member of the Immigration Appeal Board, has maintained excellent contacts among politicians and civil servants and has long followed and written about our immigration policies and practices. This book will raise the predictable cries from the immigration industry and its powerful lobbies, but concerned Canadians should read it and judge for themselves."

—*Trevor Lautens,* Vancouver Sun *columnist.*

ABOUT THE AUTHOR

Charles M. Campbell served on the former Immigration Appeal Board for ten years, eight of them as vice-chairman. Since his retirement in 1983, he has been an advocate for immigration reform and has developed a profile that makes him the recipient of government documents not normally made available to the general public. He has spoken widely, and his 1989 booklet "A Time Bomb Ticking: Canadian Immigration in Crisis" was published by the Mackenzie Institute. His articles have been published in the *Globe and Mail,* the *Ottawa Citizen* and the *Vancouver Sun,* and he has frequently been interviewed on radio and television; he appeared many times with the late talk-show legend Jack Webster.

Campbell was born in the mining town of Phoenix, B.C. in 1913. After graduating from the University of British Columbia with a degee in engineering in 1938, he worked for thirty-five years in the mining industry at all levels, from mucker to mine manager, in Quebec, Ontario, British Columbia and the Yukon. He has served as a school trustee in Quebec, a member of the Senate of the University of British Columbia, a vice-president of the Canadian Institute of Mining and Metallurgy and president of the British Columbia Branch of the Liberal Party of Canada.

For two summers, while a university student, Charlie Campbell walked miles through northern British Columbia as a member of the first geological mapping survey of that area. This experience, together with his work and travels across Canada, helped to fuel his passionate commitment to his country, a commitment leading ultimately to the writing of this book.

Betrayal & Deceit

The Politics of Canadian Immigration

Charles M. Campbell

JASMINE
BOOKS

Canadian Cataloguing in Publication Data
Campbell, Charles M., 1913–
Betrayal & deceit

Includes bibliographical references and index.
ISBN 0-9686738-0-5
1. Canada–Emigration and immigration–Government policy.
2. Refugees–Government policy–Canada. I. Title.
JV7233.C34 2000   325.71   C99-911305-4

Editor: Neall Calvert
Text Designer: Fiona Raven
Cover Designer: Gordon Finlay
Proof Reader: Ann Paulsen
Indexer: Catherine Bennett

First printing February 2000

JASMINE
BOOKS

Published by
Jasmine Books
West Vancouver, B.C.
e-mail: Camp107@ibm.net

Printed in Canada

Distributed by **Gordon Soules Book Publishers Ltd.**
1359 Ambleside Lane, West Vancouver, BC Canada V7T 2Y9
PMB 620, 1916 Pike Place #12, Seattle,WA 98101-1097, US
Web site: www.gordonsoules.com E-mail: books@gordonsoules.com
604-922-6588 Fax: 604-688-5442

CONTENTS

Foreword .... *v*

Preface .... *vi*

List of Figures .... *viii*

List of Tables .... *viii*

Chapter I   Immigration Debate—
                 The Impossible Dream? 1

Chapter II   The Five Immigration Myths 13

Chapter III   The Root of the Problem 27

Chapter IV   Refugees: Canada's Longest Lineup 65

Chapter V   A Wide-open Back Door 97

Chapter VI   Administrative Collapse 131

Chapter VII   The Consultation Fraud 143

Chapter VIII   Citizenship Fire Sale 177

Chapter IX   The Australian Solution 195

Chapter X   What We Must Do 203

Principal Sources and Selected Readings 215

Index 221

LIST OF FIGURES

Figure 1 Average income comparison between immigrants and Canadians, 1984 National averages for males age 35–44 21

Figure 2 Average earnings of foreign-born individuals who landed in 1981 and 1985, by immigration category, 1988 55

Figure 3 Success rate for refugee claims, 1983–1992 123

LIST OF TABLES

Table 1 Percentage comparisons of earnings of post-1980 and pre-1981 immigrants with earnings of Canadian-born citizens, based on 1991 census data 23

Table 2A Refugee Status Advisory Committee record of refugee claims from India, Jamaica and the Dominican Republic in the period 1977 to 1988 .. 84

Table 2B Immigration and Refugee Board decisions— Record of refugee claims from India, Jamaica and the Dominican Republic in the period 1989 to 1998 85

Table 3 Backlog breakdown of refugee claims by region and nationality 90

Table 4 Honduran refugee claims processed in Vancouver, 1996–1999 (first quarter) 129

Table 5 Canadian attitudes towards immigration levels, 1975–1987 144

Table 6 Chilean refugee claimants, 1995–1997 160

FOREWORD

In no area of Canadian public policy has there been such a complete lack of sustained and informed national debate in recent decades as has been the case with immigration and refugee policy. Many Canadians sense that there are serious problems with both. Whenever serious discussion has been attempted, however, those who benefit from the existing state of affairs have shown themselves remarkably adept at applying pressure on successive governments to discourage open debate and avoid major reforms.

During the 1960s and 1970s Canada provided an example to the world of an immigrant and refugee receiving country that could boast genuine and substantial progress in building a tolerant and compassionate multiracial society. But with immigration and refugee policy now largely under the control of special-interest groups whose objectives have little in common with the needs of Canada, we are now placing at risk these noble achievements.

The public focuses attention from time to time on immigration and refugee problems, as in the case of the recent arrival of boat people from China. For the most part, however, Canadians do not regard these as pressing issues. They do not realize that our policies in these areas have profound implications for what kind of country Canada is to be in the years to come, and that we may well be looking at a national disaster happening in slow motion.

The time is long overdue for an open and continuing national debate over immigration and refugee policies. Charles Campbell's book makes a key contribution to this debate. He provides valuable documentation on how current policies evolved, as well as important insights into how successive governments have put a positive spin on developments, in deference to special-interest groups with little reference to the concerns of Canadians in general. His book is a wake-up call for all of us.

—Martin Collacott, former Canadian Ambassador
to Lebanon, Syria and Cambodia, and former
High Commissioner to Sri Lanka.

PREFACE

My ten years' service on the Immigration Appeal Board generated a consuming interest in Canada's immigration policies and their administration. Over the sixteen years since 1983, I have gathered related official and semi-official government reports and other documentation, some of it confidential, as well as ministerial statements and press releases. This record of recent immigration history has provided the foundation for this book.

It is a pleasure to acknowledge that the preparation of this post-sixties immigration chronicle has been undertaken in response to widespread support and encouragement received during several years of public appearances before service clubs, and in the media. Encouragement has also come from members of the Immigration Ministry with whom I had contact, and, more particularly, from those with whom I worked, including Bruce Howard, my old colleague on the Immigration Appeal Board in Vancouver.

Throughout the process there was guidance from my editor son, Charles, and retired *Time* correspondent Paul Hurmuses. At the production stage, valued contributions by publisher's representative Jo Blackmore and her talented team of editors and designers contributed much to the quality of the book. There has been continuing support from Gordon Gibson, Daniel Stoffman, Kean Bhatacharia, Trevor Lautens, and retired ambassadors Martin Collacott and William Bauer.

My dear wife, Dorothy, has not only lived with my commitment to immigration reform in Canada, but has produced on her computer thousands of pages of speeches, media articles and now this manuscript, always editing judiciously and effectively with appropriate advice and counsel when she recognized the need.

To all I extend my great appreciation.

—Charles M. Campbell

CHAPTER I

IMMIGRATION DEBATE —
THE IMPOSSIBLE DREAM?

"It is clear that for much of Canada's history, it has been natural increase, not immigration that has driven the growth of population. This conclusion casts considerable doubt on the proposition that history proves that Canada needs immigration. Only a few periodic bursts of immigration were needed—not sustained inflows.

"The same conclusion applies with respect to the country's economic prosperity: a historical perspective gives little or no support to the view that Canada needed immigration to become a wealthy nation."

The Economic Council of Canada, 1991

"We go about congratulating ourselves for our over-exuberant acceptance of mostly bogus refugees, with the rest of the world snickering at us for the suckers we are."

British Columbia and Yukon Immigration Officers'
1994 report to Immigration Minister Sergio Marchi

Public-opinion polls frequently assure us that Canadians accept and welcome immigrants and refugees. Of course we do, but only if their entry is handled in a fair and controlled manner. Instead, we have been let down by our politicians because what is happening is neither fair nor controlled. Current immigration and refugee policy exhibits contempt for the will of the majority of Canadians. Canadians resent their government's tolerance of tens of thousands of illegal immigrants; the uncontrolled opportunities for systematic abuse and growing criminal activity; the discrimination against the able; and the mismanagement of the process.

In March 1992 in a news story presaging the above-cited report by frontline British Columbia and Yukon immigration officers, the *Vancouver Sun* sought comments from several former members of the Immigration Appeal Board (IAB), including the present federal minister of the environment, David Anderson. Mr. Anderson was quoted as saying: "The system is corrupt and the Immigration Board has become a wretched monster that's out of control."

In commenting on the notion that members of the present board might suffer from "compassion fatigue", Mr. Anderson offered an alternative suggestion: "Perjury fatigue is more like it because they have seen the rule of law subverted so often." He pointed to the dramatic difference between Canada's acceptance rate of refugee claimants, then 64 per cent, and the far lower rates of other countries (21 per cent in Britain, 14 per cent in the United States and 7 per cent in Australia):

> Clearly something is wrong. *Either everyone else in the world is wrong or we are out of line*, and I think it's us [emphasis added]. There is too much pressure on our board members who deal with cases, to let people in. The underlying premise is that if someone lied well enough to get here then they'll do well.[1]

Too bad he didn't share this wisdom with his Chrétien Cabinet colleagues, Mr. Marchi and Madame Robillard.[2] Then again, perhaps he did.

The March 4, 1991 issue of *Maclean's* magazine quoted one senior immigration officer, who said that almost all of the refugee backlog claimants in Canada were "queue jumpers". Another twenty-year veteran was even more emphatic: "The last system was bad enough, but this one is a joke."

An officer in Immigration's Intelligence Branch put it this way: "The system has become so open that when a refugee gets in, the word goes out and his whole village floods in behind him." One Immigration and Refugee Board (IRB) member stated: "We get people who all repeat the same story about how they were involved in a coup. It's a fabrication—but we can't prove it. They have friends who have gone through the system and coached them".[3] Another was equally blunt: "You wouldn't believe how the system is abused. If the public knew, there would be riots in the streets."[4]

According to several immigration officers in Toronto, their department managers had instructed them not to challenge claims at the initial-inquiry stage from about twenty-five countries, including Sri Lanka. As a result, they explained, these refugee claimants received approval based on little more than the material on their application forms. This was so, even when they arrived with no identification, or whatever they produced was probably fake. As one Refugee Hearing Officer (RHO) observed: "We no longer protect refugees. We just let in any liar who comes along."

Of course, except for the fact that the sources here were active, frontline immigration officers, none of the above was new information. For example, J. C. Best, who had been the department's executive director of immigration and demographic policy from 1978 to 1985, and Canadian High Commissioner to Trinidad-Tobago from 1986 until his retirement at the end of 1988, had provided details chapter and verse in a lengthy and extremely thoughtful public statement in March 1989.

This retired, broadly based public servant was not optimistic. Recognizing the importance of maintaining the integrity of the system, he found it inconceivable that any claimant from Trinidad and Tobago could even remotely have a true refugee claim. Mr. Best emphasized that universal access to Canada was the main cause of the problem and that the key legislation was the Charter of Rights and Freedoms.[5]

In 1978, the federal government instituted fundamental changes in our immigration legislation. The result has been a disaster. For those in Montreal, the problems began in earnest in 1983 with the arrival of Iranian refugee claimants with ties to the vigorous Southeast Asian heroin trade. Five years later, by police count, there were at least 300 of them linked to drug rings in the city, and the number of local addicts had tripled. More than 100 of these refugees had been convicted of trafficking, and many had been implicated in violent incidents, including murders. Yet none had been deported.

Iran is one of those countries whose laws deal decisively with drug dealers. Since Canada opposes capital punishment, deportation to countries where severe punishment is part of the legal process is not even considered an option. Thus, an invitation is extended to the criminals of the world to take advantage of our generosity, and in the process the destruction of Canadian lives is tolerated by the Canadian government.

On August 25, 1998, the *Vancouver Sun* carried a front-page story, headlined "Thousands of People Smuggled into Canada", in which it cited a new study prepared for the federal government to the effect that:

> As many as 16,000 illegal immigrants are entering Canada each year with the help of smugglers, costing taxpayers hundreds of millions of dollars. . . . Experts consider most people who arrive in Canada without proper documentation to be linked to smugglers. . . . The trafficking of illegal immigrants has become big business, police say. Syndicates operate in Canada, the United States, Iran, India, China, Sri Lanka, Pakistan, Hong Kong, Thailand, Nigeria, and Brazil. They charge clients up to $50,000. . . . Police report that some illegals become involved in drug trafficking, prostitution or theft once in Canada in order to pay their smugglers.

One RCMP officer was quoted as saying, "We've got them coming in ships. They're coming across land by buses, through the bush." He estimated that a single refugee claimant costs the Canadian taxpayer $50,000 in social benefits. His solution: "Stop them before they get on the plane."

Had anyone in authority been prepared to take seriously the leaked 1994 observations and recommendations of Canada's frontline immigration officers cited above, perhaps we wouldn't be in crisis today. These career people, having toiled on a daily basis with immigrants, refugee claimants and the government policies that make every abuse of our system workable, fully understand what is wrong. They have a major contribution to make in fixing it. Is anyone listening?

Certainly, we, as Canadians, accept our obligation to take in our fair share, or more, of those of the world's genuinely persecuted who are in need of resettlement. But we also know that, with only one-half of 1 per cent of the world's people, Canada cannot solve the population problems of all the developing nations. What we can do is to assist them on their own ground. However, should our government continue along its current irresponsible path, not only will it prejudice and jeopardize the multi-ethnic society that has emerged in Canada over the last generation, it will place in further peril our nation's great potential.

In the past, people came to Canada to work, to make such contribution as they could, and to build a place for their families in a new country. There was no social-security net to attract them. Their only incentive was the opportunity to succeed. Their attitude is expressed most eloquently by a postwar refugee from Europe. Mr. John Bruk, now a distinguished Canadian, put it clearly in a letter to the editor of the *Vancouver Sun* at the time of the landing of illegal immigrants on the shore of Nova Scotia in July 1987:

Thirty-five years ago I came to Canada as a political refugee from Yugoslavia. I am thankful that Canada accepted me, and I find Canada a good country. I am referring not only to the physical grandeur and natural wealth but more importantly to the quality of life, which includes a fine attitude of Canadians toward the less fortunate of this world, especially those oppressed by physical or political forces beyond their control. Suffice it to remember the generosity of Canadians toward the Vietnamese refugees and victims of the Ethiopian drought.

. . . When I applied to come to Canada as a refugee, in a European refugee camp in Italy where Canadian Immigration had an office, we all knew that we were not entitled as of right to be admitted to Canada. It was accepted that refugees had to satisfy very demanding tests.

> Those tests included confirmation of status as political refugees, and
> meeting of health, character, and other qualifications, which were
> much more stringent for Canada than for other countries. We came to
> Canada with an expectation of performing to those high standards.

This book tells the sorry story of political betrayal by governments elected to serve the interests of the country which, instead, have favoured immigration policies that flout "those high
standards", and of how ministerial deceit and duplicity have
abetted such abuses.

The thrust of any national immigration policy must be to
serve the best interests of the nation. In Canada, immigration
has been integral and crucial to the process of nation-building—
a determining factor in the shaping of our relatively young
country. Our future depends upon the wise implementation of a
carefully reconstructed immigration policy suited to a realistic
assessment of Canada's needs. But for years there has been a
progressive deterioration of that principle in the regulations, the
statutes and the administration of our immigration program.
One result of these diminishing standards over the past three
decades has been the rise of systemic discrimination against potential immigrants with the skills and talents Canada has
needed. Ironically, and in parallel, we have provided an overwhelming advantage and benefits to those least qualified to
adapt successfully to a productive life in our society.

That the foundation of past excellence was crumbling became particularly evident following the proclamation in 1978 of
our current Immigration Act. This legislation tipped the balance
in favour of sponsored family members having entry into
Canada in vast numbers without consideration for either skills
or literacy. Then, in 1989, there followed the creation of the new
Immigration and Refugee Board, which allowed the acceptance
of refugee claims at a rate five times that of other refugee-
receiving countries.

Until the mid-1960s, the overwhelming majority of both immigration and refugee admissions were judgment calls made by
experienced visa officers at Canada's overseas consular posts.

That a nation has the right to decide, prior to their arrival at its border, who can come in was the operative principle. The system wasn't perfect, but, by and large, it worked. Following the 1968 election, the Trudeau government began the quiet transfer of visa offices from traditional source countries to the Third World. The immediate effect, long understood, was finally acknowledged in the 1995 majority report of the House of Commons Standing Committee on Labour, Employment and Immigration, *Economic Impact of Recent Immigration*: "The initial earnings of both male and female foreign-born workers who entered Canada prior to 1971 were found to be comparable to those of Canadian-born workers. Foreign-born workers arriving after 1971 had lower relative initial earnings." This report estimated those earnings to be 10 to 20 per cent lower by 1986.

In a democracy, one of the fundamental principles of policy development is public debate. It is a necessary element in the process of developing public awareness, informed opinion and government policies. This usually extends to policy development at political-party conventions where, without approval of the leadership, clearly expressed opinions can be disregarded, as happened at the 1991 Progressive Conservative Party policy convention. Or they can be effectively stifled, as happened at the 1992 Liberal Party policy convention.

At their 1991 convention, the Progressive Conservative Party membership showed its dissatisfaction with the Mulroney government's immigration policies through its responses to various immigration and multicultural resolutions:

1. A resolution advocating rigorous application of immigration-sponsorship regulations, and penalty enforcement where financial commitments were not met, passed at 82 per cent;
2. One demanding a review of "administrative weaknesses" to assure cost-effective immigrant and refugee processing passed at 83 per cent;
3. One demanding effective screening of the criminally and medically ineligible passed at 66 per cent;

4. A resolution requiring that all immigrants be admitted to Canada on their own merits passed at 90 per cent;
5. One demanding revisions of multicultural policy to foster "a common national identity for one people living together in harmony as equal citizens loyal to the Canadian ideal" passed at 89 per cent;
6. One requiring that funds devoted to existing multilingual programs be redirected to introducing immigrants to Canadian institutions, history and cultural norms, including such indoctrination prior to arrival in Canada, passed at 79 per cent;
7. And finally, 58 per cent of these convention delegates indicated they would dismantle the Department of Multiculturalism altogether.

The governing Tory Party membership had overwhelmingly rejected an expansive immigration program, initiated that year following a process of arranged consultations designed to justify that expansion.

On the other side of the political fence, in anticipation of the 1992 federal Liberal Party policy convention, the Capilano–Howe Sound party association prepared a resolution on immigration policy. Of the British Columbia provincial quota of twelve resolutions, ten would be dealt with in workshops and two would be directed to the plenary session to ensure that they received consideration by the full convention. At this provincial convention, called to make their decisions, the following immigration resolution was selected by the British Columbia membership for plenary-session status:

BE IT RESOLVED that the Liberal government in Ottawa would review and implement immigration and refugee policies that contribute to the economic welfare of Canada and the social well-being of the immigrants and refugees by:
a) encouraging the admission of those who meet the current and changing needs of Canada;
b) re-evaluating the criteria for family sponsorship;

c) reinstating the UN definition of a refugee as a basis for determining refugee status; and

d) taking all other measures necessary to meet our obligations to genuine refugees including legislation to provide the claimants with fair, expeditious, and compassionate treatment.

However, a strange thing took place on the way to the convention floor. The party executive overrode the decision of the membership with the consequence that, at the national convention, this lone, four-item resolution on immigration was directed to a workshop on education, thus avoiding the plenary session. The Liberal opposition immigration critic, Warren Allmand, did not attend, and there was no debate. Though it passed with a show of voting cards, it quickly found its way to a convenient wastebasket. This cleared the way for the Liberal platform committee to include this deceitful passage in its "Red Book" policy statement: "We should continue to target immigration levels of approximately one percent of the population each year, as has been the case for more than a decade." It hadn't been. Not nearly.

Since both the governing and opposition parties had either completely disregarded the expressed opinions of their memberships, or failed to allow these opinions to be expressed, it is not surprising that in the following 1993 federal election campaign, not a word was uttered on the vital issue of immigration by either the Conservatives or the Liberals. "Immigration Goes Undiscussed" was the *Globe and Mail* headline following the 1993 election. Following the 1997 election, a *Vancouver Sun* headline (over the reprint of an *Ottawa Citizen* article) announced: "Immigration Ignored in Election Despite Its Impact on the Future."

Why? Because neither party was prepared to court the displeasure of the so-called "ethnic vote", which was sufficient to tip the balance in thirty or more constituencies. Those seats often determine which party gets to govern. It is called "politics".

In today's atmosphere of leadership control and the politicians' concern for the ballot box, the privileges and responsibilities provided by Question Period in the House of Commons are never invoked over official or commissioned government reports on immigration. In today's power-driven politics, it does not matter how seriously such reports reflect on immigration policy and its administration.

- Why was there no floor debate when the 1982 Auditor General's report listed extensive and unacceptable abuses of Canadian immigration regulations, or when, in releasing his 1990 report, this same Auditor General described the operations of the nearly new Immigration and Refugee Board as "close to collapse"?

- Why was there no debate in 1991 and 1992, when the Law Reform Commission of Canada, in special reports covering the refugee-determination process, exposed extensive failures in that administration, or in 1997, when a new Auditor General exposed serious shortcomings in the Immigration and Refugee Board administration?

- Why was there no debate when successive Immigration Ministers disregarded a 1989 report of the Department of Health and Welfare that established, among other critical considerations, that a larger population will not benefit Canadians?

- Why was there no debate over the fact that, in 1997, 5,800 aliens (23 per cent of the 25,300 who claimed to be refugees) immediately enjoyed the right to all the privileges of Canadian citizenship, including social welfare and medical care, although none had any intention of appearing at a required refugee hearing?

- Why was there no debate over the fact that, in 1993, 40 per cent of the children entering English as a Second Language (ESL) classes in the Greater Vancouver school system were born in Canada, yet still spoke no English? And that four years later that figure had risen to 50 per cent?

- Why didn't the generally sensible recommendations of the recent *Not Just Numbers* report, prepared for the Minister of Immigration, initiate a national debate beyond the minister's consultations program when they were released in early 1998?

- Why is there no debate over the fact that elected Immigration Ministers continue to repeat the fallacy that Canada needs more immigrants to balance declining births, when there are thirteen births per thousand population annually and only seven deaths, resulting in a substantial natural growth? And why have those figures not become public knowledge?
- Why do so many ordinary, decent Canadians accept immigration policy errors so shocking that duplicity now drives the formulation and application of this country's immigration and refugee rules and regulations?
- And finally, why is it that the truth about Canada's immigration policies has become so politically unacceptable? Why indeed!

At this stage in our history, the information already available to ensure sound policy decisions is both extensive and convincing. Any government has the opportunity and responsibility to re-examine immigration and refugee policy in the light of that evidence, to explore and develop new policies that meet the needs and obligations of our country and to provide the leadership to sell that program to an as yet largely uninformed and misinformed electorate.

Yet, following publication of *Not Just Numbers*, Immigration Minister Lucienne Robillard began her series of public consultations in Vancouver on February 27, 1998. In a *Vancouver Sun* interview following the opening of those meetings, the minister was quoted, "I would like to be able to table legislation at the end of this year (1998). And 1999 will be a year of consulting on government policy; from that point the government will hold new hearings."

That will make it twenty years since then Immigration Minister Lloyd Axworthy first opted for study, and there is still no evidence of the political will to pursue, legislate and regulate in our nation's interest. The minister was scheduling three more years of political talk. With the legislation she promised in the fall of 1998 now expected in the fall of 1999, Madame Robillard was already a year behind her schedule. There was no sign of any legislation when she was succeeded by the Honourable Elinor Caplan as the leaves of 1999 began to fall.

Welcome to Canada as this country enters the new millennium!

ENDNOTES

1. The *Vancouver Sun*, March 17, 1992.
2. Sergio Marchi became Minister of Citizenship and Immigration on November 4, 1993, and held the post until he was replaced by Lucienne Robillard on January 25, 1996.
3. There were more than "friends" to coach them. The author, who spent ten years on the Immigration Appeal Board (eight as vice-chairman), recalls one lawyer in Calgary with a large refugee clientele, whose prepared statement of claim was the same for every one of them.
4. The author, as a still emerging immigration critic, experienced universal encouragement from public servants at all levels in the ministry. On one occasion in particular, as a member of a panel discussion at the UBC law school, at the morning break a senior immigration official sent from Ottawa to participate on the panel approached him: "You should know that I agree with nearly everything you say, but I cannot say it."
5. The *Globe and Mail*, March 10, 1989.

Chapter II

THE FIVE IMMIGRATION MYTHS

*"Whether the Canadian population in 2036 is 27 million, 30 mil-
lion, 34 million or 41 million makes very little difference to the
income per person or household."*

*"These explorations indicate that it is not so much the number of
people that will affect Canadians' economic well being as their
skills and the effective deployment of those skills."*

Canada's Health & Welfare
Demographic Review, 1989

For decades, Canada's immigration policy has been justified
and supported by a series of interrelated myths propagated by a
succession of immigration ministers; by members of the immigration industry, including members of the immigration bar; by
non-governmental service organizations; and, all too often, by
the media. Under constant and unchallenged repetition, these
myths have come to be accepted as fact by a largely uninformed
Canadian public.

MYTH #1—

CANADA'S ANNUAL IMMIGRATION RATE
HAS BEEN 1 PER CENT OF THE POPULATION

Not true.

The 1-per-cent figure was used in the first edition of the Liberal "Red Book" (1993) to justify that party's immigration
policy: "We should continue to target immigration levels of approximately one percent of the population each year, as has
been the case for more than a decade." The *Vancouver Sun*, in an

August 19, 1997 editorial, declared that "Canada's policy used to be to let in one percent." *It never was.* And there have been no studies or competent analyses of population needs of Canada that would allow one to determine the appropriate number of immigrants that should be admitted on an annual basis. The sole motivation for today's rate of immigration, and for Canadian immigration policy generally, appears to be political advantage.

From 1960 to 1993, the average intake of immigrants was 0.63 per cent of population. It was 1.1 per cent in 1967 only, averaging 0.9 per cent between 1965 and 1969, and 0.88 per cent between 1973 and 1975. These figures reflected large refugee-settlement movements. For twenty-four of the years from 1960 to 1993 it averaged 0.51 per cent, and in the 1983–85 Liberal-to-Tory-government transition period it averaged 0.35 per cent. Then, arbitrarily, the Mulroney government increased it to 0.60 per cent between 1987 and 1989, and to 0.86 per cent from 1990 to 1993, the year of that government's downfall. In the four years 1995 to 1998, the intake averaged 215,000 persons, or 0.73 per cent of population. A fictional history of immigration levels at 1 per cent of population is no basis for creating immigration policy.

MYTH #2—

OUR LOW BIRTH RATE
DEMANDS HIGH IMMIGRATION

Not true.

Advocates of high immigration levels have asserted that Canada has just 1.6 births per productive mother, and that a balanced population, allowing for early deaths, depends on 2.1 births per mother. They draw a picture of an aging population supported by steadily declining numbers of younger people and thus a decline in the necessary tax base to finance universal social programs. The extreme pessimists project that picture indefinitely until there will be no Canadians left! This would all make sense if the evidence supported their case. It doesn't.

There are two measurements for natural growth in population:

the *fertility rate* and the *birth rate.* The fertility rate is a relative term, believed to be based on the number of births per woman between the ages of fifteen and forty-nine. This has been gradually falling in advanced industrial countries for five decades. In recent years, the fertility rates for Canada, the United States, Japan, Germany, Britain and Denmark ranged from 1.44 in Germany and Denmark to 1.82 for the United States and Britain. For Canada it has remained practically unchanged at 1.6 births per woman for several years.

The birth rate is the number of births per 1,000 population. Statistics Canada recently published the 1993 Organization for Economic Cooperation and Development (OECD) birth and death statistics for twenty-four industrialized countries, including eighteen in Europe, plus Iceland, Japan, Australia, New Zealand, Canada and the United States. Of these, only in Germany did the death rate, at 11.0 per 1,000 population, exceed its birth rate at 10.0. In Sweden, a country with a mature and balanced population, there were 13.5 births versus 11.1 deaths per 1,000 population. For Canada, the figures were 13.5 births versus 7.2 deaths. Although the fertility figure of 1.6 versus 2.1 births per productive woman makes a convenient case for immigration advocates, taken alone it is not a sound foundation for population planning.

The fact is that in the five-year period 1991–95, there were an average of 389,000 births in Canada and 206,000 deaths, for a natural annual increase of 183,000. But after subtracting emigration of approximately 44,500 per year, this leaves a natural annual growth in those five years—with zero immigration—of 138,500.

However, there are factors that must be understood. Statistics Canada provides helpful information in the study *Demographic Situation in Canada* (released on June 24, 1998). Natural growth declined between 1990 and 1995 from 7.7 to 5.7 per 1,000 population.

Canada is still a young and growing country. Those whose natural life span is ending come from a population base of less than half of today's thirty million. As the population matures, as it has in European countries, the Canadian births/deaths gap will narrow, with the expectation that limited natural growth will continue as it has in Europe, where births exceed deaths in all countries except Germany.

In Canada in 1996, natural growth accounted for 47 per cent of total growth, and immigration for 53 per cent. What advantage was there to the receiving population of the immigrant phase of this growth? What justification is there for that rapid growth to continue? Why the hurry? Why not depend on natural growth alone and so extend for another twenty or thirty years the development of a balanced and mature population? And why, if Canada is the dynamic and vibrant society we believe it to be, in addition to being "the best place in the world in which to live", is population growth from outside considered essential? It is long past time our policy makers seriously examined these questions to ensure our policies serve the real interests of the future of Canada.

Charting Canada's Future, the December 1989 report of the three-year Demographic Review initiated by Canada's Department of Health and Welfare to contribute to sound policy development, concluded that "Sweden, a prosperous and dynamic country, now has an age pyramid resembling that projected for Canada in 2031." Canada is still a young country and must expect gradual changes in the age profile of its citizens. The Health and Welfare report concluded that the future for Canada is that of a society with a larger population of older people and a proportionally smaller population of young people but, with proper planning and careful utilization of resources, it need be no less dynamic and prosperous than it is today.

MYTH #3—

CANADA NEEDS A LARGER POPULATION

Not true.

Charting Canada's Future also concluded that:

The consensus among those economists who have considered the question is that, within broad limits, population growth or sheer numbers of people is not a major factor in economic growth or economic well being in modern economies that play an active role in world trade. Canada is such an economy. . . . Comparing the rate of change of economic growth and that of population growth of the 22 OECD developed economies during the period 1960–1985 shows no relationship between them.

The larger the economy the more stress we can expect to place on the environment. . . . The critical question is how effective we will be in ensuring that the growth is sustainable in terms of our environment.

In support of these well-reasoned conclusions, the Demographic Review cites a 1972 report of the United States Commission on Population and the American Future: "We have looked for, and have not found, any convincing economic argument for continued national population growth. The health of our economy does not depend on it. The welfare of the average person certainly does not depend on it."

In 1991, the Economic Council of Canada in two studies, *New Faces in the Crowd* and *Economic and Social Impacts of Immigration*, reached similar conclusions. In examining the historical record, the council observed:

It is clear that for much of Canada's history, it has been natural increase, not immigration that has driven the growth of population. This conclusion casts considerable doubt on the proposition that history proves that Canada needs immigration. Only a few periodic bursts of immigration were needed—not sustained inflows.

The same conclusion applies with respect to the country's economic prosperity: a historical perspective gives little or no support to the view that Canada needed immigration to become a wealthy nation. In the 19th and 20th centuries the fastest growth in per capita real income occurred at times when net immigration was zero or negative. In the 1950's and 1960's real incomes were again growing rapidly as was immigration, but in the 1980's similarly high levels of immigration coincided with low rates of per capita income growth. Clearly there is no sustained correlation between immigration and economic growth.

The Economic Council of Canada supported this position by citing the 1985 Macdonald Royal Commission: "A broad consensus is that high levels of immigration will increase aggregate variables such as labour force, investment and real gross expenditure, but cause . . . real income per capita and real wages to decline." The council did waver in the summation of their findings in the Canadian literature on the subject with the conclusion "that there is little or no effect of immigration on the per capita income of existing residents; there may even be negative effects, but these results may be attributable to the failure of researchers to allow for economics of scale." In the meantime, the North American Free Trade Agreement has seriously diminished the significance of economies of scale in Canada's domestic market.

In making its recommendation on immigration levels, the council considered the major effects of recent immigration:

1. Economic—for which its conclusions were neutral;
2. Political, in terms of the effect of a larger population on Canada's relative world status—on which it took no position;
3. Social—although it found no solid evidence that greater racial diversity brought net social benefits, it was not prepared to dispute the widespread presumption of such benefits (only that they remained unproven). The council then acknowledged that it favoured such diversity because, "in our opinion, it will make Canada a more interesting and exciting society, and that is a substantial non-measurable advantage."

Unlike Health and Welfare's 1989 Demographic Review, which cautioned that "growth must be sustainable in terms of the environment", neither the environment, nor the costs of immigrant settlement, nor the quality of life in Canada were considered by the Economic Council. Instead, it advised that immigration be increased gradually from a benchmark figure of 0.63 per cent of the population (the average rate of immigration for the previous twenty-five years) to 1 per cent of the population by the year 2015. In doing so, the council freely conceded

that "the humanitarian aspect weighed quite heavily in our recommendation. . . . We might have felt differently had we evaluated diversity less positively."

On May 15, 1990, when Shirley Seward of the Institute for
Research on Public Policy appeared before the Commons
Standing Committee on Immigration, she presented the results
of the institute's study of the effect of structural changes in the
economy on the immigrant labour force. Its research, based on
the 1986 census, found that pre-1971 male immigrants from traditional source countries and post-1981 female immigrants
from non-traditional sources were disproportionately represented in declining industries. Each faced the challenge of re-
training for re-employment. The men, being earlier immigrants,
were older, spoke English or French but had only limited elementary education. The women were lacking English or
French and, like the men, had limited elementary education. It
was essential to provide basic educational upgrading and literacy training for these vulnerable immigrant workers. With
that background, the institute found in its research that:

> For many decades immigration had been perceived as a tool for im-
> proving the quality of the labour force, and had played a role in facili-
> tating structural change by filling certain skill shortages. However,
> immigration policy had become less selective in the past 15 years and
> there is recent evidence to suggest that several groups of immigrants
> in the labour force may face special problems of adaptation in the fu-
> ture. . . .
>
> The long term benefits associated with a better educated and more
> highly skilled labour force would more than offset the immediate
> costs involved in a comprehensive labour adjustment program.

Put more directly, the message was that immigrants must be
literate and skilled and these disadvantaged citizens must be re-
trained.

Five months later, Ms. Seward, anticipating the annual announcement of immigration levels for the following year, set
out her views in the *Financial Post* (October 22, 1990):

Any day now, Employment and Immigration Minister Barbara McDougall is likely to announce the government will increase the number of immigrants permitted to come to Canada over the 1991–1995 period. This, in spite of compelling evidence that many immigrants and Canadian born workers are already facing serious adjustment problems which are likely to worsen as Canada slides into a depression. . . . There is no compelling logic for higher immigration levels. . . . It is far more important to assist workers in coping with uncertainty rather than to increase the size of the labour force with higher immigration levels. Let's get our priorities straight!

MYTH #4—

IMMIGRANTS EARN MORE AND RETURN MORE TO THE CANADIAN ECONOMY THAN CANADIAN-BORN CITIZENS

Not true.

In 1988, Professors Roderic Beaujot and J. Peter Rappak of the University of Western Ontario were engaged by the Health and Welfare Department's Demographic Review to undertake a major study, entitled *Role of Immigration in Changing Socio-Demographic Structures*. Messrs. Beaujot and Rappak divided immigrants into "Traditional Immigrant Groups" and "New Immigrant Groups", and compared their respective incomes, in five-year age groups, from ages fifteen to sixty-four, and sixty-five plus, based on arrival periods from pre-1946 to 1984.

Figure 1 shows the figures for the 35-to-44 male age group, based on the 1986 census. The steep decline in incomes for the 1980–84 arrival period reflects the crucial legislation which came into effect in 1978, drastically reducing admission standards. It also reflects the short adjustment period. The relative relationships found in the other age groups vary, but there is a common trend. The chart also demonstrates the immediate effect of the change in direction taken late in the mandate of the Pearson government. More significant is that while this was happening, the number of immigrants in the traditional group declined from 95 to 35 per cent, and those in the new group increased

FIGURE 1

AVERAGE INCOME COMPARISON BETWEEN IMMIGRANTS AND CANADIANS, 1984

National averages for Males, 35–44 age group

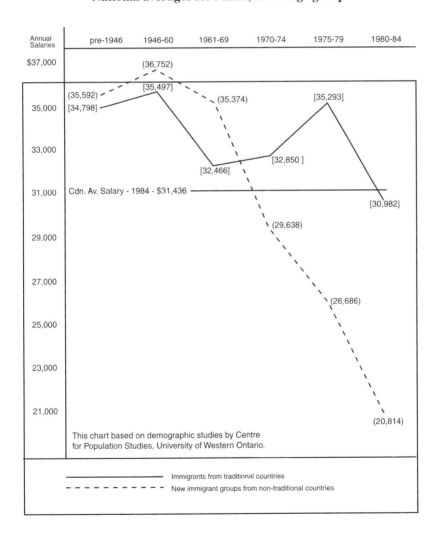

This chart based on demographic studies by Centre for Population Studies, University of Western Ontario.

——————————— Immigrants from traditional countries

– – – – – – – – – New immigrant groups from non-traditional countries

from 5 to 65 per cent. The result was that by the 1980–84 period the new immigrant group's average earnings were only two-thirds of those in the traditional group, yet they comprised nearly double those from traditional sources accepted in that period.

The message that "immigrants do much better economically than Canadian born" originated with a doctoral thesis based on 1981 Canadian census figures by Ather Akbari, a mid-1980s doctoral student of Professor Don DeVoretz, a specialist in immigration economics at Simon Fraser University. The fact is that most pre-1981 immigrants with a record to check would have entered Canada before the 1978 legislation drastically reduced admission standards. It is not surprising that the selected people in Dr. Akbari's study registered average incomes exceeding the average of the broad range of the Canadian public. The immigration industry and its political supporters have never allowed Canadians to forget those findings.

They would have found much less convenient the testimony of Dr. DeVoretz before the House of Commons Standing Committee on Labour, Employment and Immigration on February 13, 1990, in which he discussed the effects of the 1976 Immigration Act (proclaimed in 1978), and the consequent change in the composition of immigrants by class of entry:

> The rise in the family class of immigrants has produced a new disturbing trend for this post-1978 group of immigrants. The most recent wave, 1978 on, of Third World immigrants has not replicated the experience of past Third World immigrants. This recent immigrant group's income has not caught up to their resident born cohorts' income. And our most recent study using census data indicates that the post-1978 immigrant may never equal earlier immigrant income performance. This recent trend can have serious consequences on future assessments of the economic performance of immigrants.

> Our finding for tax performance, use of public services and savings behaviour are all predicated on rapidly rising immigrant income after their arrival. We are now finding just the opposite. Years of residence in Canada are coupled with a decline in relative earnings for this recent immigrant vintage. There is one important and instructive exception

to this trend in earnings degradation. Namely, those post-1978 immigrants who are highly trained continue to outperform highly trained Canadian workers. After ten or less years in residence this highly trained immigrant group's income surpasses the highly trained native born group. For the semi-skilled and unskilled post-1978 immigrant group the opposite pattern for earnings emerges. These less trained immigrants are falling further behind similarly trained Canadians with each year in residence.

Five years later, the consequences of the 1978 changes were even more measurable. In a speech to the Association of Professional Economists of British Columbia on September 29, 1995, Dr. DeVoretz confirmed his 1990 findings. Using 1991 census data, he compared productive ability in terms of the earnings of Vancouver/Victoria immigrants of the pre-1981 and post-1980

TABLE 1

PERCENTAGE COMPARISONS OF EARNINGS OF POST-1980 AND PRE-1981 IMMIGRANTS WITH EARNINGS OF CANADIAN-BORN CITIZENS, BASED ON 1991 CENSUS DATA.

Age	Cdn. Born	Pre-1981	Post-1980	Post-1980 vs. Pre-1981	Post-1980 vs. Cdn. Born	Pre-1981 vs. Cdn. Born
25–29	$34,676	$45,032	$25,858	58%	75%	144%
30–34	41,267	47,888	27,091	57	66	116
35–39	46,171	49,067	27,950	57	61	106
40–44	49,389	49,889	28,436	57	57	101
45–49	50,921	49,914	28,548	57	56	98
50–54	50,767	49,142	28,286	58	56	97
55–59	48,926	47,573	27,651	58	57	97
60–64	46,958	46,249	27,090	59	58	98

Source: These figures were originally published—although not in this form—by Dr. Don DeVoretz of Simon Fraser University, in September 1995.

periods with those of Canadian-born. Again, his analysis, based on five-year age groups, from age twenty-five to sixty-four, compared equals. As shown in Table 1, the post-1980 immigrants earned about 58 per cent as much as their pre-1981 cohorts and about 60 per cent as much as Canadian-born citizens. These are averages. They include those highly trained, post-1978 selected immigrants whom Dr. DeVoretz's studies found to outperform highly trained Canadian workers. How many of the others are responsible for the depression of Canada's historic standards by 40 per cent; what is their level of performance; who are they and why are they here?

This table illustrates the extent to which the 1978 legislation and subsequent amendments seriously diminished the quality of Canada's immigrants in the post-1978 period. The superior performance of pre-1981 immigrants, particularly in the 25–29 age group, reflects the fact that this group entered Canada between infancy and age eighteen. They are children of selected parents, some having received their total education in Canada in prosperous and favourable times. It may also be that what is possibly a small sample reflects a modest number of high achievers.

A great many factors influence a society's productivity, the quality of the workforce being one of them. By 1991 Canadian immigration was heavily Family Class. The difference between these immigrants and the principals in the Independent Class, who came on merit, was that the Family Class came without consideration of anything, save health and criminality. This was hardly a situation conducive to immigrants earning more, or returning more to the Canadian economy than native-born Canadians.

MYTH #5—

IMMIGRANTS CREATE
MORE JOBS THAN THEY TAKE

Not true.

Communications Framework for the Immigration Program was developed by the Public Affairs Branch of the Immigration

Commission with the objective of selling immigration policy to the public. The publication was distributed internally in 1989 preliminary to introduction of the five-year program of planned increases in immigration admissions.

The Immigration Commission's own research indicated that:

> In the initial stages of the program, messages and themes tied to the economic benefits of immigration are most likely to be accepted by the public at large. However, this will be difficult to achieve because there is little substantive data available. . . .

> However, there is little hard data to support the claim that immigrants create more jobs than they take.

Be that as it may, the program of immigration expansion demanded support, so the program provided that:

> Phase II will include initiatives to inform Canadians about the contribution of immigrants, particularly the economic contributions.

*   *   *

The evidence is overwhelming:

1. That the politically favoured folk tale of immigration at 1 per cent of the population is deceitful propaganda;
2. That Canada's alleged low birthrate is not one that puts our future at risk;
3. That a larger population will not benefit Canada's existing citizens;
4. That today's immigrants do not, on average, contribute more to the Canadian economy than do native-born Canadians; and
5. That the government's own studies can find no evidence that immigrants create more jobs than they take.

Faced with an increasing need to deal with these truths, the immigration-industry spin doctors have been kept busy. Recognizing an information crisis, the solution of politicians, immigration lobbyists and lawyers, and others less visible, is to perpetuate these fabrications, as if, through their endless repetition, hard facts can be denied; and as if Canadians, in consequence, will accept that large-scale immigration is necessary and beneficial. Perhaps they will. Indeed, perhaps they already have.

CHAPTER III

THE ROOT OF THE PROBLEM

~

"It is in Canada's interest to accept and if need be to encourage, the entry to this country each year of as many immigrants as can readily be absorbed. To remain of positive value immigration policy must be consistent with national economic policy in general and with national manpower and social policies in particular, and it must be related to the conditions of national and international life in 1966 and the years ahead rather than to past events."

The 1966 White Paper

In the post–World War II period the Canadian economy was doing well, unemployment was below 5.0 per cent (considered by many to be full employment), and there was a perceived need for a larger population. Changes began with the admission of immigrants on a non-discriminatory basis in the early sixties, and the rationale for a new policy appeared in the form of the 1966 White Paper. This document initiated the principles and policies the government believed should be part of new immigration legislation, and it sent a clear message.

The White Paper acknowledged that sheer numbers themselves were not beneficial and considered it essential that immigrants have the ability to integrate by becoming economically productive members of Canadian society. The emphasis was on attracting as many well-educated and well-trained immigrants as the country can absorb. The emphasis would be a response to "need with excellence". In 1967 it was all incorporated into a new Department of Manpower and Immigration under the leadership of the Honourable Jean Marchand. This association of manpower and immigration signalled an emphasis on the economic well-being of the nation. The conveyed impression was that in this period of economic prosperity, Canada would ride this wave with quality.

The establishment of the new ministry formally placed Canadian immigration policy on a universal selection system with objective selection criteria based on the principles set out in the 1966 White Paper. Potential immigrants would be divided into four groups—Independent applicants, Nominated Relatives, Sponsored Dependents and Entrepreneurs. Selection was to be based on a points system weighted towards productive ability. For the Independent applicants, factors of education, training, skills, demand for those skills, and age were together worth 70 points. Arranged employment, language ability, relatives in Canada and area of destination were worth 30 points. The required pass mark was 50 points.

Nominated Relatives also faced the education, skills and age 70-point requirement; the nature of the settlement arrangements provided by their Canadian resident family could augment that score by from 15 to 30 points. Entrepreneurs, an immigrant class committed to creating jobs, was introduced with these 1967 regulations. They faced similar point requirements to those of the Independent Class but with the automatic allotment of 25 points in lieu of the 10 and 15 points for skills and skills demand. The rationale was based on economic advantage.

Then came a denial of the expectation of high standards in the selection process, a denial that has prevailed for thirty years. For the sponsored or accompanying dependents there was no assessment beyond health and criminality. The only requirement was to have a relative in Canada, at first a citizen or, years later, a permanent resident committed to the care and maintenance of their sponsored relative in Canada for ten consecutive years. With neither limit on the numbers, nor assessment of literacy or skills of what was to become the Family Class, this was the first break with the expectation of excellence. Quality in immigration would not be universal.

The second break with the high objectives came later in the sixties. Until then it had always been a requirement for potential immigrants to Canada to make their applications to Canada's visa officers in embassies or consular offices abroad. That allowed for a reasonable opportunity to check on the applicant's background and history. Then, with no apparent justification, the government by regulation established the right for visitors to Canada to apply for landing in Canada *while visiting in Canada*. But, of greater significance was the provision that those rejected, having failed to meet Canada's admission standards, would have the right to appeal that decision to the newly appointed Immigration Appeal Board. This meant remaining in the country beyond the expiration of their "visitors' permits". It would all have made such good sense in Ottawa. These visitors need not be put to the trouble and cost of returning to Europe or India or the West Indies, or to other places where they originated, and where their records were available, when their application could be processed so easily right here in Canada.

As is so often the case with immigration and refugee legislation and regulations, this approach lacked adequate provision for either its administration or its consequences.

This opportunity to gain a foothold in Canada was immediately recognized around the world. The Immigration Appeal Board was swamped. Predictably, by mid-1973 there were 20,000 appeals lodged by visitors still in Canada who had been rejected because they were found to be unsuitable. Faced with an impending crisis, notice of the decision to cancel the opportunity to apply from within Canada was published in the *Canada Gazette* thirty days in advance of its effective date of August 15, 1973. Immediately, to beat that deadline, family heads in disadvantaged countries responded to urgent messages from relatives or friends already in Canada, and quickly abandoned their immediate families for the earliest flight to this country. Ottawa, having granted an amnesty to rejected economic migrants, advertised to the world that our door remained open for another month. It was the initial signal to all and sundry that we Canadians had lost control of our border.

To meet the onslaught, the Immigration Appeal Board was augmented with temporary members to process and admit for landing those applicants not otherwise inadmissible for reasons of health or criminality. These applicants would be followed, by right and without delay, by members of their immediate families, and, on becoming citizens, they would have the privilege through sponsorship to bring in additional family members.

One 1973 amnesty immigrant was joined in Canada by his family, including four children. As they matured, and as was their custom, father returned to the homeland to negotiate arranged marriages for each young adult. Initially on obtaining citizenship and later on grant of landing, each new spouse would enjoy the privilege of sponsoring his or her nuclear family; thus a broad base was established for pyramidal population growth, subject only to health and criminality checks. Some would do well. Some would not. And as we shall see, the statistical income averages proved unacceptably low.

In the years 1973–1975 there was an upward blip in both the number of immigrants received and the number of those listed as Independents. This suggested that reprieved amnesty candidates (having failed to meet Canada's admission standards) were included in this upscale category. They had to belong somewhere.

Canada accepted an average of 197,000 immigrants in each of those three years—1973, 1974 and 1975—of amnesty receptions. The average admissions in the two years immediately preceding and the two years immediately following the amnesty period was about 127,000. That annual average increase of 70,000 in those three years meant 210,000 new Canadians in excess of what had been a downward trend at a time of increasing Canadian unemployment.

The more significant statistic is that Canada accepted an average of 92,500 immigrants in the Independent Class over that period, when the annual trend had been 46,300. This suggests that about 140,000 unplanned-for new Canadians were part of this improvident movement and listed in the Independent category when it is unlikely they were examined for either skills or literacy.[1]

A March 1988 departmental publication, *Canada's Immigration Levels and the Economic and Demographic Environment*

1967–87, beautifully describes this disaster in these uninspired and unedifying terms:

> Certain new economic factors intervened between the period 1968 to 1978. As a result the level of immigration for the three year period 1973–1975 was unusually high. This was the result of a number of visitors who arrived before the summer of 1972 with their status adjusted to landed immigrants in the years that followed. (Between 1967 and 1972 it was easy to apply from within Canada for landed immigrant status. Many citizens and landed immigrants brought their relatives from home as visitors, and once these relatives were in Canada they applied for landed immigrant status).

With the benefit of seven years' experience with the new rules, and with the consequences of the White Paper experience, the government, in 1974, produced *Immigration Policy Perspectives: A Report of the Canadian Immigration and Population Study*, a Green Paper to be the basis of debate in the development of a new Immigration Act.

The literature of the period is dominated by two basic considerations: a low mortality rate and a declining fertility rate. The first results in an increase in the elderly to be cared for, and the second in a perceived decline in the number of producers to provide for them. This was described as an increasing dependency ratio, and interpreted by many as reason to increase immigration rates. There was no recognition of the difference between fertility rates and birth rates, and the fact that in Canada there were 13.5 births per year and only 7.2 deaths ensures continuing growth without immigration.

Then the Green Paper acknowledged that the population would not stabilize at its [then] level of approximately 23 million. There was significant momentum for growth from natural increase built into the present age structure. This, of course, didn't mean the immigration lobby would abandon the fertility-rate argument. Twenty-five years later it remains both as strong and as invalid as ever.

As a discussion paper, the Green Paper presented both the

advantages and disadvantages of immigration. In one instance, acknowledging that the Canadian economy benefited from immigration, it also stated that:

> It would probably be a not unfair assessment of our understanding of the economic consequences of higher against lower population growth rate for a country in Canada's present position to conclude that the evidence in favour of higher rates is uncertain.

Uncertain they were. They weren't exactly flying blind, but wearing dark glasses under cloudy skies. They did their best without the guidance later available in the detailed reports of the Economic Council, the Health and Welfare three-year Demographic Review and the work of Shirley Seward of Canada's Institute of Research on Public Policy. All of these reports could have supported a renewed attack on the legislation fifteen years later.

The new Immigration Act, presented to Parliament in 1976, had as its first listed objectives "to support the attainment of such demographic goals as may be established by the government of Canada from time to time in respect of the size, rate of growth, structure and geographic distribution of the Canadian population." Twenty-three years later those goals have yet to be established and immigration policy development continues to be an exercise in ad hockery, dominated by the pressures of domestic political advantage.

*   *   *

The 1976 Immigration Act came into effect on April 10, 1978 and, as amended in 1985 and 1992, applies today. It brought order to the various regulations that had accumulated since the previous Act was passed in 1952, and incorporated, among other things, the 1967 Immigration Appeal Board Act and establishment of the Refugee Status Advisory Committee (RSAC).

Our concerns here are with the terms, conditions and process under which immigrants were now to be welcomed to Canada. Section 6.(1) of the Act states that:

> Subject to this Act and the regulations, any immigrant, including a Convention Refugee, a member of the family class and an independent immigrant may be granted landing if he is able to establish to the satisfaction of an immigration officer that he meets the selection standards established by the regulations for the purpose of determining whether or not an immigrant will be able to become successfully established in Canada.

Section 6.(2) of the Act provides that Convention Refugees and others, to whom Canada's humanitarian tradition with respect to the displaced and the persecuted applies, could be admitted subject to regulations which exclude assessment of their ability to become successfully established.

The conditions for admission of the several classes of immigrants (all of them subject to health and criminality checks) are outlined below—in order of priority processing. Family Class (or Sponsored) immigration was now effectively established as *the first priority of the federal government.*

THE FAMILY CLASS

Every Canadian citizen and every permanent resident in Canada who is at least eighteen years of age, and who gives an undertaking to support a member of the Family Class and accompanying dependents for ten consecutive years, may sponsor applications for landing made by his/her spouse or fiancé(e), unmarried children under twenty-one, and by his/her father and mother, and by grandparents over sixty years of age, or under sixty if incapable of gainful employment or widowed, and certain other children orphaned or needing care. Sponsored parents may bring with them as accompanying dependents their unmarried sons or daughters under the age of nineteen.

It was this provision that new Canadian citizens (and, later, landed immigrants) could sponsor these family members without any consideration, beyond health or criminality, of the skills or literacy of any of them, that defined the Family Class. This process was described as "reunification of family in Canada". This is in contrast, for example, to New Zealand and Australia where "family reunification" requires skills and literacy and is facilitated only when a majority of what those countries' immigration regulations define as "family" are already legally domiciled there. Thus, if the majority of one's immediate family lives, say, in China's Szechuan Province, they would have to qualify individually until a majority of them were in New Zealand or Australia before the balance would be sponsored. Not so in Canada, where it appears that every economically disadvantaged family in the world is keenly aware of Canada's unique immigration opportunities.

* * *

A June 1994 "National Consultation on Family Class Immigration", convened by the Department of Citizenship and Immigration at York University's Centre for Refugee Studies (Refugee Law Research Unit), indeed suggested what a Canadian definition of "family" might be. (This astonishing statement is included as much for the quality of the dissertation as for the contribution it makes toward policy development.)

(Family) . . . might logically include those persons critical to the work of reproducing ethnicity and culture within a materially and emotionally dependent or interdependent unit, as well as those persons necessary for more traditional forms of social reproduction. A construction of this kind is arguably in keeping with the Charter of Rights and Freedoms' commitment to the interpretation of rights in a manner 'consistent with the preservation and enhancement of the multicultural heritage of Canadians.'

The challenge is to recast eligibility for family class immigration in a way which eschews unthinking reliance on definitional generalizations of questionable social validity. By avoiding facile categories and moving to a contextualized, functional definition of family, it is possible to achieve significantly greater social and cultural inclusiveness. If the underlying premise of privileging the admission of family over the immigration of other would-be immigrants is the need to maintain the integrity of emotionally bonded economic units in which relations of dependency or interdependency facilitate the provision of social reproduction, then the criteria and procedures for family class admission should be reconfigured to meet this goal.

This anticipated policy recommendation was to be favoured by the minister five years later with a new Citizenship Act, proposing "the recognition of common law and same sex relationships through regulatory changes. . . ." With this regulation, the thriving practice of convenience marriage entered into for immigration purposes only was no longer necessary.

ASSISTED RELATIVES

An Assisted Relative is a relation other than a member of the Family Class for whom a Canadian citizen gives an undertaking of support for five years, and who successfully passes a modified points test in which factors of arranged employment, designated occupation and language ability are excluded. This results in immigrants whose productivity level matches that of the Family Class.

ENTREPRENEURS

An Entrepreneur is an immigrant who intends, and has the financial resources, to establish or purchase a substantial interest in the ownership of a business in Canada, whereby employment opportunities will either be created or maintained *for more than five Canadian citizens or permanent residents* (exclusive of members of the Entrepreneur's family), and to engage in the management of that business. The requirement to assure employment for what was in effect a minimum of six people didn't work and was later reduced to two, and then to one. Having made those decisions, the politicians continue to tout the benefits of this immigrant class to Canada. The fact that the publicity for this innovation originally referred to "more than five citizens or permanent residents" ignored the possibility that one or more landed immigrants might well arrive on the same plane as the Entrepreneur and meet that requirement. (See Chapter VIII, Entrepreneurs and Investors.)

INDEPENDENT IMMIGRANTS

These immigrants, who enter Canada on merit, have demonstrated their ability to successfully establish themselves in Canada to the satisfaction of a Canadian immigration officer by way of a points test based on education level, vocational training, experience and occupational demand, arranged employment, location, age, language ability, personal suitability and the support of a relative in Canada.

*   *   *

In 1982, under the pressure of rising unemployment, Minister of Employment and Immigration Lloyd Axworthy froze the entry of Independent Immigrants (with very limited exceptions). On January 1, 1986, this means of entry would be restored but in the context of very restrictive occupations lists. These occupations lists, intended to assist visa officers in selecting Independent Immigrants, were based on job vacancies on a province-by-province basis and were revised by Minister Bernard Valcourt in 1991.

The General Occupations list was based on the thousands of jobs described in the *Canadian Classification and Dictionary of Occupations*. Mr. Valcourt's 1991 list included only 506 of these and only 56 were allotted the full 10 points for skills. These included nurses, 32 varieties of medical and dental technologists, 18 varieties of cooks and chefs and 5 mechanical designations.

The Designated Occupations list was to be used, the publicity release said, to promote "independent" immigration. This was the priority list, presumably reflecting real need. There were 1,085 jobs—based on 1,500,000 unemployed, approximately one for every 1,500 Canadians then looking for work. Canada, it seemed, needed 305 medical therapists, 295 engineers, 315 computer specialists, 40 head chefs, 20 farmers and 110 mechanical people. This moderate need was in decline.

When promoting immigration policies, politicians have two constituencies: the ethnic vote and established Canadians whose concern is that immigrants have the skills, literacy and the ability to succeed and integrate into their new country. No time like New Year's Eve to respond to the latter group. In a December 31, 1992 news release the minister announced ". . . one more step towards enhancing the benefits that the immigration program brings to Canada."

The release can best be described as headline-grabbing:

> In 1993, some 41,000 independent immigrants will come to Canada along with their dependents. Of these some 33,500 will be skilled workers (including assisted relatives) with qualifications in critical need nation wide.

The "critical need", as expressed in the Designated Occupations list, was updated effective the next day, January 1, 1993, but not in the form of a news release. It would not get headlines during the Christmas holiday season. The updated list was to fill 768 jobs—not 33,500.

Immigration politics is a great game, particularly at election time. Doug Lewis became the Tory minister of public security, and Mr. Valcourt minister of human resources and labour. On August 23, 1993, just two months in advance of the 1993 federal election, the two ministers jointly announced "an expanded 1993 General Occupations list and updated Designated Occupations list." The spin people were busy. The new general list nearly doubled to 953 the job descriptions at the 10-point level. It recognized the expanding need for computer programmers and confirmed the continuing need for paramedical therapists and culinary specialists. However, the principal addition to the 10-point category was 46 varieties of repairmen, including quilting-machine fixers, gum-wrapping-machine repairers, tobacco-machine adjusters, shearing-machine fixers and 42 other similar trades.

However, the new designated list, reflecting actual requirements, was restricted to 267 jobs for paramedical specialists. By November 1, 1994, under Mr. Marchi, the new minister, the list was down to 54 occupational therapists (30 in Ontario and 24 in Alberta).

With that, Mr. Marchi announced the impending replacement of the *Canadian Classification and Dictionary of Occupations* with the *National Occupational Classification* as a basis for a new single General Occupations list. He didn't hurry. Thirty-one months later, on May 1, 1997, it became effective. It contained only 275 job descriptions, of which only 95 were allotted more than 1 point in the assessment scale. Only 19 got the full 10 points, this time 11 varieties of medical therapists, plus executive chefs, chefs' cooks and sous chefs, millwrights, heavy-duty mechanics and computer programmers. In the new Liberal General Occupations list, that reflected critical needs. The opportunities for gum-wrapping-machine repairers and their colleagues had obviously been filled.

REFUGEES

A Convention Refugee is any person who has a well-founded fear of persecution for reasons of race, religion, nationality, membership in a particular social group or political opinion, and is outside his country of nationality and unable or unwilling, because of such fear, to avail himself/herself of the protection of that country. (See further material on refugees in Chapters IV and V.)

*　　*　　*

There are many cases where the initial supporting evidence available to immigration officers resulted in the refusal of a particular sponsorship application, but when a full family hearing took place before the Board, a favourable award proved justified. On the other hand, Federal Court precedents have allowed flagrant abuse of our generosity as a nation.

Take the case of the young man who, when visiting his married brother in British Columbia, decided that he too would like to be a Canadian. To expedite matters, a marriage was quickly arranged with a family friend, an accommodating middle-aged spinster. They took no other shortcuts. The young man returned home, where all immigration documents were appropriately filed. The wary Canadian immigration officers rejected them: it didn't take a Sherlock Holmes to recognize that this was a marriage of convenience, whose purpose was to circumvent Canadian immigration laws. There were, for example, no letters, postcards or telephone calls; no evidence of even the slightest communication between this newly wedded couple after the husband's return home. The Canadian "spouse" had never approached the immigration people in her home city to express anxiety, or simply to inquire about the progress of her husband's application. His Canadian brother did that, as this woman of limited means enjoyed extensive and expensive travel. Based on precedent, the Immigration Appeal Board allowed the appeal.

A dissenting opinion in the IAB judgment encouraged the Department of Immigration to appeal the decision favouring the sponsorship. The Board decision was upheld by the Appeal Court. For them, a marriage was a marriage and there was nothing in the statute requiring an examination of its intent.

A classic and curious example of the validity of marriage for immigration purposes, whatever the circumstances, was that of yet another family. An elder daughter, betrothed to a Canadian, entered Canada, married and subsequently arranged to sponsor her parents. The parents arrived in Toronto accompanied by their dependent children except for one daughter. Already married, she did not qualify under the definition of a dependent. To complete this family reunification, the original sponsoring couple went through divorce proceedings, as did the daughter who had been left behind. The four then joined forces in their homeland, where each sister married her former brother-in-law. The original "Canadian couple" were now free to sponsor their new legal partners for admission to Canada, with no indication by suggestion or need for any adjustment in their personal relationships.

Ultimately, the legal definition of "marriage" was rewritten to exclude marriages entered into solely for the purpose of achieving landed status in Canada. It still remains for an examining visa officer to detect and gather the necessary evidence to prove the fraud in a court of law—often not an easy task.

*   *   *

Today's Immigration Appeal Division, like the Immigration Appeal Board before it, has a particularly important responsibility with respect to appeals by landed immigrants from deportation orders made against them. It is the duty of immigration-enforcement officers to issue deportation orders when the conduct and behaviour of a landed immigrant under the law justifies this action. It is, however, reasonable that a separate body determine if sufficient compassionate or humanitarian considerations exist to justify modifying such decisions. Appeals often involve teenage members of good immigrant families, who, having failed to adjust to a new environment, find themselves in trouble with the law. There is always a concerned family to plead these cases and usually the decision is to "stay" the execution of the deportation order (the option to deport remains) for two years to allow such young persons to change their behaviour—a worthwhile exercise that usually solves the problem and illustrates the value of the work of this section of the Board.

It is noteworthy that, in framing the definition of the various immigrant classifications, no restrictions on entry other than health and criminality were placed on the admission of members of the Family Class beyond authenticating the required relationship with the sponsoring Canadian resident. The government thus had regulated away our nation's right to select those who would become Canadian citizens.

For refugee claimants, there is an obligation for Canada to accept all claimants who satisfy the UN Convention definition of a refugee.

*   *   *

In 1980 Canada was facing a severe economic depression. Unemployment had increased and Immigration Minister Lloyd Axworthy found it necessary to reduce immigration levels. It may or may not have come as a surprise to him that Family Class immigrants and refugees entered Canada by right—their admission was not only demand-driven but they also enjoyed primary and secondary priority in processing. As we have already seen, Minister Axworthy was limited to imposing restrictions on Independent Class immigrants, those selected for their ability to integrate and contribute economically to Canada.

There is the example of the young man who, having completed his apprenticeship as an upholsterer, wished to emigrate to Canada. He circulated his credentials to prospective employers in Canada, offering his services free of charge for two weeks to demonstrate his competence, with the proviso, if found satisfactory, he would be offered employment. An established Vancouver upholsterer, Ian Andrews, took a chance and not only found the performance of his new recruit superior but recognized the young man's potential for supervisory responsibilities. Job guarantee in hand, this enterprising young fellow applied to be admitted as an Independent Immigrant. However, the new rules required that his job offer could only be considered relevant to Canada's needs. This required the failure of a nation-wide advertising program to produce a Canadian applicant potentially suitable to Mr. Andrews' needs.

A response might come from Atlantic Canada, requiring fares to be paid without guarantees. It might come from someone already employed as an upholsterer, which would not serve the national need. Or it might come from someone just fired, which might not serve Mr. Andrews' needs. Faced with all this, both Mr. Andrews and his prospective employee gave up. Meanwhile, tens of thousands of Family Class immigrants and refugee claimants, many without skills or literacy, legally poured across our borders.

In fact, there is little in our immigration regulations to accommodate young immigrants from countries with a level of economic development parallel to that of Canada. Imagine, for example, that a Canadian Rhodes Scholar at Oxford University falls in love with a fellow student (Oxford students have a worldwide base) and that, on graduating, they marry and settle in Canada. Imagine also that the foreign partner to this legal union has siblings pursuing their education at the same level and who, on graduation, wish to build their lives with their newly Canadian brother or sister in Canada. This too could be called "family reunification", but our system doesn't welcome them. Also, the parents of these potential immigrants, who are most probably busy in their own country with their own careers, are unlikely to be free to respond to sponsorship by their offspring in Canada.

The obvious and appropriate route for the admission to Canada of such siblings should be as Independent Immigrants, whose acceptance is based on the merit-point system. The young and well-educated, fluent in English or French, with good academic standing, personal suitability, potential to adjust to a rapidly changing economy and with close family in Canada, ironically enough face the handicap of the restrictive Designated Occupations list. Because of their youth they have little job experience, which virtually guarantees their refusal by Canadian visa officers.

*   *   *

There are, however, several alternatives to the merit process for young people wishing to emigrate to Canada:

1. Genuine marriage (including engagement) to a Canadian, which has gone unchallenged.
2. Convenience marriages, available to those lacking in charac-ter, which are increasingly popular and generally successful as a route to citizenship. As the 1982 Report of the Auditor General observed: "engagements and marriages of conven-ience, even pregnancies of convenience, unverifiable or du-bious family relationships and false or altered documents are some of the methods used; the form they take varies with the year and the country of origin."
3. The "Courier Parent" scheme is also usually effective, but unacceptable to persons of integrity. To quote from the Audi-tor General's Report:

Many of these ploys are designed to obtain landed status for young people about to enter the labour market. . . . The phenomenon of 'courier parents' is a common example of this. When parents obtain immigrant visas, dependent children under 21 [now under 19] are al-most always granted immigrant visas as well. In addition, many dependents over the age of 21 are granted landing by Order-in-Coun-cil so that they can accompany the person who supports them in Canada. According to estimates by a major immigration office abroad, approximately 50 per cent of parents with children around 21 years of age return to their country of origin as soon as or even before their children settle in Canada. Thus, a procedure designed to reunite families actually has the opposite effect.

4. The fourth option is to claim refugee status, an effective and popular means of entry into Canada both for legitimate refu-gees and for those willing to lie about their circumstances. Still, it is difficult to imagine the siblings of our theoretical Oxford graduate following the example of the countless thousands of economic migrants who have taken advantage of such easy opportunities.

*   *   *

Soon after the 1978 proclamation of the new Immigration Act, evidence of the sort of abuse cited above prompted Kenneth Dye, the Auditor General, to dispatch his auditors to Canadian immigration stations worldwide. The thirty-three-page section on immigration included in his annual report for the year ending March 31, 1982 (published in December 1982 and referred to above) is a devastating condemnation, both of the Immigration Commission and of government immigration policy. Mr. Dye's conclusions were based on information pro-vided by serving Canadian immigration officers. They were unanimous in their criticism of the system in which they worked. However, his report's warning of impending disaster was disregarded by the Trudeau government and, strangely enough, evoked no criticism from either of the two federal op-position parties. (The ethnic vote must not be disturbed.)

Except for a radio interview with the late Jack Webster, the distinguished Vancouver talk-show host, the report appears to have received no other media reference. Not surprising, for Mr. Dye told Mr. Webster that he was the only media person in Canada to question him about this report on immigration practices.

Indeed, even the Economic Council of Canada appears to have been ignorant of its existence. In its 1991 study, *The Economic and Social Impacts of Immigration*, the Report of the Auditor General for 1990 is listed, but not the one for 1982.

There have been many changes in the intervening years, but Canadians and their representatives in Parliament should be familiar with at least some of the additional highlights of this significant document (and its continuing implications for our country), particularly those which relate to Family Class immigration:

7.4 . . . Canada is looked on as one of the countries most accessible to foreigners.

7.20 The purpose of immigrant selection is to ensure that immigrants are able to establish themselves successfully in Canada, as required by the Immigration Act. The process should thus contribute to Canada's economic and cultural development.

7.37 The family class has accounted for approximately 40 per cent of the total flow of immigrants to Canada in recent years. According to an internal Commission report, a significant portion of the movement in the family class does not correspond to the generally accepted definition of the family reunification principle. This class, as defined in the Regulations, includes many people who are not dependent on their sponsors and who establish separate households as soon as they arrive in Canada.

7.39 Recent studies . . . have shown that members of the family class are not well prepared to participate in the Canadian labour market. Although at least a third of the immigrants in the family class say they want to work when they arrive in Canada, the Commission's studies indicate that the proportion who actually enter the labour force is even higher. However, there are generally no jobs waiting for them, and they have less training, work experience, and knowledge of the official languages than immigrants in other classes. They often belong to occupational groups whose skills are in low demand in Canada and to age groups where the rate of unemployment is high.

These studies raise questions about the ability of a significant proportion of the members of the family class to adapt to life in Canada; this could have repercussions on social programs and on the labour market.

7.40   The Commission has not conducted studies to determine whether the selection criteria used for these immigrants and their sponsors provide any assurance that the immigrants will be able to become successfully established in Canada, as required by section 115(1)(c) of the Act. Nor do the Regulations define the expression 'successfully established in Canada'. However, Immigration officials told us that they consider any immigrant not on social assistance or otherwise a burden on the state to be 'successfully established' in Canada.

7.42 The selection process for members of the family class contains loopholes and thus lends itself to abuse, because the only specific criterion is the sponsor's undertaking to help the immigrant become successfully established in Canada. The process has been greatly simplified in order to promote the family reunification objective set out in the Act. Moreover, this class of immigrant is given priority in processing.

7.46 Because Headquarters does not systematically collect data on the nature of the abuses and loopholes that come to the attention of Immigration officers, it can neither analyse nor assess the magnitude of the problem. However, every Immigration Centre (CIC) and post we visited during our audit reported such practices.

7.47 Without an information and analysis system, Headquarters cannot curb these practices. To do so, it would have to pass judgment on the intentions of applicants, and such judgments have often been challenged successfully before the Immigration Appeal Board and the courts.

7.48 The Commission should implement a system for gathering information on the nature of abuses and loopholes in the system for selecting family class immigrants, analyse this information, and take the necessary measures to close loopholes and curb abuses.

The one body that could not simply ignore the Auditor General's damning criticism, of course, was the Immigration Commission. Unabashed, they responded to Mr. Dye's report by promising that "Information the Commission has been collecting will be organized in a systematic way, and regular analysis will be conducted and reported so that appropriate corrective action may be taken where necessary." Nothing of the sort happened; instead, there would continue to be modifications in regulation to favour the Family Class. That perception of the importance of the ethnic vote is never abandoned by vote-conscious politicians.

Auditor General Dye's 1985 follow-up report records the Immigration Commission's failure to do more than merely accept the status quo. He again cites the commission's senior civil servants' astonishing acknowledgment that immigrants with much less potential for settlement are admitted; that keeping off welfare is the only measure of adaptability; and that the Immigration Commission believes "it would not be worthwhile to make any more rigorous assessment of whether members of the family class have the ability to become established." Were they reflecting the preferences of their political masters?

*   *   *

In the meantime, the Trudeau government on June 27, 1983—just six months after publication of the Auditor General's highly critical 1982 report—established the Special Committee on Visible Minorities in Canadian Society with a mandate to seek positive ideas for the improvement of ethnic minority relationships in Canada and recommend positive programs to promote racial understanding.

With an election due in a year (September 1984), this would require a political report to be produced, but without examining the extent to which Canada's immigration policies were responsible for such problems as existed. It would never occur to politicians that shutting off the skilled and literate in the Independent Class in favour of welcoming increasing numbers of Family Class immigrants might create a negative reaction.

The following immigration figures for 1981 set out the formula for the development of racist attitudes. Recognizing that those emigrating would be accepted in countries with standards based on merit, these figures speak for themselves. It has been an uneven trade.

Immigration	128,611
Emigration	71,551
	57,060
Family Class	51,019

The Committee on Visible Minorities reported on schedule, on March 8, 1984, six months before the election. *Equality Now* was an elaborate, 150-page political document complete with photographs containing eighty recommendations for change to improve the lot of visible minorities in Canada. It was produced with considerable expenditure of public money.

Although this report emphasized evidence of immigrants of all races who successfully overcame the barriers presented by language and culture shock, it also offered testimony to the disaster of Canada's immigrant-selection processes. The executive director of SUCCESS, the United Chinese Community Enrichment Services Society, compared the problems of adjustment and language faced by a Chinese professional and a Chinese rice farmer.

There is a long process of adjusting, not only to life in a strange city, but also to work which requires totally different skills from the agricultural ones they knew in China. Their agricultural background prevented many Chinese from being exposed to much formal learning. To be thrust immediately into a language class for six hours a day is beyond their ability to concentrate. . . . Chinese immigrants come from many places around the world. Some language classes may have a lawyer or a doctor in the same class . . . with a rice farmer. We need to have two kinds of language classes to recognize the different abilities to learn.

The real and unrecognized failure was not in language training, but in our selection of these immigrants. We are not dealing
here with anyone who abused the process, but is it fair either to
Canada or to Chinese rice farmers, so ill-equipped for North
American city life, to even expose them to such trauma, or to
the likely failure of their expectations of life in Canada?

The report referred to the Regent Park community of Toronto, where the unemployment rate in 1978 was 57 per cent of
non-visible-minority youth, fifteen to twenty-four years of age.
Among visible-minority youth in the same age group it was 87
per cent. What's more, there was "no evidence . . . to suggest the
situation had changed or would be significantly different elsewhere."

This all-party Parliamentary Committee had discovered part
of the problem, but this was no time to tinker with Family Class
regulations. The problem was not race, either with respect to the
57 per cent non-visible-minority youth or the 87 per cent visible-minority young people. The committee opted for more bor-
rowed money to assist unemployed immigrant youth—at a time
when the country was failing unemployed Canadian youth.
Then, with Recommendation 29, they zeroed in on the solution:

> Employment and Immigration Canada should conduct a comprehen-
> sive study of the current situation with respect to immigrants who
> have been admitted to Canada through the family reunification plan
> to determine whether or not there are substantial differences between
> them and other immigrants in terms of their ability to successfully in-
> tegrate into Canadian society.

Wasn't that the essence of the original mandate of the Commons Committee? What a pity that not one of the seven MPs on
this anti-racist panel, selected presumably for their interest in
the subject, appears to have known of the existence of that 1982
Report of the Auditor General, *published only fifteen months
earlier.* And not one of the fifteen members of the Parliamentary
Committee staff seems to have told them about it. Of course, the
government's promise to follow through on this one sensible
recommendation was lost forever in the events of the 1984 federal election.

In the meantime, by the end of 1984, Canada's new Conservative government was experiencing the usual need of new governments to demonstrate an aggressive attitude toward administrative economies. Accordingly, Deputy Prime Minister Eric Nielsen, himself sufficiently aggressive, undertook to chair a task force comprised of both public servants and private citizens to examine the administration and operation of every government function, and to recommend necessary changes.

The immigration segment of the Nielsen Task Force, made up of representatives of business, labour and an immigration official, failed in its approach to recognize the political significance of the exercise. Instead, they concentrated on the fortunes of the nation.

In its October 1985 report, the Nielsen Task Force set out the principle that an acceptable immigration level is "highly dependent on its being seen to consist of people who readily adapt and contribute to Canada's economic and social list." But, noting that this was less and less the case, it found that "Since 1982 [the year of the Auditor General's report] Canada has stopped selecting Independent immigrants on the basis of occupations in demand in Canada" and "the most qualified immigrants are effectively barred while large numbers who are potentially less adaptable continue to arrive." In fact, it also discovered that "Selected [Independent] immigrants [had then] declined from 30 to 14 per cent of an annual movement."

The Nielsen report summed up reality with the following valid recommendations and observations. They would reorient the system towards a positive selection by Canadian visa officers abroad and increase the number of Independent immigrants with the required ability to adapt and succeed in Canada. They would raise the age of sponsorable parents to sixty; reduce that of dependent children to under eighteen from twenty-one; and require Assisted Relatives to meet the same standards as Independent immigrants, with a bonus of 10 points for family support. Further, they would emphasize procedures to prevent entry of inadmissible persons and provide for the expulsion of those in Canada without legitimate status.

It is not surprising that not one of these recommendations

would be acceptable to the political agenda. Like the Auditor General's 1982 report, they went unreported by the media, and with this failure they were unknown to the public. Indeed, like Mr. Dye's earlier work, all two linear feet of Eric Nielsen's magnum opus were quickly relegated to the shelves of our nation's libraries, where they rest to this very day, gathering dust.

In addition to their foregoing recommendations, the Nielsen study team warned that ready accessibility to social-welfare programs would serve to attract additional illegal entries, ultimately inviting another amnesty. If the selection system was altered to invite larger numbers requiring language training, settlement cost to the taxpayers would expand accordingly. They pointed out that for many years, available polling data had indicated that increased immigration was opposed by the majority of Canadians, and reflected some degree of tension and resentment, possibly racial in origin, in Toronto, Vancouver and Montreal. All of this, predictable as it was, accurately described only some of the problems that would arise in the 1990s.

On the other hand, the Nielsen report noted that virtually the entire body of organized opinion (lawyers' groups, immigration aid groups, etc.) tended to favour more immigration, relaxation of criteria and amnesties. They were describing what has become an immigration and refugee industry, perhaps the principal beneficiary of Canada's immigration policies, and, with that public profile, the usual source of media comment. Yet, like the Auditor General's 1982 report, the real significance of those comments went unnoticed by the media.

Incidentally, at the Nielsen study team session in Vancouver, one of the members, an upper-middle-level immigration official, referred to large numbers of people carrying Canadian passports with little or no active connections with Canada, but benefiting from the services of our embassies and consular offices throughout the world. She felt something must be done. Fifteen years later, in December 1998, a new Citizenship Act would finally be tabled in Parliament.

*　　*　　*

The Honourable Flora MacDonald began her term as Prime Minister Mulroney's first employment and immigration minister in September 1984. When announcing that immigration levels for 1985 would be set at between 85,000 and 90,000, she gave the usual assurances that the new government would undertake a major review of immigration policy before establishing levels for the longer term. The minister emphasized the political imperative that *reunification of family members remained a first priority*, reminding us that "There are no restrictions on the number of eligible family class members who can be admitted if they qualify."

Independent applicants would continue to face the three-year-old Axworthy requirement to have arranged employment on entry. Yes, freedom of entry to 45,000 Family Class without reference to skills or literacy and restricted entry for 13,000 (including their families) having the ability to contribute and support themselves. A crazy way to build a nation!

The minister, however, held out the usual prospect of positive change. She promised: "This temporary policy, in place since May 1982, will be more closely examined as part of the direction of immigration policy."

*   *   *

In October 1985, a Parliamentary subcommittee published *Equality for All*, a curious report recommending that special benefits usually reserved for citizens be extended to those who have rejected Canadian citizenship. The committee expressed concern that some landed immigrants might not accept citizenship after three years in Canada because advantages they enjoyed "in their country of origin may be seriously jeopardized."[2] In consequence, the committee concluded "that a permanent resident who is eligible for citizenship should not be disadvantaged because of failure to become a Canadian citizen." It recommended that the regulations "be amended so that a permanent resident who has been in Canada for at least three years is entitled to sponsor a parent without regard to age, ability to work, or marital status of that parent, as is the case if the sponsor of a parent is a Canadian Citizen."

Perhaps not understood by the committee is the effect of this proposal: it would be a denial of "equality for all", the chosen title of their report. It would, indeed, make landed immigrants quite unequal, possessed as they would be of all the benefits and advantages of their original citizenship, plus all of the benefits and advantages of Canadian citizenship, but without its accompanying responsibilities. Certainly the rest of us would be unequal by comparison. Although this strange proposal was set aside for further study, it would not be forgotten.

*   *   *

At the end of October 1985, Walter McLean, a new minister of state immigration, announced projected immigration levels for 1986 and 1987. These were set in response, he explained, to an anticipated "need to consider in the next two years significantly higher levels of immigration if we are to sustain our population growth and economic development." Though population growth was not a problem, it had become an essential part of the spin of the new Tory government and the intake for those years would be 115,000 and 125,000 respectively.

More important, following four years in immigration purgatory, skilled applicants would be returned to grace through a slight thaw of the 1982 freeze on Independent Class applicants. It would no longer be necessary to have an arranged job in Canada in order to be granted landed status. Effective January 1, 1986, the minister further announced there would be screening of Independent applicants based on Canada's occupational skills requirements.

In the meantime, following the Auditor General's 1985 report, the Immigration Commission published the paper *Family Class Immigrants to Canada, 1981–1984: Labour Force Activity Aspects*. This study, based on a consultant's telephone polling of 1,400 randomly selected immigrants, began by denying the importance of successful settlement of the Family Class. "The primary goal of Family Class immigration is social," it stated, and added that "initially their labour force participation rate is low since they are destined to a close relative who has *guaranteed to support them for up to 10 years* [emphasis added]. Therefore, when they decide to join the labour force it is often by choice and not by necessity." Its report then acknowledged reality:

After six months in Canada (Family Class) still had an unemployment rate close to double the rate of all immigrants. . . . At 16.5 per cent it was highest for the age category 35–64 . . . and highest for those from Africa, Asia, Central and South America and the Caribbean.

Not unexpectedly, Family Class immigrants earned substantially less than Independent immigrants. . . . Family Class . . . have always been at a disadvantage in terms of earnings compared to those selected for economic reasons.

Their figures were dependent in part on the 1976–77 survey covering a period before the sponsorship admission rules were broadened under the 1978 legislation. This survey showed that even then, "family class immigrant males had more than twice the unemployment rate of independent immigrants." Of those responding to the 1985 survey, 42 per cent earned below $20,000 (the low-income cutoff rate in 1985 for a family of four), and another 38 per cent earned below $10,000 (the cutoff rate for the unattached). All this the Immigration Commission apparently judged superfluous. For them, concerns that Family Class immigrants become a burden on society were unfounded, and though they registered a higher unemployment rate than other immigrants, they knew instinctively that their relatives provided the necessary economic support. Not surprising, but nonsense nevertheless. The sponsor's ten-year commitment to maintenance was meaningless for several reasons:

1. Its legal effect would be doubtful after the Sponsored immigrants achieved their Canadian citizenship—normally after three years;
2. The Department of Immigration had no enforcement capacity,

so collection of welfare by Family Class immigrants was, and is, unrestricted;

3. Like all Canadians, recently unemployed Family Class immigrants collect Employment Insurance benefits (or UIC as it was then known); and

4. Many Family Class immigrants from lands without official vital-statistics records often are able to backdate their birth dates to establish early eligibility for Canada's universal seniors' benefits. On one occasion the IAB denied a sponsorship appeal involving parents who had advanced their ages ten years so they might benefit in Canada from the Old Age Pension at fifty-five (as though they were insured with London Life). That Board decision was shot down on appeal by the Federal Court. Dishonesty about age, once accepted on an immigration document, became reality in Canada.

*　　*　　*

The continuing need to publish political reports favourable to the family carried on unabated. Next came the June 1986 *Family Reunification Report* of the Commons Standing Committee, replete with fifty-nine recommendations for streamlining policies and procedures. It not only summarized the problem, it provided a clear statement of the uncritical, indeed self-serving, political thinking of the day:

Family class immigration is based on statutory entitlement. Provided an immigrant falls within the specified categories of family class, and meets the other statutory requirements of good health, and background required of all immigrants, he or she may be landed. Family class processing, therefore, should be viewed as a largely clerical exercise. But why does the average family class take six or seven months just to process abroad and why do some cases drag on for years?

[That 1982 Auditor General's report provided part of the answer.]

In May 1982, labour market restrictions were introduced which prevented significant numbers of independent immigrants from qualifying to come to Canada. Since then, the family class has assumed even greater importance as it became the only avenue to Canada of most people.

A 1995 report of a successor Commons Committee would include an important graph, included here as Figure 2, showing relative earnings in 1988 of the immigrant classes that arrived in the years 1981 and 1985.

FIGURE 2

AVERAGE EARNINGS OF FOREIGN-BORN INDIVIDUALS WHO LANDED IN 1981 AND 1985 BY IMMIGRATION CATEGORY, 1988

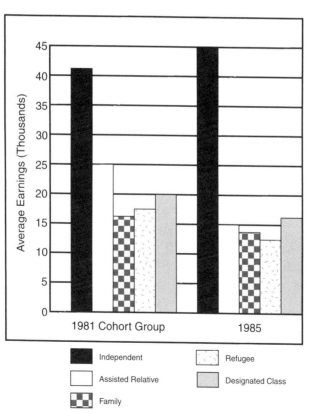

Figure 2 shows that the average annual 1988 earnings of Family Class immigrants in the workplace was $16,000 for those arriving in 1981; for the Independents it was $41,000. For those Family Class arriving in 1985, the average annual 1988 earnings was $14,000; for the Independent immigrants $45,000. This 1995 chart shows the Assisted Relatives' average incomes in 1985 to be $15,000. Assisted Relatives are essentially another categorization for Family Class immigrants.

The procedure with these committee reports is that there be a response from the government by the minister, in this case the Honourable Gerry Weiner. The following examples illustrate the emphasis on family immigration and explain the political agenda:

Committee recommendation No. 48

In its planning, External Affairs and CEIC [Canada Employment and Immigration Commission] should consider the geographic distribution of posts abroad and immigration centres in Canada. Efforts should be made to shift resources to high-volume family class posts.

The minister's response

As the number one priority in immigration processing, the Family Class category is staffed on a priority basis, both in Canada and abroad. The processing of this category abroad is carefully monitored and if there is an indication that backlogs may develop, additional officers are assigned to posts both through redeployment and from incremental sources.

Committee recommendation No. 52

Increasing the resources devoted to other immigrant categories, such as entrepreneurs, must not be at the expense of the family class.

The minister's response

The government is in full agreement with the Standing Committee's perspective.

Committee recommendations Nos. 5–10 inclusive

had to do with an involved reorganization of the whole Family Class/ Assisted Relative group designed to broaden their admissibility.

There would be a new Assisted Family Class to consist of parents with dependents, siblings and non-dependent children. Non-dependent children translated into those over nineteen and unmarried, with or without children. Those familiar with the system may be left to imagine a flood of middle-aged bachelors, some with children, arriving from those countries not having reliable vital statistics records, and followed by widows or single moms with their children to consummate recently arranged marriages.

The minister's response:

The government is sympathetic to the rationale . . . which relates to the need to provide opportunities for adult siblings to join their relatives in Canada. This movement was severely curtailed in April 1982 when a 'freeze' on independent immigrants was imposed in light of reduced labour market opportunities. Further modifications to the selection system are now being considered.

This admissibility question surfaced again on February 24, 1988 at a meeting of the Standing Committee. Attending in the role of witness was Kirk Bell, director general of immigration, policy and program development. Committee member John Oostrom, MP (Toronto Willowdale), anxious about new regulations covering recommendations 5–10 above, asked the question. Mr. Bell replied:

I think I can speak to it in enough detail to reassure you, Mr. Oostrom. The Ministers went to Cabinet, and Cabinet supported the notion that we should expand the family class. But rather than doing it in the way the committee proposed, which is to have another type of assisted relative where you had to make some economic thing, if we were going to help people, the way to really help family reunion is to expand the family class per se and to give more scope for people to be able to fit within the family class, particularly sons and daughters over 21 and any offspring they may have providing they are not married. That is the direction that is taken.

I think it makes it simpler, and it makes it easier to expand the family intake without getting caught up in points and that sort of thing again.

So I hope all the committee members will find the government's decision very positive.

They did! On May 17, 1988, near the beginning of her term as immigration minister, Barbara McDougall[3] announced the "never-married sons and daughters of any age" regulation to be effective on July 8, conveniently just four months before the November 1988 federal general election.

Fortunately for Canada this political gambit lasted only four years. The regulation was reversed in 1992, a change that was neatly described by the 1997 Immigration Legislative Review Team:

> In 1988 the Family Class was expanded to include all "never married" children. Since this could and did include a large number of effectively independent children with common-law spouses and children of their own it gradually came to be seen as contrary to the program's intent.[4]

On October 17, 1988, however, just twenty-five days before the November federal general election, Minister McDougall announced acceptance by the government of the earlier mentioned *Equality for All* recommendation extending sponsorship privileges to landed immigrants. The effect of this was that landed immigrants who had consciously rejected Canadian citizenship for their own reasons and interests were now able to sponsor parents of any age who, in turn, could bring with them all of their never-married children, and any never-married children these never-married children may have had, without regard to the ability of any to adapt to life in Canada. Further, the required ten-year commitment of support for them was now to be accepted from one who pledged neither fealty to nor continued residence in Canada. And still we continued to turn away good people who had demonstrated their ability to succeed and whose skills and expertise were in demand, even though that demand was limited.

*   *   *

On September 6, 1990, the *Vancouver Sun* carried a story about Mark Andrew, a British butcher. In the late 1970s, his wife's mother, married to a Canadian, was terminally ill in Vancouver. The Andrew family came to Canada as visitors so that Mrs. Andrew could care for her dying mother. After Mrs. Andrew's mother passed away they returned to England, leaving her stepfather in Canada. Three attempts to return as Independent immigrants failed. Immigration said there were no job vacancies for butchers in British Columbia. And despite the close personal relationship, a stepfather is not close enough to sponsor Family Class immigrants.

In 1989, Mr. Andrew obtained a temporary work permit allowing him to spend twelve months in British Columbia. His job would be to teach European butchery specialties to Canadian trainees at a Vancouver Shop Easy store owned by Mr. Au Leung. Back in Vancouver that October, the Andrew family found accommodation, and the three Andrew children, ages ten to fourteen, were enrolled in school. According to Mr. Leung, meat sales at his store soared; customers were delighted. He offered Mr. Andrew a three-year contract as senior butcher. However, as Mr. Andrew explained to the press: "I'm not allowed to take it. I've also had about ten other positions offered." To fulfil Canadian immigration requirements, there was the usual demand that his job be advertised nationally. Two applicants—one was a chef and the other someone looking for part-time work—were unsuitable. Asked about the various job offers to Mr. Andrew, Lynn Jackson of the Canada Employment Centre referred to the butcher-training program at Vancouver Community College as a source for firms seeking meat cutters.

A three-year contract offer, ten other job offers, a failed national advertising program and a storekeeper's need for an experienced butcher were rejected in favour of an unknown prospective graduate from a college, which, according to its principal, had no difficulty in placing its graduates. The Andrew family again returned to England, where Mr. Andrew said he would learn French to build his eligibility point score. For all we know, he is still studying French.

*   *   *

Janet Gabites,[5] also employed in Canada under a work permit, is a graduate in science from a New Zealand university. She entered Canada as a student in 1980 and subsequently won her master's degree at the University of British Columbia, where she was employed under permit as a research assistant in the Department of Geological Sciences.

In 1984, established in Canada, she applied for landed status and was rejected. In the summer of 1988 her work permit was cancelled. For her to remain in Canada, her job would have to survive the usual trans-Canada advertising program. Because the research project in Earth and Ocean Sciences in which she was engaged depended on annual grants, there was really nothing to advertise, and certainly no money to pay the costs of transporting applicants from around the country to interviews in Vancouver. A victim of the system, Ms. Gabites fought to stay. Meanwhile, her job, protected for a Canadian, was not filled.

After a year without income, and hundreds of hours of bureaucratic time devoted to attempting to send her back to New Zealand, she was finally landed and she returned to her job. She is one case of a good immigrant who managed, where so many others had failed, to beat back a regime of regulations prejudiced not only against her but against the future of Canada. Ten years later, she is established as a valuable university employee.

* * *

The admission of the Andrew family would have been consistent with the general view of the 1985 Macdonald Royal Commission on the Economic Union and Development Prospects for Canada. The commission's section on immigration emphasizes the desirability of relatively young, well-qualified, educated applicants, better suited to exercise flexibility in employment than candidates with more specific occupational qualifications. The Macdonald Commission recommended that "Canada should now place more weight on general labour-market skills of potential immigrants, and less on narrow occupational requirements", stressing that the "criteria for selection of immigrants facilitate their absorption into Canadian society."

The Macdonald Commission's general position was reinforced in a 1989 joint publication of Employment Canada and the British Columbia government entitled *Job Futures—An Occupational Outlook to 1995*. This report focussed on the impact of technology on the workplace and the increasing need for improved levels of basic skills, and emphasized that those with greater knowledge would be more adaptable to the changes necessary for tomorrow's jobs. None of these considerations would be given priority in existing immigration policy.

* * *

While Ms. Gabites and Mr. Andrew were fighting their battles to stay in Canada, tens of thousands of Family Class immigrants passed easily through immigration, to say nothing of the thousands of bogus refugees who "were being landed under the Administrative Review on the same day they were being evaluated."[6]

When the Refugee Backlog Clearance Program was announced in 1986, the minister gave assurance that all claimants would have work permits, and that those found not to be refugees would enjoy compassionate consideration. Under this latest amnesty or so-called Administrative Review, Ms. Gabites, for example, could have been accepted. She need not have lost over a year's work. After eight years legally in Canada, and with her favourable employment record, compassion might have applied—but only if she had made a fraudulent refugee claim. Political persecution in New Zealand? Why not? The Immigration Appeal Board and its successor tribunal, the Immigration and Refugee Board, have heard everything else.

* * *

Thousands of applications are denied on the convenient premise of preserving jobs for Canadians. Yet under sponsorship we admit tens of thousands of immigrants annually without reference to the ability of any of them to take a job. The 1990 government immigration target was 200,000 (213,334 were admitted).

It would swell to 220,000 for 1991 (232,020 were admitted) because of increasing numbers of sponsored refugees and sponsored (Family Class) relatives, we were told, and an increase in the average family size of these applicants.

In August 1990, the government announced a two-month hiatus in the issuing of visas. Because of the priorities enjoyed by Family Class and refugee applicants, however, presumably those cut would be the Independents. Indeed they were the ones. Five months later, on January 29, 1991, Minister McDougall announced that the General Occupations list for Independent applicants would be temporarily closed as of January 30, 1991. Nothing made sense any more!

*　　*　　*

For several years, immigration ministers received advice from the Canada Employment and Immigration Advisory Council. This august body consisted of twenty-six members selected from across Canada, a staff of ten, plus twenty-eight professors and four others each with special qualifications who were all listed as consultants. In March 1991, having been disbanded in one of Finance Minister Mazankowski's budgets, this council submitted its final report to the immigration minister. Two paragraphs of this astonishing document confirm that this expensive fringe organization had outlived its purpose:

> With regard to the economic cost-benefit aspects of immigration, it is found that expensive econometric studies based on huge macro-models, unless carefully modified, are incapable of producing useful or reliable conclusions, as has been shown by study after study of that nature since the 1970s. The conclusions of these studies, as is very well known to economists and policy makers, are more dependent upon the assumptions made than upon the structure of the model. If the assumptions are unrealistic (e.g. immigrants have the same labour force participation rates as residents and the same levels of education) or ignore crucial variables (such as billions in investment capital brought into the country, or the different consumption patterns of immigrants in their initial years), the results of such studies can only

misinform and confuse. Even experts face doubts on the findings of such studies.

When all micro-economic factors point in one direction, that immigrants contribute positively, how could macro-economic studies say that at best the impact is neutral? There is ample evidence that immigrants create more jobs than they take, contribute more to the treasury than they receive, start more enterprises than the average Canadian, are more educated and mobile, and eventually have comparable levels of income and lower unemployment rates. Yet the public at large is not fully cognizant of these facts and no communication strategy designed to inform and educate the public is in place.[7]

Another campaign to market and sell immigration policies was well beyond the planning stage. In 1993, as the Mulroney era ended, immigration would rise to 255,939.

An Angus Reid Associates study, prepared for Mrs. McDougall (see Chapter VII), revealed, among other things, that the public remains both uninformed and misinformed about both immigration and populations issues. This book is aimed at closing, at least in part, this information gap, and starting a long overdue public debate on a matter crucial to Canada's future. It is not targeted at those who, having recognized the advantages and benefits of Canadian citizenship, have taken advantage of our government's ludicrous immigration policies.

ENDNOTES

1. Immigration to Canada, 1969–1978

1969	161,531
1970	147,713
1971	121,900
1972	122,006
1973	**184,200**
1974	**218,465**
1975	**187,881**
1976	149,429
1977	114,914
1978	86,313

2. The Citizenship Act of 1976 provided that adult permanent residents might apply for citizenship after three or more years, thus reducing the number of years from the traditional five.

3. Mrs. McDougall was to serve as minister of employment and immigration from March 31, 1988 until April 21, 1991.

4. Robert Trempe, Susan Davis, Roslyn Kunin, *Not Just Numbers: A Canadian Framework for Future Immigration,* pp. 404–424.

5. Ms. Gabites has agreed to the publication of this account.

6. 1987–1988 Annual Report, Employment and Immigration. Ottawa, p. B4.

7. *Immigration in the 1990s: Canada Employment and Immigration Advisory Council.* Ottawa, March 1991. Pp. 9–10.

CHAPTER IV

REFUGEES: CANADA'S LONGEST LINEUP

"Headquarters is aware of unlawful means used by prospective immigrants to gain entry to Canada. However, the Commission has not established an information and analysis system that would permit it to assess the extent of the problem and take the appropriate steps to curb abuses."

Report of the Auditor General of Canada
for the year ending March 31, 1982

Canadians who remember the 1980 revelation by Immigration Minister Lloyd Axworthy that Canada's refugee-determination system was in trouble, will also recall the subsequent nine years of tortuous progress towards a new refugee policy, involving two governments, seven ministers, three independent advisory reports and a plethora of back-room spin doctors scurrying to generate acceptable explanations for it all. Those Canadians will also recall that 1988 legislation, effective January 1, 1989, creating the Immigration and Refugee Board (IRB), promised to solve for all time the immigration and refugee problems that had so beset the nation. Once again the participants failed.

Kenneth Dye, the Auditor General, again dealt with immigration in his report for the year ending March 31, 1990. When publishing that report, covering only fifteen months' operations of the new and revised IRB, he described those operations as "close to collapse" and, yet again, there was a reaction from neither the government nor members of the opposition nor the media. The Board, unperturbed, has continued operations in its "close to collapsed" state with little hope of resuscitation.

In this context, there is reason to wonder how we have arrived at the point where, ten years later, another Auditor General reports the Immigration and Refugee Board to be in crisis—and a minister's Advisory Committee, appointed to provide solutions for all the problems, recommends a complete overhaul of Canada's immigration and refugee policies.

*   *   *

In 1978, the new Immigration Act established a formal definition of a refugee in Canadian law as that set out in the 1951 United Nations Convention, and as amended by the 1967 Protocol. It appears as Article 2(1) in the Act.

'Convention refugee' means any person who, by reason of a well-founded fear of persecution for reasons of race, religion, nationality, membership in a particular social group or political opinion,

(a) is outside the country of his nationality and unable or, by reason of such fear, unwilling to avail himself of the protection of that country, or

(b) not having a country of nationality, is outside the country of his former habitual residence and is unable or, by reason of such fear, unwilling to return to that country.

It is important to understand what this means. The definition deals with "any person . . . unable to avail himself" of the protection of his or her country's laws. The definition refers to individual circumstances, but does not apply to those suffering distress resulting from internal civil conflict.

Ambassador William Bauer, a distinguished public servant, was honoured by the Baltic Federation of Canada and the Canadian Polish Congress for his work in the cause of freedom. He was a recipient of the prestigious Raoul Wallenberg Award for work on behalf of Soviet Jews and in the cause of human rights. In 1991, retired, he joined the Immigration and Refugee Board. Dissatisfied with Board performance, he resigned in 1994, and wrote at some length about its operations in a November 12, 1994 article in the *Globe and Mail*. In his article he analysed the definition of a refugee:

> The law does provide for exceptions. If, for example, claimants committed atrocities, engaged in criminal conduct or were persecutors, they do not deserve protection and must be deported. If they received protection in another country, they do not need Canadian protection and should not receive it.
>
> We all know of the masses of people—Rwandans, Afghanis, Ethiopians, Somalis, Sudanese, Bosnians—who have fled famine, civil war or the cruelty of their fellow countrymen. Twenty years ago, UN records say, there were about 2.5 million such people; today there are 26 million.
>
> Most of these people do not fit the legal definition of refugees. They may be victims of immense hardship. They may suffer persecution or death. But if they have not been singled out because of one of the five grounds—if, for example, they have not been starved because they are of a certain ethnic origin or religion—they are not refugees under Canadian law.

Three years earlier, on October 7, 1991, the question before the United Nations High Commission for Refugees (UNHCR) meeting in Geneva was whether to broaden the Convention Refugee definition to include those suffering as a result of civil strife in their home countries. Refugee advocacy groups and their lobbyists from African and Latin American countries had sought a wider interpretation so that refuge could be provided to more of those in need. Gerald Shannon, Canada's Permanent Representative to the UN in Geneva, substituting for an ailing Immigration Minister Bernard Valcourt, presented Canada's position in unmistakably clear and specific terms. In cautioning that the international community must "resist forcibly"[1] any such view, Mr. Shannon said:

> To expand the convention, in an era of severely restricted resources,

would serve only to disadvantage those who are most in need by further diluting available funds. . . . If the refugee definition is drawn too broadly we risk defining the problem into complete unmanageability.

Order and control must be reestablished over migrating movements. Not to do so will result in the loss of domestic public support, which is so critical in our efforts to assist true refugees.

Mr. Shannon told the UNHCR meeting that Canada supported the idea of international agreements requiring countries to adopt standardized refugee-screening procedures to prevent "asylum shopping" and "to ensure that the convention is applied fairly and efficiently." He emphasized the generous nature of Canada's refugee-determination system, and added:

. . . Can we tolerate the inefficiency, in fact the implicit inhumanity, of spending thousands of dollars each on individuals who manage to reach our territory, whether or not they are the most deserving of our help?

The reality is that the many millions more who never succeed in moving more than a few kilometres from home receive only a few dollars from the international community. We must ask ourselves whether, in good conscience, we should allow this kind of distortion to continue.

Canada's contribution to the United Nations High Commission on Refugees was then $35 million;[2] the budget of the Immigration and Refugee Board was $79 million. In addition, there are the costs of the parallel services of the Immigration Department and the expenditures by all three levels of government for welfare, health care and ESL to the thousands waiting in the wings.

Following nearly three years of operation by the Convention Refugee Determination Division (CRDD) of the IRB, Mr. Shannon, the Canadian diplomat, had set out on behalf of Canada a policy that little resembled the agenda of Canada's government. What would the presentation to the UNHCR have been had the minister, and not the diplomat, represented our country?

* * *

To separate the genuine refugees from the fraudulent, the 1978 Act established an elaborate, time-consuming and expensive process for determining refugee status. For the refugee claimant it began with an "Examination under Oath", during which the claimant was led through a series of questions and given an opportunity to state the basis of the refugee claim—always with the right to counsel and the opportunity to edit the transcript for accuracy.

That transcript was examined by the newly established Refugee Status Advisory Committee, working with United Nations advisors. RSAC findings were in the form of recommendations to the minister, in whose name these decisions were made. As such, RSAC recommendations were never published. For those whose claim was rejected by the minister, there was the right of appeal to the Immigration Appeal Board. The applications for refugee redetermination were read by three members of the Board and hearings granted if only one of those members felt there was even the possibility the appeal might succeed. The hearings were seldom granted and, when they were, almost never succeeded. But then, success before the Board was seldom the objective of filing an appeal.

The right to such appeals of these decisions had been quickly recognized as an opportunity for fraudulent claimants to remain in Canada for extended periods of time, perhaps forever. That opportunity came in two stages, the first described above. The second stage was the right of appeal from negative Board decisions to the Federal Court of Canada. The extent of the abuse of this right is reflected in the hearing lists of that court. The list in the Toronto court for the period August 15 to September 26, 1983 reports that of 238 scheduled hearings, 224 were immigration appeals. This was the final opportunity for bogus claimants to legally extend their stay in Canada. But with no legitimate case to present, there was no advantage in keeping their date with the court. The court, in turn, scheduled hearings at up to twenty a day in a single courtroom.

Most appellants had either returned home, fraudulently obtained a duplicate citizenship card from a look-alike relative or gone underground in Canada. The backlog would continue to grow out of control, and one more amnesty was predictable.

*   *   *

Having recognized a problem, then Immigration Minister Lloyd Axworthy had earlier appointed a Task Force on Immigration Practices and Procedures, chaired by Vancouver lawyer W. G. Robinson.[3] Its report, *The Refugee Status Determination Process*, was released by the minister on November 18, 1981. Significantly, it included a detailed submission by the Canadian branch office of the United Nations High Commission for Refugees. The UNHCR emphasized the importance of an oral hearing for every claimant. Consistent with this counsel, the task force recommended establishment of a full hearing process at the first level of refugee determination, and the replacement of the three-stage refugee-determination process by a single body to hear and decide all refugee claims. That significant recommendation was to percolate for another eight years.

On releasing the report, the minister said: "There is real need for change in procedures and I am prepared to respond to that need by implementing some of the report's recommendations now." Several positive procedural changes were listed and there would be a national symposium on the protection of refugees in Canada. All this, however, would take time, a lot of time. The backlog of claimants was 1,500.

Seventeen months later, on May 2, 1983, in response to a friendly query in the Commons about progress in processing refugee claims, the minister assured the House that, commencing that day, in Toronto and Montreal, oral hearings would begin before members of the Refugee Status Advisory Committee. He said this would "make a substantial inroad into the backlog." The backlog was then 3,500.

Another seven months later, on November 25, 1983, a new

immigration minister, John Roberts, issued an effusive press release. He had instructed his officials to develop new measures to improve the system for assessing refugee claims in order "to reduce the current backlog by the end of 1985." His department would prepare a series of new policy options. The backlog had nearly trebled to 9,000. The system didn't work. The minister was only seeking options.

Remedial steps included $1 million to provide work for 2,500 claimants in Montreal; $50,000 to serve the indigent among them; welfare costs would be shared with the provinces; and overtime for staff was approved.

Having described a looming disaster, the minister felt confident to assert his determination to retain the strengths of what he described as the fairest and most humane refugee-claims system in the world. He appointed Professor Ed Ratushny of the University of Ottawa to study and make recommendations. Dr. Ratushny, a member of the original 1980 task force, was eminently qualified. His mandate was to develop "a new Refugee Status Determination Process for Canada."

Most people, having read the minister's statement above, would have been led to believe that the officials of the Immigration Department were doing just that. But then there was the bothersome timing of an election within a year and Mr. Roberts, in anticipation of that 1984 election, would be a candidate for leader of the governing Liberal Party.

Professor Ratushny's report was delivered to the minister in May 1984. This was yet another paper by a thoughtful, respected and knowledgable student of the subject, containing an abundance of material, potentially of inestimable value to those charged with rewriting the existing legislation. Professor Ratushny found the current process encumbered by critical shortcomings which needed to be expeditiously addressed. His report included valuable observations; however, the looming fall election would preclude any of them influencing political fortunes.

Professor Ratushny underlined the unfortunate vulnerability and attraction of refugee-assistance programs offering survival benefits to migrants not at risk of persecution but seeking improved economic conditions. He highlighted the serious and well-known problem of non-meritorious refugee claimants, suggesting the need to limit direct access to Canada as a place of refuge in order to ensure that asylum is available to those in real need. And he used as an example the near crisis in 1980 when Canada faced an influx of people from "one region in India", all of whom made refugee claims, each of which was found to be manifestly unfounded. The delays and the threat of collapse of the system had been avoided by the imposition of visitor visa requirements to travel from India, a strategy immigration ministers are increasingly hesitant to use.

Professor Ratushny particularly emphasized the importance of early oral hearings with the observation that "a central focal point in almost any assessment of the fairness of the existing process continues to be the absence of any effective oral hearing." Despite this authoritative emphasis it would be another year before the Supreme Court of Canada reached a similar conclusion, compelling attention, if not immediate action, to correct this injustice.

The professor also emphasized the importance of the quality of the decision-maker and credited the members of the Refugee Status Advisory Committee with specialized knowledge and experience. To this he added the importance of participation, in an advisory capacity, of permanent representatives in Canada of the UNHCR. (Yet, when the new Immigration and Refugee Board finally began its operation on January 1, 1989, many RSAC members and experienced and competent members of the Immigration Appeal Board were eliminated, and their United Nations advisors completely sacrificed.) In the meantime, with the 1984 election on the horizon, and presaging what was to become a tradition with immigration ministers, John Roberts dodged his responsibility and opted for still another study.

The minister asked Rabbi Gunther Plaut of Toronto to assess public reaction to Professor Ratushny's findings and to present a final report suggesting, if necessary, yet another new refugee-determination process. To those the minister had requested to participate in a dialogue with Rabbi Plaut, he wrote of his long-held concern with the problems created by the existing refugee-determination process in Canada, indicating that legislative and regulatory change might be required. He was right about that.

It was now nearly four years since Minister Axworthy, in September 1980, had correctly discerned an impending disaster and created the first task force. Under Minister Roberts the backlog had expanded from 9,000 to 15,000.

Rabbi Plaut, a refugee from Nazi Germany and a recipient of the Order of Canada, is a distinguished Canadian. Taking his duties seriously, he failed to recognize that he had been drawn into the time-honoured political game of delay and avoidance. In July he asked those who had shown interest to make their submissions by August. The matter, he wrote, "was urgent and pressing." His thoroughly competent report was in the hands of the new Progressive Conservative immigration minister, Flora MacDonald, as 1984 was ending. She shelved it. On April 4, 1985, the Supreme Court, in the *Singh* decision, ruled that oral hearings were required in every refugee-determination case.

*   *   *

The *Singh* decision of the Supreme Court of Canada signalled the urgency of major changes in the legislation, and it is important that it be understood. This decision involved six Sikhs and a Guyanese. The Federation of Canadian Sikh Societies and the Canadian Council of Churches were interveners.

Six of the appellants were citizens of India who claimed Convention Refugee status on the basis of their fear of persecution by Indian authorities as a result of their political activities and beliefs, particularly their association with the Akali Dal Party, which was demanding independence for the Indian state of Punjab. Harbhajan Singh, Sandu Singh Thandi, Charanjit Singh Gill and Satnam Singh had been refused admission at the border; Paramjit Singh Mann eluded inquiry when he came to Canada in July 1971; and Kuwal Singh arrived as a "visitor" with temporary status in 1980. Irandi [full name], the Guyanese, came in 1979 on a false passport and was granted visitor status until November 30, 1979. She was arrested in March 1981 for working illegally.

Each had claimed refugee status in Canada. All had been denied by the minister on the advice of the Refugee Status Advisory Committee. The Immigration Appeal Board denied subsequent applications for redetermination, and the Federal Court of Appeal refused their applications for judicial review of these decisions.

In its turn, the Supreme Court of Canada heard the appeal from these refusals on April 4, 1985. Based on the principles of fairness and fundamental justice and invoking the Canadian Charter of Rights and Freedoms, the court found that these rights apply to any person in Canada, regardless of their status. Thus the right of refugee claimants to an oral hearing of their refugee claims was finally established in law.

This obvious requirement had been found necessary by the United Nations High Commission on Refugees and had been recommended in the 1981 Robinson report, in the 1984 Ratushny report and in the 1984 Plaut report. It would be neglected by a succession of immigration ministers, except for token application, for four more years until it became fully effective in the new legislation on January 1, 1989.

The form of the hearing was, fortuitously, dealt with six weeks later in a decision of Chief Justice Nathan Nemetz of the British Columbia Court of Appeal. A related case, in which the *Singh* decision applied, involved administrative tribunals and the scope of a hearing necessary to meet the requirements of fairness and fundamental justice. The Court of Appeal recognized that the circumstances of the case could require a full formal hearing or, at minimum, a simple hearing involving the opportunity to respond to and have notice of the case to be met.

Because of the significance of these decisions, pertinent extracts of the reasoning of each court are set out in the notes.[4]

The well-reasoned judgment of the Supreme Court of Canada and the similarly clear decision of the British Columbia Court of Appeal did two things. First, the Supreme Court solidly confirmed the 1981 conclusions of Mr. Axworthy's task force, as well as the conclusions of the 1984 Ratushny report commissioned by Mr. Roberts, of the need to introduce oral hearings into the refugee-determination process. Second, the reasoning of Chief Justice Nemetz established that the circumstances of the case determined the scope of the process. The principles of fundamental justice require a hearing, notice to the subject of the case to be met and the opportunity of the subject to respond. All of this should be sufficient for competent officials at the border to conduct a face-to-face hearing across a desk and immediately separate the purely fraudulent and frivolous claimants from those whose circumstances demand a more broadly based procedure.

*   *   *

Confronted by a crisis brought about by the *Singh* decision, Minister MacDonald asked Rabbi Plaut to make appropriate amendments to his report. He did, in two weeks, returning his new report on April 17, 1985. Incredibly, the minister delayed its release until late in June, just as Parliament rose for the summer. Rabbi Plaut had produced a monumental and valuable document of 200 pages centred on three proposed models for a completely new process. His report included detailed observations, both philosophical and practical, on procedures to be followed in each stage. Six months after first receiving his report, Ms. MacDonald lavishly commended the Rabbi for his work and promised a legislative package in the fall. One more minister, one more report and one more delay. And endless waves of bogus refugees washing across our unprotected borders.

*   *   *

Canada must recover the power and prerogative to decide who shall come into this country. Clearly the legal right to be heard does not mean that thousands of migrants with specious claims should be allowed to plug our refugee-determination system. Our worldwide reputation is one of fairness. Regulations that allow for the application of this characteristic, and at the same time eliminate the flagrant abuse of our border, require no more than the political courage to ensure the strict, swift enforcement of the law.

When Premier Sterling Lyon of Manitoba insisted on including the "notwithstanding" clause in the Charter of Rights and Freedoms, it was for the purpose of recovering legislative control when Charter interpretations were in conflict with the greater interests of the nation. To recover the ability to control Canada's border and decide at the border who will and who will not enter is an appropriate function of this special clause. The "notwithstanding" clause and the procedures for its application are described in the document *How Canadians Govern Themselves: A Federal State* (apparently written by the late Senator Eugene Forsey, a recognized constitutional authority, it is available on the Government of Canada's Internet site):[5]

> The fundamental, legal and equality rights in the Charter are subject to a 'notwithstanding' clause. This allows Parliament, or a provincial legislature, to pass a law violating any of these rights (except the equality right that prohibits discrimination based on sex) simply by inserting in such law a declaration that it shall operate notwithstanding the fact that it is contrary to this or that provision of the Charter. Any such law can last only five years, but it can be reenacted for further periods of five years. Any such legislation must apply equally to men and women.

Invoking the "notwithstanding" clause with respect to entry into Canada would provide Canada's border officials with the authority to refuse entry to patently fraudulent applicants.

*   *   *

Handed down nearly two years after the recommendations of Minister Axworthy's first task force, the *Singh* decision demanded action. But tinkering with the large ethnic vote was not on the agenda of either the new government (despite its huge majority) or its neophyte immigration minister, Flora MacDonald.

Nor were they moved to action when the refugee crisis brought forth this clearly stated critical analysis in the 1985 report of the Nielsen Task Force:

> What can best be described as an assault on our system for refugee asylum and appeals has led to a situation where virtually anyone refused admission or discovered overstaying in Canada can claim recognition as a refugee. This makes a rapid determination of well-founded cases impossible.
>
> The refugee determination system is quite incapable of handling 700 new claims a month on top of a backlog of 20,000 persons. The delays are such that a claimant is virtually assured of a stay in Canada, with permission to work or receive welfare, for at least 40 months before the claim is settled. With a rapidly rising backlog, the period of grace will only lengthen. To date, only about 30% of claims are upheld, but by the time they have all been heard, it will be politically difficult to remove from Canada the by then entrenched, unsuccessful claimants. This situation not only places a costly burden on resources, it attracts increasing numbers of would-be settlers the longer it persists.
>
> Any new refugee claims determination system must be both fair and expeditious. For those truly needing protection, it should be given without delay. But fair immigration procedures should not give unlimited access to those with no well-founded claim to be refugees nor to the deceitful who purport to be visitors with the intention of becoming permanent residents.
>
> One part of the solution is for visitors' visas to be required for nationals of most countries. A more important element in the solution is to provide that claims for refugee status be made only when the person is abroad, except for those in 'hot flight' (i.e. arriving by direct transport from the country which they are fleeing).

This task force pointed out that the annual costs of pending welfare support, language training and settlement services, largely to indigent refugees, had increased in 1985 to $100 million. Further, the annual welfare cost of the then 20,000 claimants in the backlog was $38 million.

Nine years later, in 1994, the minister's deputies, in a report to the minister, listed the welfare costs for Family Class immigrants whose sponsors had failed to live up to their commitments at $700 million annually. It is probable that welfare costs for refugee claimants were also in that region, and that ESL charges would reach $350 million annually. Adult language costs and medical and dental care suggest a total bill for social benefits in the $2 billion range. If the Nielsen Task Force could see what was happening, and the bureaucracy was measuring the costs, why has a series of governments failed so completely to deal with the facts?

For the task force, two steps were necessary: first, an Administrative Review to determine how many claimants may be appropriately landed; second, the appointment of a large temporary panel to clear up the claims backlog. It recommended assembling, for two years, a task force of 50 refugee-claims judges working independently, or 150 working as three-member panels, to cost $3 million on a single-member basis or $9 million on a three-member basis.

This would have been a bargain for Canadian taxpayers, particularly in a period when deficits were also building to a crisis stage. But it was a bargain the Mulroney government wouldn't buy. It would be another eight months before an exploding backlog would force the establishment of an Administrative Review, and the yet-to-be established Immigration and Refugee Board would eventually grow to 279 members, with an annual budget of $90 million, largely for refugee determination. The Nielsen Task Force had recognized what should have been obvious to politicians: the solution to long lineups was to open more wickets.

On the other hand, it was evident to the pro-immigration lobby that a clogged system would assure another amnesty. Armed with this insight, certain unscrupulous immigration consultants peddled Canadian citizenship on the black market to the Portuguese, Turks, Trinidadians and others. A refugee claim would provide welfare, medical care and, eventually, citizenship—all guaranteed by these black marketeers. It was profitable, it worked and the "refugees" poured in.

In the fall of 1985, thousands of Portuguese began arriving at Pearson International Airport, falsely claiming refugee status on the grounds of religious persecution as members of the Jehovah's Witnesses. Walter McLean, minister of state immigration,[6] made the appropriate gestures, with the stated intention of taking legal action. He asked the director general of the Ontario region to set up a system to monitor specific cases where the so-called "immigration consultants" counsel fraud. Minister McLean said, "we want to alert people that this process is going on so they think twice before they enter into these kind of dealings." He ordered the move because of "deliberate and persistent abuse of the refugee determination process in Canada." If this abuse continued, he was considering placing a visa restriction on travel from Portugal.

This minister of the Crown couldn't let himself get close enough to those involved in a gross abuse of Canada's border to even rap the knuckles of either the Canadian or Portuguese abusers, so he allowed the abuse to continue for another eight months before taking action.

Immigration officers, working long and stressful days clearing the airports of refugee claimants, pleaded repeatedly for visa restrictions at the source. Finally, Cabinet, overcoming the fear of offending those whose nationals were criminally abusing both our border and our hospitality, passed an Order-in-Council imposing visa restrictions, but applicable only to Portugal-Canada travel. Meanwhile, officials were developing short-cut solutions to deal with the increasing numbers. The long delayed "Administrative Review" (obfuscatory terminology for an amnesty) would deal with all claims filed to date. Designed to accept about eight out of ten frauds, it was justified on the grounds the backlog would be cleared for new legislation to be in place on April 1, 1987. April 1st is always a significant date. The Portuguese visa restrictions and the Administrative Review were to be announced and were to be effective on May 21, 1986. The statement had already been circulated to Members of Parliament but when read by Minister McLean in the House, the Portuguese visa provision was abruptly excluded. Why?

The Ontario Tory caucus, concerned for their Portuguese votes, had reached the prime minister's office. The Order-in-Council imposing visa restrictions on travellers from Portugal was suspended. Not a single Member of Parliament challenged this government failure to act in Canada's interest. Indeed, Sergio Marchi, then Liberal opposition immigration critic, upbraided the government, exclaiming his amazement the government had even considered restrictions. "Fortunately," he said, "due to pressure, it decided to reverse itself at the eleventh hour. Notwithstanding this decision, I believe the minister has besmirched the good name of an ally and owes the Portuguese-Canadian community an apology."

The Portuguese continued to arrive, claiming religious persecution. The backlog continued to grow out of control. In July, just two months after having failed to read the visa message to Parliament, and with the Portuguese component of the backlog exceeding 5,000 bogus claims, the government resurrected that Order-in-Council and imposed the necessary restrictions on travel from Lisbon to Canada.

The foregoing story about the Ontario Tory Caucus is, of course, subject to challenge. The late Moira Farrow, the *Vancouver Sun*'s competent and responsible immigration reporter, checked with the former Tory caucus chairman, John Reimer, and in an article published December 22, 1989, reported his response:

> . . . I can tell you that I and other Ontario MPs at that time were receiving a lot of contradictory advice from our Portuguese constituents about how to deal with the situation and there was concern about offending people. . . . Feelings were very intense. However, we felt in the end that visa restrictions should be imposed and that was done. I personally agree . . . that they should have been imposed earlier.

Unfortunately, this visa decision was not to be taken as a precedent. The arrival of the first planeload of Turks at Mirabel airport late in 1986, with similar bogus claims, indicated another fraudulent operation. It was the duty of the appropriate minister, foreign affairs or immigration, to immediately advise the Turkish ambassador of at least the temporary imposition of visa restrictions on Turkey-Canada travel, to request support and to give assurance of a return to normal relations as soon as control had been recovered. Three years later, 2,600 Turks in the backlog were a measure of that particular failure.[7]

Early in 1988, larcenous Canadian immigration consultants took their message to Trinidad-Tobago, where the attractions of Canada's social-support system and the prospects of citizenship were just as appealing as they had been to the Portuguese and the Turks. A fraudulent flow of "refugees" quickly became a flood. Aircraft from Trinidad to Toronto arrived fully loaded and returned practically empty. In March, the Canadian High Commission briefed the Honourable Sahadeo Basdeo, the Trinidad-Tobago minister of external affairs. Mr. Basdeo could not understand Canada's failure to close the flow with the imposition of visa restrictions. But then, he might not have understood that there was to be a federal election in Canada in November 1988 and that there was a large Caribbean vote to be courted, some of it in the Toronto St. Paul's constituency of the latest immigration minister, Barbara McDougall.

With the advance announcement of changes in refugee-determination procedures under the new legislation to be effective January 1, 1989, the numbers in the refugee backlog continued to multiply. No one was in charge of the shop. Then, in November and December 1988, the *Globe and Mail* published a series of articles exposing the obvious contempt of Canada's ministers of foreign affairs and of immigration for Canada's border. After this, and after the election, visa restrictions on travel from Trinidad-Tobago followed on December 11, but not until 14,800 Trinidadians had been added to the backlog. It is ludicrous to think any were refugees; it is probable that few met Canada's admissions standards; and it is certain their presence represented unnecessary costs to the Canadian taxpayer. Not a single Member of Parliament spoke out with a word of criticism.

*   *   *

Roysie Francois, his wife Pamela and daughter Sharlene arrived in Canada from Trinidad on a three-month visitors' visa in the fall of 1988. They applied for refugee status on December 29. This placed them in the pre-January 1, 1989 backlog. Nearly two years later, on November 5, 1990, they were summoned to the hearing of their refugee claim before a two-member panel, one an adjudicator under the Immigration Act and the other a member of the Immigration and Refugee Board. Under the special regulations applying to backlog claimants, a favourable decision gave the right to apply for permanent residence in Canada. (Persecutions as defined by the United Nations Convention on Refugees were unknown in Trinidad.)

The Francois family claimed psychological problems caused by the two-year delay in hearing their case. The adjudicator found that, under the Charter of Rights and Freedoms, the effect of the two-year delay was to violate their right to psychological security and ruled in their favour. The IRB member rejected their claim on the basis of the evidence relating to conditions in Trinidad. Under the rule, a split decision favoured the refugee claimant.

The implications of this decision were that, as a Board precedent, it was an invitation to thousands in the backlog to make similar claims of "psychological damage" and so to win the right to remain in Canada. Under the Family Class sponsorship policy, they could then be followed by their extended families without any consideration of the ability of any of them to successfully settle in Canada.

*   *   *

There are countless other blatant examples of the abuse which has been allowed to continue since the 1978 legislation formalized the refugee-determination process, or since Minister Axworthy acknowledged the incipient problem in 1980 and opted for a course of study. From some countries there has been a steady flow of bogus refugees who have used the lengthy appeals process to remain in Canada for long periods, many permanently, and so circumvent the selection requirements of the immigration regulations.

Table 2A sets out the Refugee Status Advisory Committee record of those from India, Jamaica and the Dominican Republic. These figures are taken from the internal records of the former Refugee Status Advisory Committee. This is believed to be the first time they have been available to the public in any form.

If nothing else, Table 2A shows that by 1981 the world had recognized the absence of political will on the part of the Trudeau government to control Canada's border. Over the eleven years, 1977–1988, of the 1,480 claims from Jamaica and the Dominican Republic, none were found to be genuine; and of 3,563 from India, only six were accepted as genuine, described in a communication from the registrar of the RSAC as "special cases". Yet from each of these countries, claims continued to be filed regularly, with opportunists from around the globe following a similar pattern.

Under the succeeding Convention Refugee Determination Division of the new Immigration and Refugee Board (involving a completely new philosophy and administration), the worldwide contempt and derision for the Canadian process would be extended. The records include new statistical columns headed "Withdrawn or Abandoned". Increasing numbers of refugee claimants were filing claims with no intention of appearing for their required hearing. Canada's "open door" policy had taken on new meaning. Table 2B sets out the records of India, Jamaica and the Dominican Republic, including the new statistical heading.

Would it be a risk to speculate that the claims allowed in the post-1988 period did not vary from those rejected in the previous period, or that many of those claimants, either refused or abandoned, are still in Canada living with questionable identification documents?

The clandestine arrival of Sikhs on the shores of Nova Scotia, and Tamils in Newfoundland in 1986, offered solid opportunities for the Mulroney government to send powerful signals that Canadians were again in charge of their border. Teams

TABLE 2A

REFUGEE STATUS ADVISORY COMMITTEE RECORD OF REFUGEE CLAIMS FROM INDIA, JAMAICA AND THE DOMINICAN REPUBLIC IN THE PERIOD 1977 TO 1988.

Year	INDIA			JAMAICA			DOMINICAN REPUBLIC		
	Claims Received	Claims Decided	Claims Allowed	Claims Received	Claims Decided	Claims Allowed	Claims Received	Claims Decided	Claims Allowed
1977	9	9		1	1		1	1	
1978	14	14	1	8	8		1	1	
1979	28	28		11	11		2	2	
1980	25	25		13	13		-	-	
1981	1,047	400		55	46		42	12	
1982	1,303	1,477		94	42		71	56	
1983/84	430	853		245	227		79	89	
1984/85	128	122	4	257	197		70	59	
1985/86	133	139		257	345		102	113	
1986/87	402	297		140	93		25	20	
1987/88	596	199	1	452	130		51	14	
Totals	4,115	3,563	6	1,533	1,113	Zero	444	367	Zero

TABLE 2B

IMMIGRATION AND REFUGEE BOARD DECISIONS — RECORD OF REFUGEE CLAIMS FROM INDIA, JAMAICA AND THE DOMINICAN REPUBLIC IN THE PERIOD 1989 TO 1998.

Year	INDIA				JAMAICA				DOMINICAN REPUBLIC			
	Claims Received	Claims Decided	Claims Allowed	Claims Withdrawn Abandoned	Claims Received	Claims Decided	Claims Allowed	Claims Withdrawn Abandoned	Claims Received	Claims Decided	Claims Allowed	Claims Withdrawn Abandoned
1989	137	47	13	-	74	1	0	-	10	3	0	-
1990	135	34	11	39	59	3	0	12	8	7	0	1
1991	653	222	81	59	88	3	0	22	63	11	3	11
1992	884	558	137	62	104	76	0	22	61	42	5	6
1993	1,803	868	226	256	174	19	1	69	44	30	11	6
1994	1,128	979	520	304	214	69	2	81	38	11	2	8
1995	1,259	855	492	311	141	84	2	62	77	11	3	33
1996	1,367	890	404	447	132	89	2	59	57	15	2	33
1997	1,166	871	302	320	76	87	2	48	11	13	0	7
1998	1,157	1,188	435	339	75	44	2	37	39	20	3	11
Totals	9,689	6,512	2,621	2,137	1,137	475	11	412	408	163	29	116

from our decision-making groups should have been flown to Halifax and St. John's to deal immediately with those claimants on site. Instead, we set these people loose in Canada with virtually all the rights of Canadian citizens.

*   *   *

By March 31, 1986, the refugee backlog had grown to 21,742 claims. Yet the number of immigration personnel responsible for conducting the initial examination-under-oath stage, on which all else depends, was reduced. In the fiscal year 1985/86 only 4,099 examinations were undertaken. In the midst of another developing crisis, with that staff reduction, the system had been all but scuttled. And that wasn't all.

Normally the Immigration Appeal Board heard refugee-redetermination applications by those whom the Refugee Status Advisory Committee had previously rejected. That committee, working closely with the United Nations High Commission on Refugees, was so effective that less than 3 per cent of those applications to the Board for redetermination succeeded. The quality of the RSAC work was never in question. However, the Board's 1986 annual report included the explanation that "as a result of the government's May 21st Administrative Review policy announcement . . . the Board's workload was dramatically altered. These scheduled refugee redeterminations would first be considered under the Administrative Review." The intent, it was explained, was to "land" two-thirds to three-quarters of the claimants. In fact, rather than the usual 3 per cent, an astonishing 85 per cent would be landed.

*   *   *

By July 1986, Canada had not one but two new ministers: Benoit Bouchard, minister of employment and immigration, and Gerald Weiner, minister of state immigration. We also had 2,000 or 3,000 more refugee claimants collecting social welfare. This may well have encouraged the resurrection of that suspended Portuguese visa restriction. Apparently it was Mr.

Weiner's job to make the "emergency" system work. He quickly recognized what the immigration black marketeers had done, characterized them as unscrupulous and set the Mounties after them. Presumably the chase continues.

Under the "Administrative Review" process, however, when Minister Weiner boasted that all 20,000 in the backlog would be processed by June 1987, he was guaranteeing delivery of the citizenship promised by the unscrupulous to the fraudulent. Two immigration-policy and program-development reports published in March 1988 round out the Administrative Review story. Admissions under that review became known as "ADRs". By preliminary count there were 23,234 ADRs landed in 1986 and 1987. It was explained that these immigrants were excluded in the regular announcements of immigration levels in order "to assure consistency when comparing 1987 data with those of previous years." The annual reports did not include 23,234 landed immigrants.

In any event, ADRs were being rapidly replaced with a new statistic. The May 21, 1986 announcement told the disadvantaged of the world that Canada's back door was again wide open. They came in such numbers that, by March 1987, a brand new backlog of 24,000 was predicted for the next month. Would they too benefit from an amnesty? What would happen to the thousands who continued to arrive?

Finally, on May 5, 1987, Bill C55, the legislation designed to save the situation and on which successive governments had worked diligently for six years, was tabled jointly in Parliament by Ministers Bouchard and Weiner. This would replace the Refugee Status Advisory Committee and the Immigration Appeal Board with a new institution to be known as the "Immigration and Refugee Board", to be made up of three divisions:

1. The Immigration Appeals Division (IAD) would carry on the original work of the Immigration Appeal Board: to hear appeals arising from Immigration Department refusals of family-sponsorship applications made by Canadian citizens or landed immigrants; to hear appeals by landed immigrants; and to hear appeals made by persons in possession of valid

visas seeking admission to Canada who had been detained, or ordered removed, at ports of entry.

2. The Adjudication Division would conduct immigration inquiries and detention reviews for people believed to be inadmissible to, or removable from, Canada.

3. The Convention Refugee Determination Division would combine the functions of the Refugee Status Advisory Committee with appeals formerly heard by the Immigration Appeal Board against ministerial decisions based on RSAC recommendations. Its Backlog Subdivision would have temporary status to deal with the accumulation of refugee claims existing as of December 31, 1988.

The minister, acknowledging a 1986 backlog of 18,000 cases, was confident abuse would be constrained, that the new system would result in rapid response to genuine refugees and permit speedy removal of false claimants.

Three months later the government, facing a backlog believed to have reached 25,000, acknowledged the critical state of the refugee-determination process, panicked and recalled Parliament from summer recess—a rare occurrence. On August 11, 1987, Ministers Bouchard and Weiner introduced their Deterrents and Detention Bill. Minister Bouchard explained, once again, that: "The purpose of this Bill is to enable the government to act immediately to prevent further abuse of the refugee determination system in Canada." He said the bill had been designed to strike at the source of the abuse by establishing tough deterrents to stop the increasing number of illegal aliens posing as refugees from entering Canada.

More specifically, he acknowledged that 500 aliens per month destroyed or concealed their passports or identity documents prior to arrival in Canada (there was a report of one poor chap actually eating his passport, cover and all). There would be ten-year jail sentences and fines of $500,000 for smugglers and their accomplices; transportation companies would be fined $5,000 for each undocumented passenger arriving; and those without documentation would be detained until their identities could be established.

Over a decade later, no one appears to have suffered punishment. On March 11, 1997, Nurjehan Mawani, the Immigration and Refugee Board chairperson, reported: "A significant number of Convention Refugee claimants referred to the Immigration and Refugee Board by the Department of Citizenship and Immigration for determination, are either undocumented or improperly documented."[8]

The Auditor General established that figure at "close to 60 per cent." With the world laughing at Canada's immigration policy, no one took action.

Early in 1989 a request was made by the author to the Immigration Public Relations office in Ottawa for a list of the source countries of the refugee claimants in the backlog. The material, marked "Confidential", was duly sent (see Table 3). It provides figures for the thirty leading source countries, gives the claimants' location by province and provides totals showing the backlog to have been 101,853 cases involving 122,223 persons. There was the cautionary note that the figures were estimates and subject to duplicate registration and departures. These figures would never appear in the public records, although increasingly, backlog figures ranging from 120,000 to 140,000 appeared in news stories.

Two years later, in a January 1991 CBC-TV Vancouver news program, when Immigration Minister McDougall was faced with this document, she denied the legitimacy of the backlog figures obtained from her own department's public-relations division. She stated that she was not going to argue about the number of cases. The information she had was that there were 85,000; she added that there were lots of memos floating around making assessments of what might be out there, but the best information they had was that there were 85,000 cases.[9]

However, on May 9, 1989, twenty months before Minister McDougall would categorically deny its validity on television, the *Globe and Mail* published the confession of her officials to the House of Commons Standing Committee on Employment and Immigration. Senior Immigration Department officials had confirmed that there might be 40,000 more refugee claimants caught up in a bureaucratic backlog than they had earlier believed.

TABLE 3

BACKLOG BREAKDOWN OF REFUGEE CLAIMS BY REGION AND NATIONALITY

COUNTRY	BC/YUKON	ALTA/NWT	SASK	MAN	ONTARIO
1. Trinidad & Tobago	0	10	0	22	13,777
2. Sri-Lanka	216	11	0	12	6,518
3. Iran	665	9	2	6	5,136
4. El Salvador	435	192	25	63	3,098
5. Portugal	2	16	0	21	5,515
6. Ghana	21	8	1	3	3,025
7. India	390	65	6	30	2,753
8. Nicaragua	275	283	0	37	2,242
9. Lebanon	38	23	0	4	1,272
10. Guatemala	155	49	3	21	892
11. Turkey	10	7	1	1	607
12. Somalia	9	16	0	5	1,404
13. Jamaica	0	11	0	1	2,379
14. Fiji	1,064	666	7	12	849
15. Chile	17	48	0	11	774
16. P.R.C.	574	49	8	5	1,717
17. Brazil	0	4	0	6	2,176
18. Panama	30	1	0	1	681
19. Pakistan	61	31	21	9	1,040
20. Argentina	3	1	0	6	1,576
21. Poland	340	42	11	14	439
22. Honduras	163	19	1	4	459
23. Haiti	1	0	0	0	10
24. Bangladesh	39	0	0	3	199
25. Yugoslavia	18	1	0	0	1,116
26. Guyana	1	4	0	0	1,057
27. U.S.A.	32	15	2	0	433
28. Peru	3	6	0	1	289
29. Mexico	16	7	1	0	414
30. Ethiopia	3	10	2	5	314
Others	354	175	18	148	8,278
Total	4,935	1,779	109	452	70,439

NOTE: The above numbers represent persons. (Total cases are calculated as 1.2 persons per case.) As the data also include duplications, disappearances and finalized cases, the actual totals are lower.

TABLE 3

BACKLOG BREAKDOWN OF REFUGEE CLAIMS BY REGION AND NATIONALITY

QUEBEC	N.B.	N.S.	P.E.I.	NFLD.	TOTAL PERSONS	TOTAL CASES
978	0	0	0	0	14,787	12,323
4,281	0	6	0	1	11,045	9,204
3,393	0	4	0	2	9,217	7,681
4,106	13	1	0	0	7,933	6,611
191	0	0	0	0	5,745	4,788
2,071	8	0	0	0	5,137	4,282
706	0	0	0	0	3,950	3,303
890	0	5	0	0	3,732	3,110
2,302	4	68	0	4	3,715	3,096
1,850	22	0	0	0	2,992	2,493
2,000	0	0	0	0	2,626	2,188
1,179	0	0	0	0	2,613	2,178
207	0	1	1	0	2,600	2,167
1	0	0	0	0	2,599	2,166
1,746	0	0	0	0	2,596	2,163
131	1	0	0	0	2,485	2,071
260	0	0	0	0	2,446	2,039
1,342	0	0	0	0	2,055	1,713
820	0	2	0	0	1,984	1,653
172	0	0	0	0	1,758	1,464
786	0	17	0	7	1,656	1,380
970	0	0	0	0	1,616	1,347
1,138	0	0	0	0	1,149	1,124
1,033	0	0	0	2	1,276	1,063
83	1	0	0	0	1,219	1,016
76	0	0	0	0	1,138	948
405	0	0	0	0	887	739
457	0	0	0	0	756	638
306	0	0	0	0	745	621
354	0	2	0	0	690	575
9,833	3	36	0	7	18,852	15,710
44,067	52	142	1	23	121,999	101,854

These figures should be interpreted only as estimates and are subject to revision. Some regions have subsequently reported lower totals by age and sex.

Gordon Barnett, director of the immigration program division, told the committee that "the backlog has gone nowhere but up since January 1st." Officials kept finding people they didn't know about.

Did the bureaucracy fail to report these discoveries to Minister McDougall, who apparently didn't read either the *Globe and Mail* or her copies of the proceedings of the Commons Standing Committee on Immigration?

*   *   *

Since the nature of its work was simply to advise the minister, the Refugee Status Advisory Committee did not publish annual reports. A single request by the author produced a binder containing the complete records of committee decisions from 1977 to 1987/88 fiscal year-end, with charts, diagrams and analyses of their decisions! There has always been a remarkable willingness on the part of concerned members of the bureaucracy at all levels (when they have the opportunity) to ensure that the truth be told. As a result, it is possible to set out the details of the crises facing the new Immigration and Refugee Board when it assumed responsibility on January 1, 1989.

In 1977, the first year of the Refugee Status Advisory Committee's mandate, there were 522 decisions. Influenced by both the 1978 legislation and the increasing recognition of the advantages provided by a "made in Canada" refugee claim, decisions increased steadily over the eleven years of the life of the committee to 6,078 in the 1987/88 fiscal year as the backlog increased disproportionately. During the first three years the acceptance rate was 35 per cent until, with the increasing entry of advantage seekers, it dropped to 24 per cent with an average of 27 per cent of the 30,000 claims decided over the life of the committee. It was during this period that Canada was awarded the Nansen Medal by the United Nations for service to refugees, specifically for the acceptance of a large quota of Vietnamese boat people. Surely an acknowledgment of a fair and acceptable record of decision-making.

The post–Administrative Review backlog facing the new

Board on January 1, 1989 had grown to 101,000 claims involving 122,000 people. As this backlog was building, the committee, working with United Nations advisors, accepted 2,700 of the 11,300 claims considered. That 24 per cent acceptance rate, based on an 11-per-cent sample representative of the backlog, was a clear indication of the massive number of impostors in the backlog. Since there had been no serious criticism of the work of the committee by the immigration and refugee industry, it was an indication of the results to be expected of the Convention Refugee Determination Division of the new Board. That is not what happened.

The critical statistics are the backlog numbers. Following the Administrative Review, claims filed in the thirty-one months between May 1, 1986 and December 31, 1988 resulted in a backlog buildup at the rate of 3,300 cases per month, or 4,000 persons per month. A projected annual workload increase from 6,000 to over 40,000 demanded major planning. When the minister responsible denies that reality, as Minister McDougall did, then adequate planning was not likely to happen. And it didn't.

Beginning in 1991, Daniel Stoffman, the well-known Toronto writer, spent a year examining Canadian immigration policy under a *Toronto Star* Atkinson Fellowship. His extensive, valuable and revealing report was published by the *Star* in 1992. Among other revelations was the work of Informal Consultations, a Geneva-based secretariat monitoring refugee movements worldwide and supported by the sixteen industrialized countries that are major destinations for asylum seekers. Canada is one of them.

The average acceptance rate for those sixteen countries was 14 per cent. In Canada, from 1989 to 1992, it had ranged from 75 per cent down to 54 per cent. An analysis of 250,000 asylum seekers arriving in those member states found 16.8 per cent were Geneva Convention Refugees, 19.2 per cent were non-Convention Refugees and 64 per cent were not in need of protection. Curiously, this Canadian-supported organization, and the results of its work, are never mentioned in Canadian official or semi-official reports. There may be a reason. Canada's record was either one of extreme generosity or of serious political failure.

ENDNOTES

1. The *Globe and Mail*, October 8, 1991.
2. The *Globe and Mail*, October 8, 1991.
3. Other members of the task force were Carter Hoppe, a Toronto immigration and refugee lawyer, Dr. Ed Ratushny, a University of Ottawa law professor, and Ms. Manon Vennat, a Montreal lawyer.
4. The Supreme Court of Canada in its decision reasoned that:

"Although appellants are not entitled at this stage to assert rights as Convention Refugees, having regard for the potential consequences for them of a denial of 'that status' if, in fact they are persons with 'a well founded fear of persecution', they are entitled to fundamental justice in the adjudication of their status."

The court then invoked the Canadian Charter of Rights and Freedoms and the requirements of fundamental justice, concluding that, although

"the administrative procedures of the Immigration Act require the Refugee Status Advisory Committee and the Minister to act fairly in carrying out their duties, they do not envisage an opportunity for the refugee claimant to be heard other than through his claim and the transcript of his examination under oath. Further, the Act does not envisage the refugee claimant being given an opportunity to comment on the advice the Refugee Status committee has given the Minister. Under the Act, the Immigration Appeal Board must reject an application for redetermination unless it is of the opinion that it is more likely than not that the applicant will be able to succeed. An application, therefore, will usually be rejected before the refugee claimant has even had an opportunity to discover the Minister's case against him in the context of a hearing. Such procedures do not accord the refugee claimant fundamental justice and are incompatible with the Charter."

In a case unrelated to immigration, but employing the precedent set in the *Singh* decision, the British Columbia Court of Appeal released its judgment on May 22, 1985 in *Pritipal Singh Hundal* v. *the Superintendent of Motor Vehicles,* in which the Honourable Chief Justice Nathan Nemetz dealt with the scope necessary for a hearing to meet the requirements of fundamental justice. He wrote:

"First of all, the principles of fundamental justice do not require that administrative decision must always be made after a formal oral hearing: Singh v. Minister of Employment and Immigration (unreported S.C.C., April 4, 1985). The content of the principles of fundamental justice required in a given case will depend upon the circumstances of that case. Thousands of administrative decisions are made daily impinging on the rights of the individual. It would be folly to suppose that the principles of fundamental justice demand a full oral hearing in every case. (See generally [Mr. Justice] H. J. Friendly, 'Some Kind of Hearing' {1975} 123 U. Penn. L.R. 1267). The key will always be whether the decision maker has acted fairly in dealing with the citizen's rights. In some cases only a full, formal, oral hearing will suffice to comply with duty of fairness; in other cases the duty will not demand so much. At a minimum, however, the principles will always require some kind of hearing, even if it only involves the most rudimentary ability to respond to and have notice of the case against you."

5. http://www.parl.gc.ca/36/refmat/library/forsey/fedstate-e.htm.
6. He was the junior minister. Flora MacDonald was the senior minister.
7. From the Immigration Department document *Backlog Breakdown by Region and Nationality,* May 1989.
8. *Commentary on Undocumented and Improperly Documented Claimants,* IRB Legal Services, March 11, 1997, p. 5.
9. From tape of the CBC program.

CHAPTER V

A WIDE-OPEN BACK DOOR

"Canada's generous refugee system is open to abuse—and foreign crooks know it. Under the Charter of Rights and Freedoms, anyone who arrives claiming to be a refugee has the same legal rights as any Canadian. That can mean a lengthy sequence of hearings and appeals, while the newcomer remains in Canada, living on social benefits . . . or crime."

The Economist

The abysmal history of Canada's largest quasi-judicial body, the Immigration and Refugee Board, really began with the appointment of Gordon Fairweather as its chairman-designate on November 1, 1987, fourteen months before it became operational. With the framework of the new law available, and subject only to final amendment, it was his job as head of a special transition team to assemble the new Board. Unfortunately, in the process, and with the personal sanction of Prime Minister Mulroney and Immigration Minister Benoit Bouchard, Mr. Fairweather was to become a chairman like no other. Indeed, the media instantly and appropriately dubbed him "Canada's immigration czar".[1]

Certainly the government's appointment of Mr. Fairweather was well received by the immigration industry and accepted without objection by the opposition parties in the House of Commons. Still, one may wonder at the decision of the prime minister and his immigration minister to circumvent the democratic process by abandoning the right and the responsibility of government to decide the rules for refugee determination.

It may be that the Mulroney crew were trying to distance

themselves from a no-win political situation by placing Mr. Fairweather in the public hot seat. But if it was often difficult to determine who was in charge, Mr. Fairweather or the current minister, Mrs. McDougall cleared that up in Question Period on December 14, 1988:

> Mr. Fairweather, I think, has done an excellent job of explaining to Canadians how his board will function. . . . He's an independent chairman of the Board.

However, it was the responsibility of the minister of immigration to make the legislation work, and it was the mandate of government to establish regulations to determine who shall enter our gates and under what circumstances. To surrender authority to any chairman (never mind an untested one) to write the guidelines under which more than 200 equally untested and independent decision-making Board members would admit to Canada hundreds of thousands of new Canadians, without at least the tabling of these guidelines for approval by Parliament, represented abdication of responsibility by government.

The independence of the chairman was emphasized during a workshop at the windup meeting in Ottawa that ended Immigration Minister Marchi's "Summer of Consultations" in September 1994. A participant asked: "Why, when the same circumstances are advanced in separate claims, are some allowed and some rejected?" The then deputy minister of immigration, Peter Harder, who earlier had functioned as Mr. Fairweather's second-in-command, explained that not only did the IRB operate with full independence from government, but that Board members enjoyed independence from each other. With that very clear explanation he confirmed the genuine concerns of the conference participants.

*   *   *

Given Mr. Fairweather's unusually wide discretionary authority, it is important to understand his views on Canadian immigration policy in general and on his new responsibilities in particular. Referring to an immigration organization devoted to assisting Europeans to enter Canada as immigrants, just as dozens of other ethnic organizations do, he took the startling position that "European immigration is blatant bigotry and the kind of thing people used to say when they said white immigration only. It's something from the past that most of us would want to forget."[2]

Under new legislation, a new Board and a new chairman with unprecedented authority in charge, the media were eager for quotes. In an early public statement, Mr. Fairweather expressed the hope that his new Board members would not be typical Mulroney patronage appointments: "If the only reason they are picked is because they are friends of the government then I am beginning on a journey that hasn't any good ending." Indicating the type of appointee he might find compatible he said: "I don't intend to be a gatekeeper in Canada at this stage in my public career." And he gave his assurance that he was "not going to see that the rules, regulations and procedures of the Immigration and Refugee Board are so onerous that no legitimate refugee can even get through." That, he said, would be turning his back on everything he believed in and everything he had fought for in public and political life. The new chairman had authority from the prime minister to develop his own guidelines in the interpretation of the United Nations Convention.

Faced with the mounting refugee backlog, Mr. Fairweather took the view that the neatest, cleanest way to get rid of what he said were the 40,000 cases involved, would be to declare an amnesty. He stated that the government was considering one. This came as a shock to Immigration Minister Benoit Bouchard, who at first denied Mr. Fairweather's assertion. Later Mr. Bouchard was obliged to confirm the IRB chief-in-waiting's expectations, thus sending yet another signal to the economic migrants of the world that the gates to Canada were open to all who could find their way here. That one could never be certain who, if anyone, was minding the store did not augur well for the operation of the new Board.

There was background for the confusion. The Cabinet Committee on Priorities and Planning, apparently failing to understand the influence of "Administrative Reviews" on Canadian immigration matters, had agreed on February 12, 1987 that the minister of employment and immigration "be authorized to implement a second backlog clearance . . . to include their estimate of 23,000 refugee claims which would accumulate during the transition period between May 21, 1986 and the actual implementation of the new refugee determination system."[3] This new "Administrative Review" was to take place only after the IRB system was in place, which would be on January 1, 1989—when the backlog of cases was not 23,000, not 40,000, but 101,000. A building contractor so unfamiliar with reality, who made estimates like that, would go broke!

*   *   *

In the thirty-one months between the first Mulroney Administrative Review in 1986 and December 31, 1988, 133,000 refugee claimants filed claims in Canada. Of these, 11,000 were dealt with by the outgoing RSAC accepting 24 per cent and leaving that backlog of 101,000 cases involving 122,000 people. Claimants had been arriving at the rate of 4,300 a month.

Following a year in office, and less than two months before the new Act was to come into force, Mr. Fairweather indicated that he knew that seven out of every ten refugee claims were bogus. In all seriousness, he promised the new refugee-determination process would make an "important statement to the world" that Canada was not putting conditions on legitimate refugees, but was closing the door to the fraudulent: "The integrity of our system is very much at stake. If our system is laughed at at home, or treated cynically by those trying to beat it, then great damage is done to Canada."[4]

He was right. Great damage was about to be done.

It is important to realize that the Mulroney government, in response to the objections of the immigration lobby in Canada, withheld the proclamation of 1989 amendments to the Immigration Act providing for the immediate return of refugee claimants from Canada to safe third countries, where they could have first made their refugee claim. This involved the application of the "first opportunity" principle, designed to discourage "asylum shopping". European countries had earlier accepted this principle in the Dublin Convention, designed to prevent refugee claimants from moving from country to country in search of the best deal.

It is a measure of the strength of the immigration lobby in Canada that it was able to have that moratorium placed on the implementation of legislation that would deny asylum shoppers access to the Canadian haven. This was especially so when a 1989 Angus Reid poll, taken during this latest refugee crisis, found that the majority of Canadians would prefer to see refugee claimants sent back to a safe third country to make their claims, if indeed they had passed up that opportunity en route to Canada.

Given Canada's generous and universal social security net, its history of immigration amnesties and, under the *Singh* decision, the provision that once a person sets foot in our country, that person has virtually all the legal rights of citizenship under the Charter of Rights and Freedoms, Canada had become a destination of choice. For economic migrants from around the world, Canada ranked up with the leaders. With advancing communications technology, the good news was heard worldwide: Canada's new Immigration and Refugee Board was using new guidelines to interpret the UN Refugee Convention, and accepting refugee claimants who would be refused in every other western country.

In fact, UNHCR professionals consider resettlement in a distant country like Canada to be the least desirable solution for most refugees. They believe the great majority are better off remaining in their region or, if obtaining temporary asylum, preserving the opportunity to return home when strife subsides. This, of course, is reflected in the Canadian policy covering the recent reception of refugees from Kosovo. Certainly resettlement is necessary for some; but for the vast majority there is concurrence with the position taken by Gerald Shannon, Canada's Permanent Representative to the UN in Geneva, that much

of Canada's huge expenditure on refugee determination and settlement would be better spent assisting at their source those
refugees and displaced persons not requiring resettlement.

*   *   *

In late December 1988, Gordon Fairweather held a press
conference to introduce his two deputy and ten assistant-deputy
chairpersons. He emphasized the long-overdue need for
changes in our refugee-determination system, and reminded his
audience that the number of claims for refugee status made in
Canada had grown in recent years to 27,000 per annum (that is,
to 2,250 claims per month). In fact, since news of the government's impending Administrative Review had spread worldwide, claimants were arriving at the rate of 4,300 a month. It
was easy to predict that planning based on one-half this figure
would create yet another backlog crisis.

Mr. Fairweather planned for 65 full-time Refugee Determination members, and for 30 in the Appeals Division. By the end
of 1989 there would be 21 in the Appeals Division, 49 in the
Backlog Subdivision and 143 in the Refugee Division, for a total of 213 members, all supported by an administrative staff of
493 and an annual operating budget of $53 million. By the end
of the third year, there would be 279 decision-makers, 793 support staff and a budget of $86 million. By the end of 1992, with
completion of the work of the Backlog Subdivision, the number
of decision-makers had declined to 233, but support staff was
maintained at 787 and the annual budget had reached $93 mil-
lion. Refugee determination had become a costly business indeed.

Under the new regime, refugee claims would be determined
in two stages. The first, to be known as the "Credible Basis"
test, was intended for early elimination of manifestly unfounded
claims. Those remaining would be subject to a full and thorough examination of their claims.

Of his Board membership, Mr. Fairweather said, "If I feel
confident in telling you that the IRB will get off to a fast start, it
is simply because we have managed to attract Canadians of ex-

perience and high calibre." He emphasized that the members reflected both the diversity of Canada and the diversity of the
IRB's clientele. Half the membership were women, many from
leadership positions; half came from multicultural organizations and, of these, 40 per cent were members of visible minorities. These were all significant factors, of course, but there was
little reference to the sort of life experience essential to making
decisions appropriate to Canada's obligations to the genuinely
persecuted of the world—a failure that would be reflected in the
statistics compiled by this new Board.

That the impact of those statistics would defy all reasonable
expectations surfaced early. On February 18, 1989 the *Globe
and Mail* reported the results of the IRB's first six weeks of operation. Of 634 post-1988 claims, only 40 failed the initial
Credible Basis test; 560 went on to the full-hearing stage; the
other 34 didn't show up. Given these odds, it is surprising that
anyone failed to appear. But then, this was the beginning of
what was to be a growing recognition that all the advantages enjoyed by landed immigrants in Canada were available to everyone else with the simple filing of a refugee claim on arrival. For
the adventurous there was no need to follow through with a formal hearing.

Of the 93 per cent who proceeded to the second stage, 113
hearings had been completed, with decisions rendered in 97
cases. Their result: 89 claimants were accepted as refugees, and
eight rejected, representing an 85 per cent claimant-success
rate. This was three times Mr. Fairweather's stated expectations,
three times the predictions of the Toronto legal fraternity, and
three times the historical record of the former Refugee Status
Advisory Committee. It was six times the 14-per-cent 1988 average acceptance rate of the sixteen countries classified as major destinations for asylum seekers. But as striking as these
figures are, more arresting still was the fact that over half the
claimants who had arrived since January 1, 1989 had yet to be
referred to the first-stage hearing. This was the beginning of
what would come to be known as the "frontlog".

With such a reversal of expectations, and such evidence that
Chairman Fairweather had made good his determination not to

become Canada's "gatekeeper", one would have expected the government to initiate a swift review to determine what had gone wrong. Instead, they seemed to take pride in this "achievement", echoing the bizarre claim of the executive director of the Immigration and Refugee Board, Peter Harder, that the healthy acceptance rate demonstrated that the new system was working to the benefit of real refugees. "Given a fighting chance," he said, "Canada can be an example to the world of how to provide a refugee determination system that meets the highest standard of humanitarian concern." This would become the party line for the government and the IRB.

*   *   *

In Mr. Fairweather's announcement of the appointments of his deputies, and in the "backgrounders" explaining the hearing and appeal processes, there was no mention of the Refugee Backlog Subdivision. This was not surprising. The process to deal with these refugee claimants (all of whom arrived after May 21, 1986—over three years earlier) had not yet been funded. Indeed, the quarterly reports of the Board, detailing the statistical record of refugee-determination decisions, would not include the backlog. The IRB annual report for 1989 acknowledged its existence and described its function, but provided no record of its accomplishments for the preceding twelve months. This at least was understandable since apparently there was little to report. Minister McDougall, theoretically in charge of the immigration shop, had as yet to secure that budget. Of course, had the amnesty occurred in accordance with Mr. Fairweather's early expectations, there would have been no need for a Backlog Subdivision.

In the meantime, Mrs. McDougall, in a press release issued March 31, 1989, had set out the rules for backlog determinations to be dealt with in a special program to begin that summer. Her planning figure was still 85,000 refugee claimants. In time, the figure 95,000 would be conceded, but not officially for nearly three years and never the 122,000 people involved in those 101,000 real claims. Minister McDougall's "backlog clearance process" would vary in its details, depending on the arrival times and circumstances of the claimants. Essentially, its stages were as follows:

Immigration officers would interview claimants to determine Family Class relationships sufficient to justify acceptance, offering the immediate right to apply for landed-immigrant status. For this, a passport, alternative identity documents and visa requirements were waived. Without identity documents, family relationships are difficult to establish, but that must not become a handicap to efficient production. Landing did depend on meeting health and criminality requirements. Ability to become self-supporting, the politically correct position, was listed though it was not made a Family Class requirement.

Those failing this test could leave voluntarily with a letter of introduction to embassy or consular offices in their home country seeking favourable consideration by the resident visa officer based on their Canadian experience. Otherwise, the next step was the backlog panel hearings, equivalent to the first-level hearings under the new refugee-determination system. These were intended to weed out the frauds, but for the backlog claimants the legal test was one of low grade and any credible or trustworthy evidence would suffice. And those failing that elementary test stage would not be rejected but would proceed to a full oral hearing before the Convention Refugee Determination Division of the IRB. At great cost and time to the Canadian taxpayer, it became virtually impossible for a backlog refugee, no matter how bogus, to fail.

But it was not over. A deportation order required an inquiry before an adjudicator to determine if deportation was justified and, if so, more senior immigration officials would again carefully examine the record, seeking humanitarian grounds to allow them to stay. Removal would only take place after a negative decision had been reached by these officials.

The power of the ethnic vote in the mind of Canadian politicians is beyond comprehension, but listen to its supporters. The Immigration Section of the Ontario Bar reacted with horror upon hearing of the backlog clearance plan. Indeed, four prominent Toronto immigration lawyers—Marshall Drukarsh, Barbara

Jackman, Mendel Green and Lorne Waldman—published a ten-page brief lambasting the program as "impractical, inhuman and improper". They estimated 60,000 to 70,000 people were subject to removal. Obviously they knew their own clients. As Mendel Green told the *Globe and Mail:* "There is no way people from Trinidad, Jamaica, Portugal, Turkey, India or Guyana will meet the Credible Basis test for a refugee claim or the humanitarian and compassionate guidelines."[5] The lawyers not only knew their clients, but they had history on their side.

In the final year of the Refugee Status Advisory Committee, *no claims* were accepted from Guyana, Trinidad, Jamaica or Portugal. Three were accepted from Turkey out of the 1,131 considered and one was accepted from India out of 199. In its eleven years, this committee considered 3,569 refugee claims from India, and accepted only six.

*   *   *

Mr. Firdaus J. Kharas, former executive director of the United Nations Association of Canada, was the assistant-deputy IRB chairman responsible for the Backlog Subdivision. In May 1989, Mr. Kharas undertook a public-relations tour, which included an open meeting and a session on talk radio in Vancouver. Employing the "official" 85,000 backlog figure, Mr. Kharas delivered a message that was designed to disarm critics in the local immigration bar. He described the standard required for those in the backlog as a low-threshold Credible Basis test, emphasizing that post-January 1989 claimants faced a much higher standard. He pointed out that if one of the two decision-makers considered there might be even the "possibility" that the subject would face discrimination at home, then the claimant was accepted. The result, he said, was that since January 1, 1989, "over 90 per cent had been found to meet the Credible Basis test, proving Canada to be the most receptive country in the world for refugees."

Mr. Kharas's most significant statement in terms of the impact of this refugee process on Canada, however, was his response to a question about Family Reunification: "I speculate that these 70,000 or so refugee admissions, under family reunification will be followed with the largest movement of migrants into Canada in our history!" As if to demonstrate further that no one was minding the store in Ottawa, he proved himself quite innovative and skilled in his reply to the question, "With over 90 per cent acceptance, why not just declare an amnesty and cut the costs?" His reply: "That would not cut the cost—cost increases with the number staying in the country. If working strictly in terms of cost, we would not allow anyone in."

Three months later, on August 27, 1989, Mr. Kharas was heard from again, this time complaining that the backlog clearance was proceeding at a "frustratingly slow" pace, and expressing his concern that most claimants would be allowed to stay in Canada anyway, making a mockery of the entire $179 million program.[6] That's exactly what was happening! This time the story referred to "124,000" claimants. Mr. Kharas stated that in the first eight months of the IRB's two-year backlog-clearance program, only 1,000 claims had been processed and that *all but two* had been accepted. He explained this 99.8 per cent acceptance rate with the assurance that "up to now the backlog program had dealt with only the most credible claimants."

Gordon Barnett, the director of immigration program delivery, later revealed that for the vast majority of claimants the Credible Basis test had been turned into a mere formality. What apparently had begun as a legitimate, if *soft*, refugee backlog-determination process, had turned out to be as close to an amnesty as an amnesty had ever been to an Administrative Review. Of course, Minister McDougall kept denying what was obvious, as she did with a twist in a March 20, 1990 press release, just eighteen months into the new system. She was adamant. "To declare an amnesty would be to tell the world that Canada tolerates disrespect for its laws. I cannot do that. Canadians live by the laws of their country, and they rightly demand that those who come here also live by those laws."

But then she also continued to repeat that false 85,000 backlog figure.

*   *   *

The minister's protestations to the contrary, this would be the fourth amnesty in modern times. The first, in the early sixties, was for 12,000 illegal Chinese plus however many dependents and relatives, real or fake. Then, in the early seventies, there were the 20,000-plus visitors who failed to meet Canada's admission standards. That turned out to be 210,000 new Canadians. In the mid-eighties the Administrative Review accepted at least 23,000 ADR refugee claimants with all of their family members. Finally, although the backlog process initially appeared to accept 90 per cent of refugee claims dealt with, the final 1992 report of the IRB reveals that of all claims decided, 32,482 (77 per cent) were accepted as refugees and 9,893 (23 per cent) were rejected. For the rejected there were still the deportation, humanitarian and risk-factor reviews. Beyond that, nearly 60,000 claims had either been abandoned, withdrawn or neglected, with the claimants disappearing into Canada or elsewhere.

One thing is certain: each refugee crisis was the inevitable consequence of a combination of legislative, administrative and political fiascos. In each case, the crisis warning signals were up. They had to be. Those numbers did not develop overnight. The political reflex action was to cut and run rather than to react head-on to what was happening.

The pyramidal provisions of our immigration laws that provided for bringing extended families into Canada meant hundreds upon hundreds of thousands of additional new Canadians for whom skills or literacy would not be a consideration. Certainly, there are many who have succeeded. But in the process, we have denied to many of them something of great importance—the knowledge of what admission to Canada once meant. Surely it must be considered a privilege. Instead, many will know that for them it is the reward of deceit. Isn't that a crazy way to build a nation?

＊   ＊   ＊

As the end of 1989 approached, it became necessary to defend the IRB record. This campaign began in late November with a cross-Canada tour by Messrs. Fairweather and Harder. In

Vancouver, they met with *Vancouver Sun* editors and reporters. The report of the meeting was headlined, "Canada's Refugee Process Touted as Model System".[7] The next day, however, another *Sun* headline read, "Refugee Backlog Cost Zooms", with an unnamed senior immigration officer describing the same process as "a goddamn total disaster". That was not real news to anyone who bothers to read the Library of Parliament's "Revised", July 1989 backgrounder, "Canada's New Refugee Determination System".[8]

Peter Harder boasted that Canada's new refugee process enjoyed an international reputation as a model system, able to make speedy refugee decisions "free of ideology". He emphasized that "Canadian refugee rules simply look at the facts of each case to determine whether the person can be considered a legitimate refugee according to the United Nations Convention on Refugees." Interestingly enough, he made no mention of the second stage of the determination process, which was intended to do just that. It did not apply to the 122,000 refugee claimants in the backlog.

Mr. Harder placed true value on these comments when he credited the new refugee system with reducing the number of claimants from countries such as Portugal and Trinidad. This fanciful claim became part of the spin program relied upon later by both Mr. Fairweather and his minister, Barbara McDougall. Until then, could anyone have conceived of the spectacle of the chairman and executive director of Canada's largest quasi-judicial tribunal travelling the country to con local media on its accomplishments?

In an early December interview with Victor Malarek, the *Globe and Mail*'s respected immigration reporter, Minister McDougall claimed that the surprise for her was how effective the new system had been "in turning off" refugee claimants from countries that had been "notorious for producing manifestly unfounded claims", such as Portugal, Jamaica and Trinidad-Tobago. "It is a pleasant surprise," she added, and "more effective than we could have even hoped for."[9]

Had Mrs. McDougall and the others completely forgotten the role she played as a member of the Cabinet in forestalling the earlier imposition of visas on Portuguese travellers to Canada? Did she forget that 14,800 bootleg Trinidadian refugee claimants were included in the backlog because she failed in her responsibility to apply visa restrictions on their travel to Canada when the first signs of this bogus movement became evident? Didn't Mrs. McDougall understand that this flood of Portuguese and Trinidadian refugee claimants became a trickle, but only after she belatedly imposed those visa restrictions on their travel to Canada? The meagre flow had nothing at all to do with the operation of the IRB.

One thing is clear. The spin culture, combined with the mess they were in, had caused this minister and her senior officials to ignore reality.

*   *   *

In the meantime, Auditor General Kenneth Dye had his auditors examining the immigration and refugee programs. At the press conference on publication of his report for the year ending March 31, 1990, covering just fifteen months' operations of the new Board, Mr. Dye described the refugee-determination process as "close to collapse". Mr. Fairweather, however, gave no indication of looming disaster in his own annual report for 1989.

In that report, Mr. Fairweather attributed that "dramatic change" in refugee-claimant admissions to post–January 1, 1989 claimants from Somalia, Sri Lanka, Lebanon, Iran, San Salvador, China, Czechoslovakia, Poland, Guatemala and Iraq.

The figures speak for themselves. Of the pre-1989 top-five countries—Sri Lanka, Ethiopia, Iran, Somalia and Chile—the pre-1989 acceptance rate was 69 per cent. Under the new Board it rose to 94 per cent. Of the next five—San Salvador, Nicaragua, Pakistan, Honduras and Guatemala—it was 29 per cent but soared to 80 per cent the following year. For the remaining twenty countries, it had been 1.6 per cent and, under Mr. Fairweather, 69 per cent were found to be genuine refugees. It is the availability of the internal record of the work of the former Refugee Status Advisory Committee that makes this significant comparison possible.

Then the chairman resorted to the chosen Harder and McDougall spin. Again, depending on figures from that "confidential" list (Table 3), the legitimacy of which the minister denied, he pointed out that during the final years of the former system, significant numbers of claimants entered Canada from countries not noted for civil-rights violations or internal strife, 20,000 of them from Portugal and Trinidad-Tobago. That too was a fact, but those claims were not adjudicated under the former system and had no influence on the earlier statistics. The Trinidad-Tobago and Portugal numbers were in that backlog list. That had to be where Harder, McDougall and Fairweather obtained them.

Though claimants were arriving at the gate at the rate of 3,300 a month, or 40,000 annually, only 21,745 were forwarded to the Board. At year-end only 6,475 hearings had been completed, and of these only 5,306 decisions rendered. In the meantime, that backlog continued its rapid growth. That gate intake was 70 per cent of United Nations' estimates of world refugees requiring resettlement!

Anyone familiar with the process would find it unconscionable that 1,169 of the hearings completed had not been decided. Board members deal with a multitude of claims based on similar evidence, difficult over time to separate in the mind. With delays, Board members require transcripts, resulting in even more delays and increased costs. Without transcripts flawed decisions would be inevitable.

*　　*　　*

Early in 1990, Mr. Justice James Jerome of the Federal Court of Appeal determined that the policy directives and criteria for immigration officers conducting the humanitarian and compassionate reviews were too narrow. In the words of the minister's March 20, 1990 press release: "He ordered a full and fair review of the humanitarian and compassionate considerations in accordance with the law and the duty of fairness." In response, Minister McDougall authorized amended directives on March 21, 1990, expanding the existing criteria for all refugee claimants in the backlog.[10] This would include 15,000 already rejected under the previous guidelines! Furthermore, Removal Orders were to be "temporarily" suspended for those persons who claimed that if they returned to their homeland, they would be put at risk because of natural disasters, political disturbances or civil strife. The temporary suspension would be rescinded, she promised, when such circumstances no longer posed a risk to the individuals concerned.

*   *   *

The IRB "News Release" of May 2, 1990, containing the highlights of that year's first-quarter report, began:

> The Immigration and Refugee Board (IRB) received nearly half as many claims during the first quarter of 1990 as it did during all of 1989.

> In its first quarterly report the IRB revealed that it received 5,987 cases from January 1 to March 31. This compared with 13,537 claims for all of 1989.

Curiously, the 5,987 reported cases received by the Board in that first 1990 quarter were compared not with the 21,745 received by the Board in all of 1989, but with the 13,537 cases opened that year. That there appeared to be a question about the validity of this statistic was to prove only a part of the actual problem.

An Immigration and Refugee Board memorandum dated "24-04-90, from/de D. Gerlitz, Director General Operations, Policy & Planning to/à Peter Harder, Executive Director; Subject/Objet: CRDD [Convention Refugee Determination Division] Statistical Report—First quarter 1990," referred to statistical data in the IRB quarterly report about to be released. It read:

> 1. CLAIMS RECEIVED
> Though these figures are not shown in the attached tables, it is useful

to recall that the number of claims received was about 4,200 in January, 3,300 in February and 3,800 in March. The month-to-month variations are a direct reflection of the numbers of claims received in the Atlantic region, mainly as a result of the Gander situation (January – 800; February – 200; March – 1,100). If the number of arrivals at Gander is controlled, our anticipated monthly intake should be between 3,000 and 3,500, or about 40,000 per year.

The "Gander situation" referred to "refugees" arriving from Europe on board the Russian Aeroflot Airlines flight to Cuba, via a fuel stop at Gander, where passengers ticketed for Havana simply deplaned and claimed refugee status in Canada.

Mr. Gerlitz' memorandum was a gentle reminder to his boss that official reporting was deliberately understating the reality of 11,300 cases by about 5,300 claimants. *Someone was cooking the books.*

However, the May 2 IRB News Release did contain this admission:

> The chairman recalled that the Immigration and Refugee Board, which began operations on January 1, 1989, was structured to process an expected 18,000 convention refugee claimants annually. But he noted that a striking increase in claims has taken place since the last quarter of 1989, which could push the 1990 caseload to 40,000 claims.

Should anyone have been surprised? Forty thousand was the rate at which claims were being filed for the thirty-one months before January 1, 1989. Obviously, nothing had changed in the operations of the Board in the ensuing fifteen months to discourage fraudulent claimants.

*   *   *

While Messrs. Harder, Gerlitz and company were struggling to reconcile their statistics, their chairperson, Mr. Fairweather, was engaged in another trans-Canada public-relations tour. It included a joint luncheon of the Women's Canadian Club and the Canadian Club in Vancouver on April 19. In what was an exceptional performance, demanding of admiration, he described the conflicting viewpoints that the new system was attempting to reconcile. "On the one hand there were traditional concerns of caring Canadians who did not want to see our humanitarian traditions hampered by 'tough' new policies that might slam our doors on people who need our sanctuary. On the other hand, there were legitimate concerns that we were losing control over our immigration policies because of the widespread abuse of the refugee process."

This was at least an acknowledgment of one part of the problem: the loss of control resulting from widespread abuse. His task was to recover that control while retaining Canada's traditional concerns for those in need of sanctuary. He assured the joint Canadian Clubs that: "After fifteen months in operation . . . the process is working as effectively as we might have hoped." He acknowledged growing pains and controversy in a system designed to deal fairly and sensitively with people of diverse cultures and languages. He judged his Board a success because:

> . . . the time from when a person first makes a claim for refugee status to when the claim is fully determined has been shortened dramatically, from a matter of years to just a few months. That means genuine refugees are granted status in Canada much more quickly while those who had hoped to use the system to get around immigration line-ups no longer have the same incentive to do so. That incentive was the length of time they might be able to remain in Canada before their claims were rejected.

Had Mr. Fairweather somehow forgotten the statistics facing Messrs. Harder and Gerlitz in Ottawa? It was important that his audience know, he told them, of the general acknowledgment both inside and outside the country that Canada now had a manageable process that was being looked at by many as a model encompassing both fairness and efficiency. He emphasized that because the management of the refugee issue within Canada was now more effective, policy makers were free to look at and reflect upon a broader range of refugee and immigration policies.[11]

The Canadian Club members were able to return to their workaday lives in Vancouver knowing that the refugee-determination process, subject of so much negative publicity, was at last in good, competent, credible hands, and those much-advertised abuses were well under control. The natives had been conned yet again.

*   *   *

Just before Christmas 1990, however, Firdaus J. Kharas questioned whether it wasn't time for Cabinet to reconsider continuing the backlog program. About one-third of the cases had been settled but only 200 fraudulent claimants had been removed from Canada. He said that it would be "very difficult to complete the program by even the end of 1991", and doubted the "prospect of large scale removals from Canada."[12]

In his annual report for 1990, Mr. Fairweather also questioned whether the program could be completed before the end of 1991, emphasizing that "almost none of the 1,630 claimants rejected under the program in 1990 had been removed from Canada." He said: "It is removals that send a clear message to the international community that Canada will not tolerate abuse of its refugee determination system." Not quite the message he had delivered in Vancouver. In this comedy of errors, nothing was to be as it seemed for very long.

*   *   *

The "Initiatives to Expedite Refugee Determination" (to be known as the "Expedited Process") was to be Mr. Fairweather's latest innovation in what was still alleged to be a quasi-judicial process. This was in place by mid-1990 in Montreal and Toronto, and to be implemented in Vancouver in January 1991. Its purpose was to identify claims which were sufficiently straightforward to allow for immediate positive determination. Essentially, it was a paper screening process to be followed by an interview and, for those considered favourably, a recommendation by a member of the Board for rapid passage to landed status.

Initially, the Expedited Process was confined to claims from countries with the highest volume of claimants and with very high positive determination rates. According to government releases, "It was assumed that there would be a correlation between the general positive determination rate for a particular country, and the proportion of claims which are suitable for expedited positive determination." IRB management considered the Expedited Process a procedure which would allow the Refugee Division to fulfil its mandate under the Immigration Act, namely, "to deal with all proceedings before it as uniformly and expeditiously as the circumstances and the considerations of fairness permit."

This appears to be acknowledgment of a Commons Committee recommendation that decision-makers be provided with the acceptance rates established under the new Board in its first year of operation. That rate had increased 37 per cent for major-source and high-acceptance-rate countries.

Would that directive result in the automatic acceptance of the 37 per cent of claimants from the high-acceptance-rate countries who would have failed pre-1989 RSAC standards, and would it result in claims filed by everyone from Somalia succeeding? Certainly it would be expeditious, informal and "fair", and it could be interpreted as conforming to Section 68(2) of the Immigration Act. Was it really the intent of Parliament that the Immigration and Refugee Board should develop expedient procedures designed only in terms of convenience and a need to accommodate a flood of questionable claimants, as opposed to just the genuinely persecuted, for whom Canada has assumed a responsibility?

*   *   *

In November 1994, a former Refugee Hearing Officer, the late Padraig O'Donahue, told the *Vancouver Sun* in an interview that when the Vancouver office's refugee-acceptance rate fell below that in Eastern Canada, there were visits by senior Ottawa-based IRB officials, who "pleaded with us not to have so many negative decisions—they said it looked bad." He continued:

"I was supposed to find out the truth—that's why I was hired. My employer wanted me to be a sort of janitor—opening the door with a polite bow."[13]

Mr. O'Donahue admitted that he was one of twelve RHOs and Board members who, earlier in the year, had been named in a plea from some Vancouver immigration lawyers to Minister of Immigration Sergio Marchi, requesting they be replaced. In response, the government now refused to renew his appointment as a Refugee Hearing Officer.

Mr. O'Donahue, Irish-born, trained in the law, had a long career in many parts of the world, including service in Africa with the British Overseas Legal Service and nine years as solicitor general in British Somalia. In Canada, he served as deputy minister of justice for the Yukon from 1967 to 1983. Certainly, in addition to his professional scruples, he brought valuable qualities to the IRB.

As he told the *Sun,* because of first-hand knowledge of many of the countries from which claimants came, he sensed when there was something wrong with a story but "the argument of the immigration lawyers was that these people should come to Canada because they were poor and afraid of a famine. But these were economic refugees. They did not meet the definition of convention refugees laid down by the United Nations." Indeed, he questioned whether he had seen one genuine refugee all the time he was in the Vancouver Board office.

*   *   *

To return to our comedy of errors. In October 1991, there was some public/media anxiety about a lack of refugee-backlog progress. This prompted the Honourable Bernard Valcourt, the last but one Tory minister of immigration, to provide assurance that the program was working well and would be completed "under budget". In fact, his October 4 press release stated that ". . . nearly 60,000 of the 95,000 claimants have been dealt with, including some 16,000 who have either left Canada or are in the removal stream"; that nearly 40,000 or 65 per cent of the individuals have been accepted; that Quebec would complete its own hearings in March 1992 and all other provinces by December 1992.

Effective January 1, 1992, an amendment to the Immigration Regulations, published in the *Canada Gazette*, stretched out the deadline for completion of the backlog clearance for a full year to December 31, 1992. Such changes must be justified and this need was explained by statistics indicating 35 per cent no-shows, adjournments of 54 per cent and an underestimated number of cases, originally thought to be 85,000. It was explained that this 85,000 figure had been set in the fall of 1988, "when refugee claimant arrivals were still increasing dramatically in anticipation of a rumoured amnesty to clear the backlog, and the new refugee determination legislation scheduled to become effective on January 1, 1989." This further confirmed what everyone knew from the outset—that the 85,000 figure was false.

So now the government acknowledged the higher figure of 95,000, and recognized that a factor of 1.2 for family members increased this to 114,000. The IRB report for the year ending December 31, 1992 would say it was "96,000". The minister's October 1991 statement said approximately 60,000 backlog cases had been decided, of which nearly 65 per cent had been accepted. The *Canada Gazette* explanation was confirmation. By the end of June 1991, over 55,000 cases had been decided, with an overall acceptance rate of 66 per cent. Then, on February 17, 1992, the *Vancouver Sun* reported that Oakley Duff, acting director of the Backlog Clearance Program, revealed that arrest warrants had been issued for more than 7,000 people who failed to show up for hearings. If, as it appears, they were part of the backlog, then most had either been in Canada for more than six years or had moved on. This same newspaper story quoted Rod Noakes, spokesman for the Immigration Department, as saying that 5,844 arrest warrants had been issued for those in the system effective January 1, 1989.

The revised backlog timetable was now due to expire on December 31, 1992, and in a moment of exuberance, just six weeks before this final deadline, Minister Valcourt again expressed his satisfaction in a November 16 press release. The encouraging news was that "the Program will be completed well within budget and I am confident that my officials will meet the December 1992 deadline for completing the bulk of the hearings. . . . As of October 1992, of the estimated 95,000 backlog refugee claims, 92,000 cases had been decided, with an overall acceptance rate of 68 per cent."

Sorry, wrong numbers! This was a great spin, but the above figures never found their way into the IRB annual report for 1992: nearly half this number of refugee claimants would be reported, but not the rest. As Ms. Mawani, who replaced Mr. Fairweather as chairperson in October 1992, was to explain:

> I am pleased to report that the Board has all but concluded work on the Backlog Clearance Program. Over the three-year life of that program, the Board dealt with almost 50,000 claimants: individuals caught in limbo for many years because the previous institutional system could not cope with demand.

To this, her report added that claims initiated by the Board in those three years were 46,514—not 55,000, not 60,000 and not 92,000. Of these, only 42,385 had been decided and 1,864 had been either withdrawn or abandoned. Of those decided, 76.8 per cent were accepted for landing. So over 50,000 either returned home, went elsewhere or are today living underground in Canada. Thus ended the backlog saga.

Not surprisingly, those who toiled in the Immigration Department were overwhelmed by confusion and discontent. This included both long-time members of the bureaucracy and relatively new appointees to the IRB.

Following then Immigration Minister Sergio Marchi's 1994 Summer of Consultations, when senior officials in Ottawa and, later, the frontline immigration officers in British Columbia and the Yukon, released their "otherwise withheld" reports to the media,[14] Canadians were reminded of that 1992 negative assessment of the IRB by the Honourable David Anderson. Mr. Anderson served on the Board from 1984 until his appointment was ended abruptly on December 31, 1988, under the legislation establishing the IRB. His comments are included in Chapter I.

An officer in Immigration's Intelligence Branch put it this way: "The system has become so open that when a refugee gets in, the word goes out and his whole village floods in behind him." One Board member stated: "We get people who all repeat the same story about how they were involved in a coup. It's a fabrication—but we can't prove it. They have friends who have gone through the system and coached them."

According to several immigration officers in Toronto, their department managers had instructed them not to challenge claims at the initial-inquiry stage from about twenty-five countries, including Sri Lanka. As a result, they explained, these refugee claimants received approval based on little more than the material on their application forms. This was so, even when they arrived with no identification, or when whatever they produced was fake.

*   *   *

J. C. Best, who was introduced in Chapter I, had been the department's executive director of immigration and demographic policy from 1978 to 1985, and Canadian High Commissioner to Trinidad-Tobago from 1986 until the end of 1988—the period those 14,000-plus bogus refugees were travelling to Toronto. Mr. Best provided a public statement less than three months into the new system's operation.[15] Because of its importance and relevance today, ten years later, it is included in full.

> It is difficult to be optimistic. No rational person will argue with the proposition that our process of refugee determination must be as fair, objective and humanitarian as possible. It is, however, equally important that the integrity of the system be maintained and that only bona fide political refugees be granted refugee status.
>
> Take, for example, the recent flood of refugee claimants from Trinidad and Tobago. Based on three years' observation (as Canadian high commissioner) of the country's political and legal system, it is inconceivable to me that any claimant from there could even remotely have

a true refugee claim. And yet they enjoy the same free access to the system as does a hard-pressed Bahai from Iran.

This easy, universal access is the main cause of the problem. The new limits contained in the latest legislation are a small improvement, but in the long run they are unlikely to prove adequate. It is highly probable that any effective limits will encounter legal problems. The key legislation is not the Immigration Act but the Charter of Rights and Freedoms.

Given the current attitude of the courts, even the limited controls in the recent amendments are likely to fail. While Parliament can exempt the process from charter control, the government is extremely unlikely to consider invoking this provision.

. . . In an era of fiscal restraint, the government will be reluctant to provide sufficient resources to operate the system more quickly.

The pressure of refugee determination will probably continue dominating policy discussions. Crisis-driven tinkering will continue, in place of a broad policy review. If this projection is correct, Canada will be the loser.

Ministers traditionally have been reluctant to open parliamentary debate on immigration except when the need to change or amend the Immigration Act becomes imperative. Even then, every effort is made to restrict the scope of change to a minimum.

Immigration policy, however, should reflect as far as possible a clear concept of our future needs in social, demographic and economic terms. This cannot be achieved by maintaining the status quo, or by limited discussion of the issues.

Tragically, the crisis-driven "tinkering" Mr. Best refers to continues unabated.

*   *   *

With the refugee backlog relegated to a perpetual limbo, it was still politically necessary to advance the image of a successful IRB. A good story would certainly help, and on May 22, 1992, a feature article appeared in the *Globe and Mail* under the headline, "Fewer Claimants Given Refugee Status", accompanied by the subhead, "Success Rate for Refugee Claims", and illustrated by a bar graph. Taken in isolation, it presented an image favourable to the Board. It showed a steadily diminishing acceptance rate between 1989 and 1992. Naturally, it told only half the story and, in doing so, provided an opportunity for refugee advocates to express their indignation at the declining acceptance rate and, otherwise, for the Board to defend its achievements. This they were able to do without any thought for the additional comparative information added to their bar graph in Figure 3.

The IRB defence was easy. The post-1988 decline in acceptance rates merely reflected changing circumstances in some countries. A Board spokesman acknowledged that although acceptances of Somalia claimants had hovered around 90 per cent for three years, the rate had dropped dramatically for claimants from Poland and China. These had followed political change in newly democratic Poland, and a decline from earlier claims from China based on the fear of potential intimidation and persecution related to the Tiananmen Square disaster of June 1989. Although the IRB administration did not concede this, both the Polish and Chinese situations were convincing arguments to support the Law Reform Commission case for temporary asylum in countries of refuge, rather than landed status leading to citizenship.

Refugee advocates, however, differed vigorously. Colin McAdam, coordinator of the Toronto-based Jesuit Refugee Service, said: "What we are seeing is more strong cases being dismissed, cases for instance that would not have been refused even a year ago and certainly not two years ago, cases which we feel are refugee cases." David Matas, Winnipeg lawyer and president of the Canadian Council of Refugees, was much more convoluted in his comments: "The Board is independent and doesn't take orders from the government but, all the same there

FIGURE 3
SUCCESS RATE FOR REFUGEE CLAIMS, 1983–1992

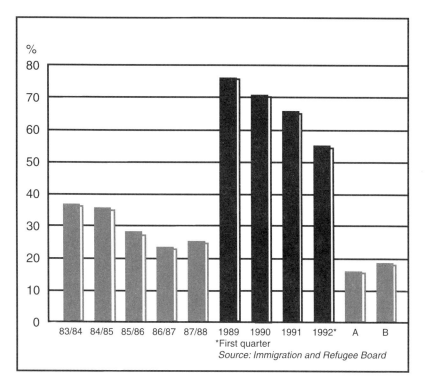

*First quarter
Source: Immigration and Refugee Board

A   Average 1988 acceptance rates of sixteen refugee-receiving countries, including Canada, as reported by Informal Consultations, a Geneva-based secretariat to which Canada subscribes, was 14%.

B   Of 250,000 claims examined by Informal Consultations, 16.8% were found to meet United Nations criteria.

is a general sentiment often expressed—and the government is under pressure because of it—that the past high recognition rate was somehow wrong . . . and I think the Board is reacting to that." Linda Read of the Quaker Committee for Refugees blamed the bar-graph decline on what she called the government's emphasis on tougher enforcement. She referred to "refugees who really need protection being deported", and spoke of a "real push to provide disincentives for people coming here, and a real push by the government to get rid of people."

All of which is proof "of a sort" that relative percentage acceptance rates are a poor basis for evaluating the work of a Board, when each decision from whatever source involves an individual, and the personal circumstances of that individual. Those percentages do have legitimacy, but only when they reflect the records of the two separate RSAC and CRDD decision-making groups, and the threefold increase in acceptances under the CRDD for both mainstream refugees and backlog claimants. They would also have legitimacy if they reflected the standards of other refugee-receiving countries as determined by Geneva-based Informal Consultations. "Column A" represents the 14-per-cent average acceptance rate for sixteen refugee-receiving countries, including Canada; and "Column B", the 16.8 per cent of 250,000 refugee claims examined by Informal Consultations that this organization found to meet UNHCR criteria. The Board and the refugee advocates conveniently neglected to recognize these facts.

*   *   *

Following the November 1993 election and the assumption of office by the Chrétien Liberals, Sergio Marchi, who had served as opposition immigration critic, became minister of citizenship and immigration. On December 30 he replaced twenty-eight Conservative government IRB appointees with his own Board members. As a new minister in a new government he was determined to reverse the trend of the Mulroney years with appointments that would set a fresh tone, and help to rebuild the immigration industry's (it couldn't have been the public's) confidence and trust in the IRB. Consequently, the new Board members were selected in consultation with the immigration and refugee lobby and vetted by IRB chairperson Ms. Mawani, who, though a Tory appointment, proved invulnerable. So far as one can tell from the news release covering these appointments, twenty-one, or three-quarters, of the new appointees had backgrounds which included professional, academic or community experience related to immigration and refugee matters.[16] The minister claimed that, overall, his appointments reflected a gender, linguistic and cultural balance, which "speaks proudly of the country's reality." Heading the list was immigration militant Michael Schelew, the new deputy-chairperson responsible for the Convention Refugee Determination Division. Described as a "leading advocate from the world of immigration and refugee affairs", Mr. Schelew had been president of the Canadian Council of Refugees.

Less than a year later, on November 2, 1994, Mr. Schelew's appointment was suspended after chairperson Ms. Mawani presented a critical report of his conduct to the minister. This followed the minister's request that she investigate the complaints of some Board members that Schelew was trying to bully them into accepting certain refugee claims. Mr. Schelew, however, refused to resign. A judicial inquiry was set up, which might well have used the opportunity to examine the entire IRB operation, had its proceedings not been foreclosed when the discredited Mr. Schelew accepted a severance settlement of $100,000. All of this led former Canadian Ambassador William Bauer, recently resigned from the Board after three years' service, to comment:[17]

> What's wrong here is far more than Mr. Schelew. What's wrong here
> is the whole culture of the Board and of late a whole lot of members
> who simply have never seen anyone they didn't think was a refugee.

Then, in June 1995, Minister Marchi appointed Inderjit Singh Bal to the Board. Mr. Bal, co-founder of the revolutionary World Sikh Youth Organization, a leading Punjabi separatist group, had served as chairman of the Liberal Party's multicultural committee after having unsuccessfully sought the party's nomination in a Southern Ontario riding in 1993. Six months later, he too found himself forced to resign from the Board. He had admitted to a House of Commons committee that he entered Canada illegally in 1976, and had entered into a marriage of convenience with a Canadian woman in order to gain landed-immigrant status, though still married to his first wife in India.

* * *

In the meantime, Minister Marchi wrestled with the vexing problem of doing something about the increasing numbers of *failed* refugee claimants who remained in Canada contrary to the law. He achieved this in November 1994 with the brilliant creation of the "Deferred Removal Order Class" (DROC). Applications to become a "DROC" could be made by those otherwise subject to deportation if, having had their refugee claim refused, they had been in Canada under an unexecuted Removal Order for more than three years. A DROC could remain in Canada on passing landed-immigrant requirements as these related to medical, criminality and security screening. Skills, literacy and language were not mentioned.

Later, a new minister, Lucienne Robillard, would discover that these regulations had the unintended, if hardly surprising, effect of encouraging failed claimants to avoid their removal from Canada until they could qualify to become a DROC. There had already been 6,244 applications, of which 5,589 had been processed—4,716 approved; 873 refused; 665 awaiting decisions. New regulations closing out this "DROC amnesty" were to be published on January 1, 1997, to be effective March 1 of that year.

In addition to closing out the Deferred Removal Order Class, the minister in her December 19, 1996 statement gave notice of modifications to the "Post Determination Refugee Claimants in Canada" (PDRCC) class. PDRCCs were failed refugee claimants who had been assessed as nevertheless facing potential risk should they be returned to their countries of origin. In 1995–96, immigration officers conducted 7,277 such reviews, accepting 473 (6.5 per cent), who were then free to apply for landed-immigrant status. Those who had abandoned their refugee claims, or who had been convicted of serious criminal offences, would not be eligible for this review, nor would it be automatic for the others. Indeed, the onus would be on the failed claimant to make a credible application. There was, however, the assurance that those ineligible because of having abandoned their refugee claim would still have the opportunity to seek special consideration through an application based on humanitarian and compassionate circumstances.

*   *   *

Canada is oceans to the east and west of today's genuine refugees and is therefore unsuited to serve as a country of temporary asylum. The United Nations' position—that most temporarily displaced people should return to their native surroundings when that is possible—is best served by asylum nearby. For example, most Tamils seeking refuge from civil strife in Sri Lanka find this among the Tamil population in southern India, from where they are able to return to their homeland. They do so in large numbers.

It would make sense for Canada to accept a fair share or more of those 59,000 refugees designated by the UNHCR who, without the necessary resources for airfare, could not make it to present their cases in person before the IRB in Canada. We could then assure their settlement and integration as productive citizens in Canada. They, in turn, would achieve their expectations of a good life as Canadians. The Convention Refugee Determination Division could be disbanded and its budget, as well as the extra peripheral costs of welfare, health, education, security, etc., appropriately redirected to foreign aid and the re-establishment of necessary funding for the health and education of Canadian citizens.

To whom will Minister Caplan and her successors listen as they contend with the attendant problems of each year's new batch of 25,000–30,000 refugee claims, the burgeoning Family Class arrivals, tens of thousands of illegal immigrants, to say nothing of the thousands dodging deportation orders? I suspect we already know.

*   *   *

On July 20, 1998, a CBC radio news item exposed an even more horrific refugee crisis. They reported that social agencies and the police were working on a new problem facing Vancouver's troubled East Side. Children from Honduras, some as young as eleven, were being smuggled in to work in the drug trade. The smugglers set the children up in apartments, helped them file refugee claims and sign up for welfare. They were then turned loose on the streets to deal drugs, primarily crack cocaine.

A media campaign followed, exposing this abuse of Canada's border and our society. There were week-long television series with cameras accompanying police on the streets of the city centre and the suburbs. We saw drug deals taking place; we saw arrests; we saw these teenage dealers entering court; we saw them back on the street again dealing drugs within a few hours of being charged and released; and we saw police frustrated in their attempts to deal with an impossible situation. We also saw an interview with an immigration lawyer publicly defending their rights.

We saw a major campaign to clean up the main street of New Westminster, with police gathering up drug dealers and dumping them out of town; and we saw attractive teenage Canadian girls fraternizing with bogus teenage Honduran-refugee drug dealers. In some cases we saw the girls dealing drugs on behalf of their new boyfriends.

Three years earlier, in 1996, knowledge of Canada's porous border, the power of its Charter and of the *Singh* decision, and a government unwilling to act in the face of disaster, had reached Honduras. In 1996 the Convention Refugee Determination Division in Vancouver processed 45 Honduran refugee claims; in 1997 the number trebled; in 1998 it more than doubled; and in the first quarter of 1999 the rate of demands on the CRDD had quadrupled. Of 754 claims received in those thirty-nine months, only 40 were accepted as refugees. At the end of the first quarter of 1999, 98 claims had been rejected, 267 withdrawn or abandoned, 240 hearings were pending and 119 had been statistically lost.

It appears of little concern to the minister or the Immigration and Refugee Board that 95 per cent of those refugee claimants were existing in an immigration and drug-infested limbo. And there could have been more of them, had the enforcement authorities in San Francisco and Portland not picked them up en route north and shipped them home.

Table 4 sets out the record.

TABLE 4
HONDURAN REFUGEE CLAIMS PROCESSED IN VANCOUVER
1996–1999 (FIRST QUARTER)

	1996	1997	1998	1999 (1st Qtr.)	Totals	
Claims received by IRB	45	132	284	303		764
Accepted as refugees	12	6	10	12	40	
Refugee claims rejected	3	9	35	51	98	
Claims withdrawn/abandoned/others	5	31	95	136	267	
Claims pending at period end	65	145	278	240	240	645
Claims statistically lost						119

How many were dealing drugs? How many were reaping the benefits of Canada's welfare and health-care programs? What were the burgeoning costs of law enforcement including police, court appearances and legal aid; and how many young Canadian lives were being destroyed through the cheap drugs dealt by these Honduran children?

Five of the six British Columbia members of the federal Liberal Caucus represent the Greater Vancouver area. With the release of the report of the minister's Advisory Committee at the beginning of 1998, four of those MPs, three of whom were Cabinet ministers, opposed the proposal that immigrants to Canada be required to speak one of our languages. But when it came to the sorry story of the Honduran drug dealers, why is it that, like the minister, these same elected representatives in Parliament for the City of Vancouver were silent on the subject of this well-publicized, gross and costly abuse of our border and our society?

ENDNOTES

1. For an example, see Richard Cleroux's article in the *Globe and Mail*, October 29, 1987.
2. The *Vancouver Province,* April 9, 1989.
3. The *Globe and Mail,* March 31, 1987.
4. The *Vancouver Sun,* November 9, 1988.
5. Malarek, Victor, "Thousands Face Deportation, Lawyers Warn", the *Globe and Mail,* April 14, 1989.
6. The *Ottawa Citizen,* August 28, 1989.
7. The *Vancouver Sun,* November 23, 1989.
8. *Canada's Immigration Program.* Margaret Young, Research Branch, Library of Parliament, January 1989, revised July 1989.
9. The *Globe and Mail,* December 7, 1989.
10. Internal IRB memorandum, April 24, 1990.
11. "Notes for remarks by R. G. L. Fairweather . . . 1:15 P.M., Thursday, April 19, 1990."
12. The *Vancouver Sun,* December 20, 1990.
13. The *Vancouver Sun,* December 1, 1994.
14. See Chapter VII.
15. The *Globe and Mail,* March 10, 1989.
16. Michael Schelew, Patricia Anne Henders, Pierre Duquette, George Cram, Brenda Parris, Jean Lanoue, Richard Lord, Daniel Paquin, Francois Ramsay, Pa Zambelli, Marcus Durant, Queenie Hum, Philomen Wright, Samuel Berman, Cornelia Soberano, Paul Aterman, Ellen Turley, Laron Hopkins, Najib Tahiri, Audrey Ho.
17. The *Globe and Mail,* November 12, 1994.

CHAPTER VI

ADMINISTRATIVE COLLAPSE

"The current process does not quickly grant Canadian protection to claimants who genuinely need it. Furthermore, it does not discourage from claiming refugee status those who do not require or deserve Canada's protection."

Report of the Auditor General of Canada
for the year ending March 31, 1997

From the beginning, the practice of granting adjournments or postponements of scheduled Immigration Appeal Board hearings, as a right, was often the first item of business at a refugee hearing. The result was that the IAB courtroom complement, consisting of three Board members, an interpreter, a court stenographer, a court clerk and the minister's appeals officer, were left with nothing to do.

Early in 1983 this was dealt with in the Vancouver office. Instead of simply summoning appellants to a scheduled IAB hearing, the staff would arrange mutually convenient times with the appellants or their lawyers. Hearings by appointment became the rule. Members of the immigration bar understood immediately that legitimate requests for adjournments or postponements would always be granted. Otherwise each case would proceed as scheduled. The members of the bar cooperated. The simple application of careful scheduling, together with firm and fair administration, doubled productivity.

What is important about this experience is that seven years later, in 1990, an extensive study of the operations of the successor Immigration and Refugee Board was undertaken by the Law Reform Commission of Canada. Their 155-page, unpublished preliminary study, entitled *The Determination of Refugee Status in Canada: A Review of the Procedure,* is dated February 1, 1991. The highlight of their research was that "Case scheduling turned out to be a crucial issue, as did practice on adjournments."

Adjudicators at large expressed their dissatisfaction with the process of scheduling, which they saw as inefficient and overly complicated. The major problems became the number of days necessary to complete a contested case, long delays before case resumption and the number of postponements.

In some offices in 1989 it took from six to nine months to process a claim, and by 1990 that period had increased to more than twelve months. With three to four months between sessions, transcripts at $5.00 a page were required to refresh the memory.

During one week in 1990, forty-six cases were opened in the Mississauga office, of which thirty-six were adjourned: twenty-two for counsel failing to arrive, arriving late or unprepared; eight for the Board member failing to attend; four when time ran out; one for both parties needing to prepare; and one for humanitarian and compassionate review.

And in Vancouver, statistics gathered confirmed that once a case is adjourned it could be adjourned again any number of times thereafter. The scheduling procedure that had proven a success in Vancouver under the former IAB had been abandoned by the new Immigration and Refugee Board.

It may not come as a surprise that this important Law Reform Commission Report, though privately distributed, was not published and presented to Parliament. Government failure to fill the vacancies on the commission left that body without the authority of the quorum necessary to publish.

Members of the Immigration and Refugee Board are charged with the daily responsibility of making critical decisions affecting the lives of thousands of individuals and their families. That responsibility includes the obligation to both Canada and the claimants to make those decisions quickly, so that the accepted may be assisted to settle and become contributors rather than dependents, and those refused may be returned home to familiar surroundings before establishing a base in Canada.

That was the real message of the Law Reform Commission Report. That this report was not formally published due to a technicality doesn't mean the message had not been received. In fact, the report was widely distributed to members of the immigration bar and others involved with immigrant and refugee policies. Members of the Law Reform Commission, along with the authors of the report, met with groups of these involved citizens in principal centres in Canada. The objective was to get their reaction in anticipation of publishing a final report. Yet none of this appears to have seeped through to the media or the public, and over a year later a draft final report, dated March 5, 1992, summarized the adjournment problem in one sentence: "Once an inquiry has been opened, adjournments top the complaints list in each region, followed by late starts and difficulties with booking resumed cases."

Yet again, Parliament and the public had failed to benefit from a critical report. In his final cost-cutting budget in 1992, Finance Minister Don Mazankowski eliminated the Law Reform Commission, and, once again, with that "economy" went the authority to publish the final document. It was distributed to members of the interested groups by mail.

Fortunately (and coincidental to all of this), Auditor General Kenneth Dye was performing an audit on the new Immigration and Refugee Board for the year ending March 31, 1990, covering the first fifteen months of operations of the new Board. It was in this report, published in November 1990, that Mr. Dye described the new refugee-determination process as "close to collapse."

Like the Law Reform Commission, the auditors found that adjournments were mainly due to two factors: the lack of availability or readiness of claimants' legal counsel, and insufficient time being scheduled for completion of hearings. Adjournments and average hearing times had not been considered in the scheduling process. In one region, 33 per cent of first hearings and 27 per cent of second hearings were adjourned and in 1989, the first year under the new Board, only 59 per cent of time allotted for hearings was used by adjudicators and IRB members.

This is a tale of gross mismanagement, but the fact that the IRB was functioning under a new system had little or nothing to do with this failure. On December 13, 1990, the IRB's chairman, Gordon Fairweather, and his staff appeared before the Commons Committee on Labour, Employment and Immigration. A particular question-and-answer exchange in those proceedings prompted these comments from Mr. Fairweather: "I saw an adjournment the other day that was the fourteenth adjournment. I believe fourteen adjournments are unacceptable and in contempt of an administrative procedure. Had it happened in the civil courts, they would have been brought to book much faster." And then: ". . . I assume they ask for adjournments based on the possibility the Cabinet at the minister's recommendation will grant an amnesty. It is a chicken and egg kind of thing."

Mr. Fairweather is a man of wide experience: former Attorney General for New Brunswick, longtime MP for Fundy-Royal, former Canadian Human Rights Commissioner and, beginning in 1988, Canada's "immigration czar". But this widely experienced political and public servant was unwilling to summon the courage to do for Canada, as chairman of the Board, not only what a judge could do without hesitation, but what had succeeded at the staff level in Vancouver ten years earlier.

In December 1997 the new Auditor General, Denis Desautels, published his report for the year ending March 31 of that year. The message of his auditors on adjournments and postponements was once again clear. Under the heading "Postponements and adjournments are a major cause of Board delays", the problem was well described. Board members and refugee-claim officers had clearly indicated that postponements and adjournments, caused by internal administration as well as by claimants and their representatives, were a major cause of Board delays. The result was that 49 per cent of scheduled hearings in 1996 had to be either postponed or adjourned.

The 1997 Report of the Auditor General effectively tells the minister, the present chairperson of the Board and all Members of Parliament the following:

- fifteen years after it was established in Vancouver that strict attention to scheduling would result in a 100-per-cent increase in productivity;
- seven years after Auditor General Dye reached the same conclusion and Mr. Fairweather had provided his assessment of this scandalous situation to a Parliamentary committee;
- and five years after the Law Reform Commission in two reports highlighted the problem;
- no one had done anything about the problem.

The obvious conclusions are that Finance Minister Paul Martin's promised restraint policies have not been respected and that the distribution of pink slips is long overdue.

* * *

The unpublished Law Reform Commission studies found that adjournments and postponements were not the only reasons for prevailing IRB inefficiencies. Chapter IV of its February 1, 1991 report, covering the commission's research into Board operations and practices, dealt with a plethora of deficiencies.

The Refugee Hearing Officers, who conduct the hearings, had complained about time wasted by all-too-frequent failure of principal participants to work responsibly. Adjudicators and Board members arrived late and unprepared, while claimants' counsel often arrived without knowing the details of their cases and requiring valuable court time for discussion with their clients. This was compounded in Montreal with delays resulting from a demand for translation of the Personal Information Form, regardless of the language on the form. These forms were an essential source of information. When given to claimants by their counsel with insufficient instructions, claimants' files lacked sufficient information for the RHO to properly prepare the case.

The most common cause of concern for the commission was "incompetent, tedious, repetitive and time-consuming case presentation by counsel." Although "local Bar Associations were aware of counsel giving less than adequate service, little was done to correct the situation." The disciplinary process for incompetent counsel was obviously ineffective.

It was the obligation of the Board chairperson, Mr. Fairweather or Ms. Mawani, to see that the system functioned. Time brought no improvement.

Five years later, in his 1997 report, the Auditor General's remarks suggest that nothing had changed. He found that "additional efforts are needed to encourage the various stakeholders in the refugee determination process to comply with the Board's rules and procedures." He repeated examples of counsel's failure to provide the essential Personal Information Forms on time. In 1996, 57 per cent of these forms were submitted overdue. Was anyone really in charge?

The findings of the Law Reform Commission reports in 1990/91, and of the 1990 and 1996/97 reports of the Auditor General, were clearly stated. In the years 1991 to 1997, claims abandoned or withdrawn increased from 6 per cent to 23.3 per cent, resulting in an apparent reduction in claims accepted to 40 per cent. Yet, of those who pursued their claims, the acceptance rate ranged between 52 and 70 per cent—still double or treble the pre-1989 experience. And in those years the backlog grew from 13,000 to 28,000. It is all indicative of the extent to which we Canadians had lost control of our border.

It testifies to an organizational dysfunction that began with the selection of Immigration and Refugee Board members on a more political basis than was the case with the Immigration Appeal Board. In the case of the new IRB, appointments went not only to those with past experience in public affairs but, increasingly, to those allied with immigrant and refugee advocacy groups in what could be described, among other things, as a possible conflict of interest. To make matters worse, if not impossible, many of those appointed were entirely without other notable accomplishments in life. The 1991 Law Reform Commission put it this way:

Most members come to the job with little or no training in law or procedure. This was observed to have a negative effect on the conduct of
hearings, for example, where lack of control contributes to unnecessary prolongation; or where disregard of basic hearings etiquette,
such as talking during testimony, results in intimidation of the claimant.

and then made their recommendation:

> Members generally should be tested for knowledge and merit. . . .
> Present selection criteria were too superficial, often bringing in the
> functionally illiterate.[1]

Certainly the appointment of suitable Board members is, beyond question, the most important factor, along with effective
management, in the success or failure of the IRB's work.
This 1991 questioning of the suitability of the prevailing appointment process did not continue in isolation. In his December 1993 report, *Rebuilding Trust*,[2] Professor James C.
Hathaway, a specialist on refugee questions from York University, made the following observations on whether Board members could handle the "activist, non-adversarial" role envisaged
by Parliament when it established the Refugee Division:

> . . . this is sadly not the case: members themselves were frank in their
> assessment that far too many of their colleagues are presently unfit to
> exercise their responsibilities by reason either of simple incompe-
> tence or a negative attitudinal disposition. Perhaps most shockingly
> was one Assistant Deputy Chairperson's assessment that, if given the
> choice, eighty percent of the members presently supervised by the
> ADC would be dismissed.

For emphasis, the professor then quoted from the 1992 Law
Reform Commission draft final report:

> Persons who are not capable of reaching reasoned and responsible
> decisions on their own should not be appointed to the board. Training
> should be provided to ensure that those who are appointed are ad-
> equately equipped to discharge their responsibilities. Individuals

who, after reasonable training, are incapable of handling the job, should be removed from the Board.

In her comments on Professor Hathaway's criticisms, IRB chairperson Nurjehan Mawani correctly pointed out that appointments to her Board are the responsibility of the minister. Certainly the findings of the Law Reform Commission, the Auditor General and Professor Hathaway are the legacy of the Mulroney government, and of Ministers McDougall and Valcourt in particular. However, none of this has inspired the successor Chrétien government, or its immigration ministers, Marchi and Robillard, to take corrective action.

Indeed, it was as if Minister Marchi had received quite contrary advice when he announced on March 2, 1995 that there would be changes in the Immigration Act to permit the Refugee Division of the Immigration and Refugee Board to conduct hearings with single-member panels. He predicted a reduction in Board membership from 175 to 112, with the annual savings of $5.7 million to be available for the resettlement of refugees from overseas. That was not and would not be a saving, even though it matters little whether the decision is made by a single or double panel.

The legislation creating the IRB reduced the traditional judicial/quasi-judicial tribunal from three members to two, with split decisions favouring the refugee claimant. When the decision is not obvious, however, this arrangement fails to assure essential discussion of the evidence among the decision-makers. Unlike a police court, which usually metes out short-term penalties, virtually every Board decision determines where those concerned will live for the rest of their lives, and positive decisions have a significant impact on Canada as a whole.

When the panel has three members, the evidence is clear and the members unanimous, the decision is immediate. Otherwise, when the members are divided, reflection and discussion are necessary to assure a just decision. Neither the single-member nor the two-member panel provides for that—which is why there are tribunals. The single-member panel is not designed to improve decision-making but to expand Board productivity and to accommodate the demands created for the Board by a "clientele" largely composed of economic opportunists. Regrettably, the flawed philosophy is such that the justice of decisions is no longer a critical factor. Whether single- or double-member panels hear claims doesn't change that circumstance.

Mr. Marchi's plan would not be a saving, but for much more significant reasons: the Board requires more members, as stated in a recommendation of the Nielsen Task Force in 1985.

In 1998 the CRDD had 166 members, down from 211 at the height of the backlog escapade. The politicians in a debt-cutting phase had sent 50 of these experienced CRDD members packing and a backlog again began to build up. The administrative organization is intact. Take the annual cost of a member with benefits as being $100,000 and ancillary staff related to that function as being $300,000. For 50 new members that totals $20 million a year. Whatever it is, that may be high. Balance that against costs. With a running inventory of 25,000 in the backlog, if only the equivalent of 5,000 require maintenance including welfare, health and dental care, at $10,000 a year, the cost is $50 million a year.

Whatever the actual figures, it is clear that mismanagement of Canada's refugee-determination program costs a lot of money. There is a clear obligation for the minister to see that the real figures are developed; to clear the backlog; and to eliminate those horrendous maintenance charges mentioned above, which only bad management has allowed to develop.

One valuable benefit of the appointment of sufficient competent and independent members to tackle this mess would be a resource of experienced people when that job is done, and the opportunity to selectively develop the strength of the organization with multi-year appointments.

There has already been reference made to the assurance of Deputy Minister of Immigration Peter Harder, at the 1994 Consultations wind-up meeting in Ottawa, that not only did the IRB operate with full independence from government interference, but that Board members enjoyed independence from each other!

The need is twofold: simple amendments to the legislation and regulations, to assure consistency in decision-making and to end the opportunities for abuse; and a complete overhaul of the management of the program at both ministerial and Board levels. Compare, for example, the conflicting reports of Ms. Mawani and the Auditor General. Each covers the one-year period ending March 31, 1997. Chairperson Mawani summed up Board performance this way:

> The Immigration and Refugee Board is reporting on performance in 1996–97 in three areas: excellence in the delivery of its services, leadership and innovation in administrative tribunal practices, and excellence in governance.

whereas the Auditor General concluded:

> The current process does not quickly grant Canadian protection to claimants who genuinely need it. Furthermore it does not discourage from claiming refugee status those who do not require or deserve Canada's protection.

Ms. Mawani's report on Plans and Priorities for the 1998/99 IRB Estimates told us that:

> It is estimated that there will be approximately 28,000 claims pending on April 1, 1998. Assuring stable intake and member complement, the CRDD (Convention Refugee Determination Division) expects to reduce this inventory over the next three years to around 19,000 claims by the end of 2000–2001.

"Claims pending" is just another term for backlog. In 1986 a backlog of 25,000 resulted in government panic and early recall of Parliament in August to deal with it. Twelve years later—the legislation, its objectives and its management having achieved complete failure—the status quo is defended as normal. This last Mawani document tells us that "allowing for an average processing time of eight months, which is the optimal norm under the present legislative regime, 19,000 claims pending is an appropriate inventory for the CRDD." Her expectation is that "the proportion of cases pending for over one year will be reduced over the course of the 1998/99 fiscal year to 10 per cent." Can anyone really believe that having 19,000 refugee claimants at large in Canada, enjoying all the privileges and benefits of citizenship except the ballot, is appropriate?

*　　*　　*

Mr. Marchi's March 1995 announcement included the formation of an Advisory Committee to assist in the selection of IRB members. It was to be headed by the redoubtable Mr. Fairweather. It would include the present chairperson of the IRB, members of the legal community and non-governmental organizations involved in refugee matters, and members of the general public. The objective was to be the strengthening of the independence of the Board in order to ensure the continued high quality of Board members. This was a fine piece of rhetoric, since a Board selected by Mr. Fairweather and Ms. Mawani, with their administrative records, and with the support of members of the influential immigration industry, did not promise change.

All of this lends credibility to the conclusion of the British Columbia and Yukon immigration staff in their "otherwise withheld" report, prepared for the aforementioned 1994 Summer of Consultations:

> We go about congratulating ourselves for our over-exuberant acceptance of mostly bogus refugees, with the rest of the world snickering at us for the suckers we are.

ENDNOTES

1. Page 39 of this report, Note 9.

2. Professor Hathaway had been appointed by IRB Chairperson Nurjehan Mawani to investigate and report on forbidden communication between IRB members and Refugee Hearing Officers. His report, however, was considerably broader in scope. See *Rebuilding Trust: Report of the Review of Fundamental Justice in Information Gathering and Dissemination at the Immigration and Refugee Board of Canada,* December 1993.

CHAPTER VII

THE CONSULTATION FRAUD

*"It must be clear who is responsible for the support and integra-
tion of immigrants whose admission is based on their tie to a
landed immigrant or citizen of Canada . . . . Thus the first basis of
support should be the family. Canadians wish to be realistic
about which costs and strains the social network can bear and
who should bear them. . . . The government cannot provide for all
needs."*

Not Just Numbers
The Report of the Minister's Advisory Group
December 31, 1997

During one of those media scrums featured so often on television, Prime Minister Brian Mulroney was heard to declare
that Canada needed a population of 50 million people. Although
not recognized at the time as a public-policy announcement,
such a goal would require the strong advocacy and management
of a persuasive public-relations program. Another new minister
of immigration to carry out the task? The Honourable Barbara
McDougall assumed that post on March 31, 1988.

Immigration policy development by managed consultations
began on December 23, 1988, when the new minister announced
her projected immigration levels for 1989. She disclosed plans
for broad consultations with the provinces and non-governmental organizations. She said the talks "would be conducted with a
view to achieving significant increases in immigration and refugee levels." Her media release was a remarkable document. The
decisions having been made, the consultations designed to justify them were about to begin.

In the meantime, the Public Affairs Branch of the Immigration Commission was busy preparing for a supportive public-relations exercise to be known as the *Communications Framework for the Immigration Program.* Their opinion surveys showed that "the economic benefits of immigration are most likely to be accepted by the public at large." Their economic research, on the other hand, established that "this could be difficult to achieve because there is little substantive data available." Expressed a little differently, they found "there is little hard data to support the claim that immigrants create more jobs than they take."

Undeterred, they commissioned the polling firm of Angus Reid Associates Inc. to review long-term public-opinion trends. The result was called *Canadian Public Opinion on Immigration and Refugees, A Review of Public Opinion Research* and was included as part of the *Communications Framework* publication. The statistical analysis is set out in Table 5 below. Though most revealing, it was probably of little comfort to those in Immigration's Public Affairs Branch.

Poll respondents over the years have consistently and persistently opposed any open-door immigration policy. The Angus

TABLE 5
CANADIAN ATTITUDES TOWARDS IMMIGRATION LEVELS
1975–1987

	Gallup 1975	Canadian Facts 1979	Gallup 1980	Goldfarb 1981	Gallup 1985	Angus Reid 1987
(%) Immigration Levels Should:						
Be Increased	10%	18%	8%	8%	14%	17%
Be Decreased	39	47	42	35	42	48
Remain the Same	43	43	44	55	38	24
Don't Know	8	2	6	2	6	6
	100%	100%	100%	100%	100%	100%

Note: The totals given in columns two and six are as provided in the original Angus Reid report.

Reid review reported "Canadians preferred a selective immigration policy rather than a completely open door policy."

Angus Reid found it appropriate to quote from the report of political scientist Nancy Tienharra. She had prepared an earlier analysis of post-war Gallup Polls for the department in 1974:

> A good case can be made for believing that, if given the option, Canadians would state themselves as being favourable to limited or restricted immigration but opposed to any massive influx of immigrants.

> Those who say that immigration levels should stay 'about the same' are more likely expressing a faith in current immigration policy and levels, whatever they may be, rather than a preference for current levels.

With respect to refugees, Angus Reid found Canadians of higher socio-economic status more sympathetic to providing refugee claimants with haven than those with less education, who perceived them as a threat to economic stability or job opportunities. However, the firm also found a general ". . . deep rooted concern over Canada's ability to . . . expedite the refugee determination process . . ." as well as ". . . concerns about queue jumping which appear to represent a fear that Canada will be unable to protect and control its borders rather than a cultural threat imposed by the refugee claimants themselves."

The polling organization observed that "Canadians are generally ignorant of immigration levels, timing and trends . . ." and "Respondents are unlikely to be fully aware of what the 'current' immigration policy is." Angus Reid's critical review quoted with approval the conclusions of demographer Chris Taylor who, in 1980, had prepared a report for the department entitled *Canadian Public Opinion on Population, Immigration and Refugees:*

> As long as Canadians continue to be misinformed and uninformed about immigration and population issues, our polls will continue to be monitors of ignorance and prejudice rather than awareness and tolerance.

All of this led this reputable polling firm to conclude that the greatest need in any Immigration Commission public-relations exercise was honest information, flowing from open discussion and unrestrained public debate in Parliament and the media about what was in the best interests of Canada. This not being a factor in anyone's political agenda, it was unlikely to be proposed. Instead, those in charge of opinion-moulding at Immigration's Public Affairs Branch decided that what was required to sell their politically motivated policies was a five-year propaganda campaign in three phases. This they set out in detail in the internally distributed publication, the *Communications Framework for the Immigration Program:*

Phase I

"Cooling the Environment" would be designed to lower public concern and provide a mass of solid, if uncritical, information on government policy and legislation. The primary goal was to restore public confidence in the government's ability to manage completely its immigration program.

Phase II

"The Contribution of Immigrants" would emphasize their positive effect on the Canadian economy. The socio-cultural contributions of immigrants, in turn, would be highlighted by the secretary of state for multiculturalism.

Phase III

"Demographic Considerations" focussed on demographic issues following release of the Health and Welfare study then underway. [That report would give little support to the political agenda.]

Focus-group testing and retesting would be used to determine the effectiveness of up to forty government publications, all designed to sell government policies. This propaganda would be supplemented with film and video presentations, magazine inserts, promotional programs in the ethnic press and speakers' kits to ensure its effectiveness. It all emphasized that the most important message for Canadians was that the government was managing the immigration program and was in control. Finally, polling would be used at various stages to determine if the campaign was achieving its ends. Their proposed budget:

Year 1	–	$1,420,000
Year 2	–	4,510,000
Year 3	–	6,120,000
Year 4	–	1,480,000
Year 5	–	1,360,000
Total	–	$14,890,000

Communications Framework, complete with the survey results, the Angus Reid report and that elaborate sales program, was distributed to frontline immigration officers in the spring. Although information is lacking on how much of it, if any, passed Treasury Board, Minister McDougall exuded confidence in her May 25, 1989 presentation to the Commons Standing Committee on Labour, Employment and Immigration. She reiterated her pledge to increase immigration levels with the assurance that the Angus Reid review, commissioned by her department, "indicates that 40 per cent of Canadians favour increased levels of immigration but in a controlled, orderly program."

That was quite different from the average 12.5 per cent of Canadians favouring an increase in immigration in the six separate polls conducted between 1975 and 1987, and analysed by Angus Reid. Mrs. McDougall's figure was close to the 42 per cent who believed levels should be *decreased* and the 41 per cent who believed they should stay the same. The 41 per cent reflected researcher Nancy Tienharra's conclusion that this opinion represents faith in current immigration policies, whatever they may be.

The minister's 1989 plan called for an immigrant increase of 25,000, described as reflecting "the government's policy of continued growth through sound management, consistent with Canada's social and humanitarian goals." She continued: "The steady rises in planning levels attests to the government's commitment to rebuild and revitalize the immigration program." All of this raises the question: Should it be the program or the needs of Canada that demand government commitment?

More emphasis was placed on family reunification, that being the centrepiece of government policy. There would be expanded admissibility of parents of any age. There would be enhanced admissibility for never-married sons and daughters, and a reduction in the points scores needed from 60 to 55 for married sons and daughters, and brothers and sisters in the Assisted Relative category.

(Readers will recall from Figure 1 that the earning record of Family Class and Assisted Relative immigrants is only one-half that of the Independent Immigrants.)

The minister reiterated her pledge to the Commons Committee that the process of consultations would "be conducted with a view to continuing to increase both refugee and immigrant landings."

These consultations, held in eight centres across Canada in the spring of 1990, consisted of selected participants meeting in camera. Sadly, the general public would not benefit from any of the "new data and valuable information" the minister had so confidently expected to emerge from these sessions. Canadians must be content with the minister's word that her meetings indicated general, though not universal, acceptance of increased immigration as an economic tool. Thus the stage was set for annual increases to be established in a *five-year plan*.

Then, a year later, on January 29, 1991, just ninety-six days after once again increasing immigration levels for that year, the minister unexpectedly revealed the need to reduce them. The General Occupations lists, the guide to selecting Independent Immigrants, would be "temporarily closed" the next day. Those skilled, literate and talented immigrants, the principal components of any economic tool, would be shut out in favour of the others.

The Honourable Bernard Valcourt succeeded Mrs. McDougall as immigration minister on April 21, 1991. He too found it necessary to stage another cross-Canada round of consultations to assist in setting levels for 1994, and he followed the McDougall formula of anonymity for the selected participants. Requests for a list of those attending and their associations was, predictably, unsuccessful. But it brought the assurance that they represented "a broad spectrum of Canadian society . . . including business, labour, officials of provincial and municipal government, representatives of the health and social services fields, ethnocultural organizations, immigrant and refugee services groups, academics, researchers, lawyers and human rights organizations." So everyone was in place, but who were they, and what did they have to contribute?

In Canada we have public galleries in Parliament, our legislatures, municipal council chambers, in the Law Courts and at Royal Commission hearings. But when it comes to politically driven immigration policy, too often it is done behind closed doors with anonymous participants. And nobody questions the legitimacy or appropriateness of the process. Not the media and not the politicians.

In 1993, at the outset of the Chrétien government's first term in office, a critic[1] wrote to Immigration Minister Sergio Marchi, setting out some of the problems the new minister faced in his portfolio. His director general, immigration policy and program development policy, was delegated to reply. She contended "that studies have shown that immigrants tend to create more jobs than they take, and that they contribute more to the economy through their taxes than they take out in government transfer payments"—fallacies already identified under Myth 4 and Myth 5 in Chapter III. In response to the suggestion that 60 per cent of successful refugee claimants don't meet the United Nations Convention criteria, the director general insisted that the "Immigration and Refugee Board's acceptance rates have been declining." In fact, they were to reach 70 per cent in 1994.

The director general further asserted that "those whose claims are successful are determined to be refugees in the sense of the United Nations Convention. It would not, therefore, be accurate to speculate that 60 per cent of those whose claims are accepted are not refugees in the sense of the Convention." The fact that the former Refugee Status Advisory Committee, working with the UNHCR advisors, accepted only 24 per cent of refugee claimants, coming from the same general sources, was not to interfere with the political program. Of course, the principal element in any immigration debate has to be numbers, but this was not an issue. The director general made it plain that the Liberal Party's election "Red Book" figures of 250,000 was established policy.[2]

Early in 1994, a Sergio Marchi news release proclaimed a consultation process more extravagant than anything ever attempted by his Tory predecessors—his celebrated Summer of Consultations. Whatever they were ultimately worth, the public consultations that followed would examine all of the issues except the most important: the number of refugees.

Ten topics were defined. Ten task forces of fifteen or more "knowledgable" people were set up to deliberate on them. Each task force would focus on one of the following:

Issue 1   –   A Vision of Canada
Issue 2   –   Criteria for Accepting Immigrants
Issue 3   –   Humanitarian Immigration
Issue 4   –   International Cooperation
Issue 5   –   Integration
Issue 6   –   Improved Coordination
Issue 7   –   Protecting Canadian Society
Issue 8   –   Economic Benefits
Issue 9   –   Partnerships
Issue 10   –   Research and Policy Development.

Reports of the resultant discussions, conclusions and recommendations would be drafted by the Immigration Commission convenors assigned to these task forces, and distributed to the 200 delegates invited to a consultations' wind-up conference in Ottawa that September. There would be prior public meetings across the country to stimulate national debate. Individuals would be encouraged to set up their own discussion groups, and to forward their findings to Ottawa.

This may all have been nothing more than a subterfuge on the minister's part, but the resulting reports contained a worthwhile collection of diverse opinions from provincial governments, academics, immigration lawyers, consultants, refugee advocacy and service organizations, school boards and health providers. Some of the observations to which Minister Marchi might have given attention, had this been as serious an exercise for the government as it was for the participants, are summarized here:

- The rationale for immigration policies must be fully and openly debated, clearly communicated and understood by the public;
- Immigration must be responsive to the circumstances in which Canada finds itself, particularly the economic circumstances, and must be limited by our capacity to commit the vital resources necessary to integrate immigrants;
- Only a small percentage of the 19 million refugees worldwide actually require protection in a third country. [In 1994, the UNHCR had asked for resettlement on behalf of approximately 59,000 persons. In the same year, the planned figure for government-assisted, privately sponsored and landed refugees in Canada was 28,300—half the world supply had they all been genuine refugees in need of resettlement.];
- There is a need to address the problem of would-be immigrants using the refugee-determination system to gain access to permanent residence in Canada;
- Canadians want their government to provide resettlement for persons overseas who require our protection, but they must be confident that inland claimants are more than simply queue jumpers;
- A school trustee, who spoke of 3,000 Somalis arriving in one condominium project in Toronto within a five-year period, explained the stress this placed on a school system completely uninformed and unprepared.[3] This particular task force included a Somali who found the trustee's observations to be an undeserved affront to her and all Somali Canadians;
- Conduct timely, focussed research on the economic impacts of immigration using current data;
- A number of provincial representatives expressed their concern

over the lack of effective consultation prior to federal immigration decisions which impact on provincial programs and costs [and this in spite of the annual rhetoric about the influence of such consultations at immigration-levels announcement time].[4]

The final gathering in Ottawa, by invitation only, was attended by 200 members of organizations concerned with services related to immigration and fairly representative of the population.[5] The fundamentals of population density, annual immigration levels, cost, absorptive capacity, industrial policy and the environment were not central to the discussions. Instead, the meeting was dominated by a well-organized group from the immigration/refugee lobby. They complained so loudly of inadequate funding to meet the challenges of immigrant settlement in Canada that they dominated the agenda— with the backing of educators unable to deal adequately with the numbers of both immigrant and Canadian-born children who spoke neither English nor French.

The workshops were efficiently organized and a great deal of dissatisfaction was expressed with current policies, but the conference failed to provide new directions.

Judith Maxwell, former head of the Economic Council of Canada, was a co-chair of the conference. In her closing statement she considered it a paradox that with immigration "the more you know the more you need to know."

In the absence of public debate, even this select group was limited in their knowledge of the topics under discussion. The final report notes that, as a result, there was a feeling of inadequacy among the participants in making judgments. Ms. Maxwell stressed the need for a more effective mechanism to deal with immigration. Would it be a Royal Commission?

The most significant aspect of that conference occurred a week later, on September 15, 1994, when a headline in the *Toronto Star* read: "Report Urges Immigration Cut of 50,000." The "leaked" document reflected the advice of a number of Mr. Marchi's senior departmental advisers. One can only assume that the conference ending Mr. Marchi's Summer of Consultations had failed to address what they considered to be the "real issues" related to Canadian immigration policy.[6]

Indeed, according to the *Star*, the senior bureaucrats' memorandum began with a one-page summary of the central messages that had emerged from these consultations, prepared for Minister Marchi. The telling points made in the summary, as quoted by the *Star:*

> There is a sense the immigration program is out of control. . . .

> Immigrants need to be better selected. . . .

> Canadians are concerned . . . that their society is becoming fragmented and that cultural and religious diversity in immigration may be exacerbating that problem.

The *Star* article summed up the leaked report:

> The immigration program can address that concern by paying more attention to integration of newcomers, being more selective about who gets into Canada. Tightening up the family class and beefing up enforcement.

It would have been the responsibility of these Immigration Department mandarins to make sure their minister was familiar with the concerns of his career civil servants. That this report had now been "leaked" to the press suggests that Minister Marchi was either not listening, or was taking his policy-making advice from other quarters.

The minister's senior mandarins offered these specific proposals following that Summer of Consultations:

1. Change the Family Class regulations so that only spouses and minor children of Canadian citizens or landed immigrants are accepted automatically. Parents, grandparents, brothers and sisters would have to meet selection criteria and "more stringent sponsorship requirements";
2. Require people sponsoring relatives to sign a bond to ensure they

will take care of their family members. Given that the breakdown of family-sponsorship agreements is costing Canadian taxpayers $700 million a year, this would ensure that newcomers are not adding to this public burden;

3. Replace Cabinet appointees to the Immigration and Refugee Board with public servants;

4. Separate the refugee program from the rest of the immigration program. Make certain the total number of refugees accepted from abroad and within Canada "reflect anticipated costs and available federal/non-governmental organization resources";

5. Change the Citizenship Act so that children of refugee claimants do not automatically receive Canadian citizenship if born in Canada;

6. Give judges the power, at the time of sentencing, to order deportation of criminal immigrants after time served;

7. Abolish the live-in caregiver program that has allowed nannies to apply for landed-immigrant status after two years. "Those admitted under this program do not adjust well. In addition, the cost benefit of the program does not favour its continuance";

8. Change the point system used to select Independent immigrants so that more emphasis is placed on their education, experience, language and long-term potential, rather than whether they have an occupation currently in demand;

9. "Privatize" health care for recent immigrants [i.e. require newcomers to purchase private health insurance for a set period following their arrival].

The immigration industry reacted. One leading Toronto immigration lawyer called the document "frightening" in its scope. Another said that it would be wrong to "abolish whole programs without consultation"; and a third: "to have developed a conclusion prior to the termination of public consultation, seriously draws the minister's credibility into question and is an overzealous bureaucratic move."

Mr. Marchi claimed he hadn't seen the document. He thought it possible some of the ideas may sound good to those bureaucrats "in Hull on the twenty-third floor, but you can't sell it in the streets anywhere."

Seven months later, a second group of civil servants, this time more than 100 frontline immigration officers, would "leak" their own likewise previously withheld Summer of Consultations report to the *Vancouver Sun*.[7] The headline read: "Rest of the World Snickering at Us Over Handling of Refugees."

A year earlier, these employees of the B.C./Yukon Region of Citizenship and Immigration (presumably like their colleagues across the country) had been invited to be part of the consultations program, and had been requested to hold discussions on the "ten issues" listed for national debate. Their report was submitted in May 1994, well before the September conference. However, reports by the ten task-force groups were printed and circulated to the conference delegates, while the observations and recommendations of those frontline immigration officers working on the west coast on a daily basis with immigrants and immigration policy were suppressed.

According to the *Sun* report, these public servants set the only standard possible for the selection of immigrants in today's competitive world: "We should start defining ourselves and our country in terms of excellence . . . and official language ability, education and 'personal suitability' must be made more important." In particular, they advocated:

1. Restricting Family Class immigration to spouses and minor children;
2. Replacing the official policy of multiculturalism with one promoting integration;
3. Selecting refugees outside, not inside, Canada; and
4. Making major changes to the Entrepreneur and Business categories to increase their economic benefits to Canadians.

Their strong opinion on the refugee program was referred to previously, but it is worth repeating here: "We go about congratulating ourselves for our over-exuberant acceptance of mostly bogus refugees, with the rest of the world snickering at us for the suckers we are." Those from the Douglas, B.C. immigration office described the refugee program as completely incapable of distinguishing between genuine refugees and those taking advantage of Canada's open-door policy. "It would seem," they wrote, "that Canada has become an economic haven rather than a safe haven for those in genuine need of protection."

Another group cynically observed: "The lawyers are making a circus out of in-Canada refugee claims. It is costly and the country can't afford it." They all agreed that: "Immigrants should not be allowed to benefit from Canada's social programs so soon after their arrival, there being so much breakdown in financial sponsorships that sponsored Family Class members should not be allowed to collect welfare." Further, they stressed the need for less political interference with their work, and faster deportation of criminals.

Thus the immigration service at almost every level had rejected the government's immigration policy, and the public, with limited background information, had seriously questioned those policies as well. Had Mr. Marchi been serious in conducting such a thorough investigation of public and civil-servant opinion, he had an obligation to respond with substantial amendments to the legislation, and amendments to the flagrantly abused regulations.

Earlier, in May 1992, and with some courage for an immigration minister, Bernard Valcourt had met with the Commons Standing Committee on Immigration, where he pointed out some of the problems he faced. He found that he couldn't set limits on certain categories of immigrants. If he planned for 25,000 Assisted Relatives and 50,000 arrived, they must be processed, and that caused backlogs, delays and the use of resources that might better be applied elsewhere. He had discovered that immigrant smuggling and counterfeit travel documents had become a multimillion-dollar business worldwide. He was shocked to discover that a customs officer could search a Canadian citizen, suspecting an undeclared bottle of perfume, but an immigration officer, who could see the passport sticking out of the refugee-claimant's pocket, could not ask to see it. Mr. Valcourt wanted to examine new measures "to respond to the challenges and provide Canadians with an immigration program that is fair, balanced and effective."

In December 1994, under the new Chrétien government, Parliament dealt with Bill C44, which was designed to correct some of the abuses in the refugee-determination process. Two years after Minister Valcourt had been shocked at the inability of an immigration officer to inspect an ill-concealed passport, his concern was dealt with. The bill gave authority to immigration officers to seize documents relating to status or identity and so eliminated this opportunity to frustrate the Immigration Act. In several areas, the bill limited access by criminals to immigration proceedings. It extended the power of senior immigration officers to redetermine eligibility to claim refugee status in case of fraudulent or repeated claims, and to make exclusion or deportation orders. Finally, it suspended the processing of citizenship applications for those subject to Immigration Act proceedings. These changes were all necessary, but still the fundamental policy issues were being ignored.

A month earlier, in November 1994, the Summer of Consulttions behind him, Minister Marchi set out a strategy

> emphasizing the admission of a greater share of skilled immigrants with the abilities to contribute directly to Canada's economic and social development. . . . Processing applications of immigrants needed to fill specific labour market shortages would be expedited and the business immigration program strengthened.

Of course, a continuing priority would be the "reunifying of spouses and dependent children along with measures to ensure that sponsors honour their financial obligations to support their family members."

And finally, "the refugee program would be managed separately from the family and economic immigration components." Which, of course, means statistical division. Yet it all meant such improved statistical results that the minister's 1996 plan allowed for 32,300 refugees; up to 187,700 immigrants, of whom 94,500 (50 per cent) would be skilled and business-oriented; 85,700 (44 per cent) Family Class; and 4 per cent divided between caregivers, DROCs (the Deferred Removal Order Class) and special humanitarian cases, for a grand total of 220,000.

A chart on page 2 of Mr. Marchi's Summer of Consultations

"Discussion Document" gave the breakdown of the government's projected 1994 immigration figures:

Independents	–	45 per cent;
Family Class	–	45 per cent; and
Refugees	–	10 per cent.

Independents were described as those selected for their skills, business expertise or investment capital. A check of the statistical breakdown of actual immigration in the 1994 levels report, however, reveals that those identified on the chart as economic immigrants included Retirees, live-in caregivers, and Assisted Relatives. If the Assisted Relatives were placed where they belong, the Family Class becomes 58.5 per cent of the year's intake; Refugees represent 11.5 per cent; businessmen, 10 per cent; Retirees and caregivers, 5 per cent. The Independent Class, then, would represent only 15 per cent! As such, Mr. Marchi's 1994 "discussion document" opened with deception and false assumption, almost guaranteeing false conclusions from whatever debate would follow.

Burying statistics when reporting them did not just encompass the separate listings for Assisted Relatives. Normally, Independent immigrants and Business immigrants had, for reporting purposes, been separated into "principal applicants" and "spouses and other accompanying dependents". Under the new Marchi regime, these immigrants were reported in bulk. There may be other reasons for this change, but to report 62,000 skilled workers in 1994 rather than 29,000 principals, or to report 19,500 Business immigrants rather than only 5,000 Investors and Entrepreneurs, did have useful political advantages.

And for statistical identification, the Family Class was to be replaced by "Spouses, Fiancé(e)s, Children, Parents and Grandparents." Whose? Obviously not those of skilled workers or Business immigrants, largely included in those totals already.

In the summer of 1995, Canadians learned of a slick advertising campaign to attract the interest of skilled people in emigrating to Canada. The literature emphasized quality of life, open spaces, educational opportunities, safe cities and a photo-

graph of people canoeing on a mountain lake.[8] In a deficit-cut-
ting year, the budget for this ad campaign had been increased
from $500,000 to $2 million. Raphael Girard, assistant deputy
minister, international operations, justified this expenditure in
fulsome terms when he explained: "We're not marketing a
brand of car. We're largely planting the seed for future immigration, to get a significant number of people thinking about moving. . . . The days of appealing on an economic basis may not be
valid. But we do have many strong advantages."

In one of those defensive spin-letters that often emerge from
the minister's office, Canadians were to be encouraged by the
success of a recent joint tour of principal cities in India by Immigration Department officials and the Canadian Council of
Professional Engineers. A check with the professional engineers' associations (both national and provincial), however, revealed no shortage of engineers in Canada. There was the
occasional opportunity for specialists, but nothing more. Apparently, the India expedition was conceived and organized in
every respect by the Immigration Department. A Council of
Professional Engineers representative had joined this expedition
simply to assure that employment opportunities in Canada were
clearly set out, but felt the entire tour to be without real purpose
beyond the politics of it all.

Although Assistant Deputy Minister Girard had acknowledged that "the days of appealing on an economic basis" were
no longer valid, a year later, in 1996, the Canadian High Commission offices in New Delhi were expanded at a cost of $26
million. India is the principal source of Family Class immigrants. Consistent with the expansion, visa officers at the High
Commission were increased from nineteen to twenty-nine.

The IRB chairperson's report for the 1996–97 year provides
a good example of how foreign-policy considerations can create
immigration complications. In August 1995, the Canadian
government, presumably in pursuit of trade, removed visa requirements on travel from Chile, with the result that many Chileans arrived in Canada claiming refugee status. During the
repressive Pinochet regime in the 1970s, 4,600 Chilean refugees
entered Canada. But even though such political repression no

longer occurred in Chile, economic migrants took advantage of free entry to Canada, as is shown in the IRB annual report figures in Table 6.

TABLE 6

CHILEAN REFUGEE CLAIMANTS, 1994–1997

	1994	1995	1996	1997
Claims referred to IRB	N/A	1,483	2,824	99
Positive decisions	21	24	37	46
Negative decisions	48	19	1,127	981
Claims abandoned	32	52	899	425
Claims finalized	101	95	2,063	1,452
Claims pending	N/A	1,476	2,245	890

Two-year totals	- Positive decisions: 83 or 2.4%
	- Negative decisions: 2,108 or 60%
	- Abandonments: 1,324 or 37.6%

Following the reinstatement of the visa requirements in July 1996, the number of Chileans claiming refugee status became negligible. However, the nearly 40 per cent of claimants, or 1,324 individuals, who abandoned their refugee claims had virtually all the rights of Canadian citizens to our social safety net, including welfare, medical and dental care during their stay in Canada.

In the spring of 1996, the Honourable Lucienne Robillard succeeded Mr. Marchi as minister of citizenship and immigration. To date, the principal feature of this minister's regime has been yet another round of consultations. This round followed release of a report by the minister's Legislative Review Committee, made up of three experts on immigration and refugee matters: Robert Trempe (chair), Susan Davis and Dr. Roslyn Kunin.[9] Their mandate had been as follows:

Canada has a tradition of fair and generous immigration and refugee programs. Based on its review, the Advisory Group will provide a series of recommendations to guide and update future immigration and refugee legislation in a way that will maintain this tradition. The review will include, but is not restricted to:

- facilitating access by legitimate visitors and immigrants to Canada
- ensuring the integrity and efficiency of our refugee determination process
- treating people with dignity and respect, and ensuring that their cases are completed in a fair and expeditious manner
- enhancing the coherence of the process
- denying access to Canada by those who would abuse our generous system
- streamlining processes to improve client service
- studying the scope and depth of ministerial discretion and the framework whereby exceptions are made to regulatory processes.

The report of the advisory group, *Not Just Numbers: A Canadian Framework for Future Immigration,*[10] delivered on deadline at the end of 1997, set the stage for Minister Robillard's round of cross-Canada consultations. They would begin in Vancouver on February 17, 1998. These meetings, with their preselected presenters and participants, were designed, we were told, to obtain public reaction to these proposals prior to the drafting of new immigration legislation.

Not Just Numbers includes 172 recommendations, many of them administrative and procedural, affecting both current operations and the underlying structure. However, in Chapter I, on page 9, we find the following sentence: "Without immigration and a rising birth rate the size of the Canadian population will begin to decline in the 21st century." Again, the birth rate, one of those Five Immigration Myths that make any rational discussion of Canadian immigration policy so difficult. However, that unfortunate conclusion on the part of the authors so early in the report should not inhibit further examination of *Not Just Numbers.*

Two quotations cited by the *Not Just Numbers* authors seem to particularly reflect the tone of their report:

Industrialized states spend billions of dollars annually to process the claims of the small minority of the world's refugee population that manages . . . to claim protection in the north. These same wealthy governments contribute less than $1.2 billion each year [Canada contributes a mere $35 million] to address the more than 80 percent of refugees remaining in the south.[11]

There is no doubt in our minds that we are headed towards an impasse and that an urgent solution must be found. To succeed in this it seems to us that we must go back to the beginning and try to identify, in today's context, the people and groups that deserve protection and find the least undesirable way of doing so.[12]

To put this into perspective, if the real costs to Canada of our immigration/refugee programs were known (a figure the government has an obligation to determine and release to the public), they would probably exceed by several times that $1.2 billion annual international contribution from northern countries to address the needs of unrelocated refugees in the south.

In 1994, the immigration mandarins, reporting to the minister, placed an annual $700 million figure on the cost of sponsorship breakdown. There is another $700 million in maintenance of refugees and refugee claimants.[13] There is the ministry budget of $650 million, the Refugee Board at $90 million, uncalculated costs of legal aid and a substantial increase in Court of Appeal costs attributed to the cost of processing appeals from failed refugee claims filed simply to prolong their stay in Canada. In 1989, 574 such appeals were filed. In 1992 there were 2,300 filed in the Trial Division and 10,800 in the Appeal Division.[14]

Related to the courts and administration of justice is the unrecorded cost of criminal activity among too many of those who have taken advantage of our porous border. The unknown scope of medical and dental costs is indicated by the $30 million provision by Madame Robillard to cover only those failed refugee claimants awaiting their humanitarian and compassionate assessment.

In 1996, 33,350 immigrant children under age fifteen arrived lacking ability in either official language. Fifty percent of ESL students in Vancouver were born in Canada. Allowing for those fifteen and over, Canadian classrooms receive an estimated 70,000 non-English- or French-speaking children annually. Assuming five years' average ESL classes alone, at $1,000 per student annually, this is another bill for $350 million. In addition, there are English or French classes for their parents. *All this is occurring at a time when there has been no hesitation on the part of Canada's governments to cut education funding for the general student body.*

Then there are the infrastructure costs of growth attributable to immigration. These come in the form of roads, bridges, schools, hospitals, parks, public transportation, sewage and water treatment facilities. Remarkably, the receiving Canadian population pays for most of it. The value of these amenities is built into the value of every housing unit. Those municipalities that impose a capital charge against every housing unit of growth provide for some of this, but regular municipal, provincial and federal taxes pay for the rest of it.

Where projected growth is 50 per cent over twenty years, there will be a 25 per cent increase in general tax revenue from that growth source over those twenty years. That 25 per cent forms 20 per cent of total tax receipts, and the resident receiving population will have been providing the remaining 80 per cent of the requirements of that growth.

The challenge is for the government to develop a clear statement of the costs of immigration in Canada. A task for the Auditor General? Immigration has become an expensive business.

Always in the background is the message of the Supreme Court's *Singh* decision that every alien, regardless of origin, personal history or criminal record, once having set foot on Canadian soil, has the right under the Charter of Rights and Freedoms to claim refugee status. Having done so, the claimant has all the privileges of citizenship except the right to vote. The *Singh* decision established a serious, though not impossible, barrier to immigration reform.

Among those claiming to be refugees, 60 per cent slip in without identification, many making the claim knowing they can exploit the loopholes in the system, abuse the costly and time-consuming appeal process, withdraw or abandon their claims and then disappear underground. That this opportunity had been recognized by bogus claimants appeared in IRB statistics for 1991, when 1,786 or 6 per cent of claims considered were withdrawn or abandoned. The ploy succeeded and those taking advantage increased. In 1993 it was 16.4 per cent; in 1995, 20.2 per cent; in 1997, 23.3 per cent; and in 1998, 6,201 or 21.2 per cent of refugee claims were withdrawn or abandoned. In spite of these increases in the abuse of the process, revealed in statistics published in quarterly IRB reports, it was not until January 1999 that it became public knowledge when exposed by a Senate committee studying terrorism.[15]

One cannot argue with the Legislative Review Committee's recognition that the determination of refugee status in Canada is "flagging badly." This is their mild way of describing a process running so completely out of control at the IRB level that it demands a total overhaul of appointments and procedures and a stiffening of the will of Parliament to see that the widespread abuses of the system are brought under control. If this requires legislative change to a clause in the Charter to deal with the consequences of *Singh*, then so be it. In reality, the government must acknowledge a crisis. It is not just a numbers game.

None of this will happen until the Canadian public expresses its outrage at the crime and corruption that Canada's preposterous immigration and refugee policies have allowed to flourish on our city streets. A prime example of this is the Honduran refugee story in Chapter V.

The major recommendation of *Not Just Numbers* is that present immigration and refugee legislation be replaced by two new acts: one for immigration and the other for refugees, the latter to be known as the Protection Act. At this point we must ask ourselves how starting at the beginning again can ever succeed when Parliament has, for twenty years, been writing and amending legislation and regulations, all the while failing to insist that what is already on the books be made to work? Administrative failures have been part of the problem, but most of the trouble has arisen because the political culture has been unwilling to deal decisively with problems only too well understood by the immigration bureaucracy. There is no need for more consultation and years of debate over new legislation when we should be making what we have now work as it was intended to.

Of Family Class immigration, *Not Just Numbers* set out its findings as follows:

> It must be clear who is responsible for the support and integration of immigrants whose admission is based on their tie to a landed immigrant or citizen of Canada. . . . Thus the first basis of support should be the family. Canadians wish to be realistic about which costs and strains the social network can bear and who should bear them. . . . The government cannot provide for all needs.

The Legislative Review Committee found that the exploitation of welfare by sponsored parents and grandparents is rising and now approaches four times that of the general population.[16] Their report recommended a three-tier Family Class:

• Tier One would limit sponsorship to spouses and dependent children, but only after the principal immigrant has become sufficiently well-established to provide independent support to the family. They made it clear that sponsorship even in this first tier cannot be automatic.
• Tier Two would consist of fiancé(e)s, parents and, when sponsors' parents are deceased, grandparents.
• Tier Three would include other close relatives and close friends, and "will with certain minimal restrictions on education and a strong incentive to become proficient in an official language at the sponsors' or applicants' expense, permit sponsors to decide who is most important to them, and who is part of what they consider family in the broadest sense."

The thinking behind this may well be that marvellous definition of "family" suggested by the June 1994 National Consultation on Family Class Immigration.[17]

The *Not Just Numbers* authors must be given credit for what, within the immigration/refugee-advocacy field, must be a radical concept: to actually monitor the programs, determine their benefits and disadvantages and modify the regulations accordingly.

However, their report emphasized the connection between fluency in one of our languages and success in Canada, when we know that it takes seven to ten years to become sufficiently proficient in English or French in order to function in today's technological society. Surely, the admission of marginal friends and relatives without either of these languages, and under minimal educational standards, just invites more abuse and is of no benefit to Canada or to the sponsors of these people.

The evidence is clear that while there are many refugees and members of the Family Class and Assisted Relatives who succeed in Canada, there are others not able to earn a living wage, who represent a lifetime burden for the Canadian taxpayer. In today's world, Canada can only afford one standard—excellence. Tiers One and Two would seem to meet this need.

The authors of *Not Just Numbers* proposed grouping Independent skilled immigrants, Entrepreneurs and Investors into a single "Self-supporting Class", in a framework of objectives that would form the foundation for a Canadian economic immigration program:

- Prosperity: Increasing economic benefits to Canada through the creation of employment and wealth.
- Stability: Using economic immigration as a long-term tool to smooth out variations in the markets for labour and capital, and for goods and services.
- Competitiveness: Raising the level of skills and resources of our pool of human capital to ensure our ability to sell goods and services internationally.
- New Technology: Attributing value to technological knowledge as an important factor of economic growth.
- Global Investment: Removing the obstacles and barriers to attracting global capital required to develop new products and services to ensure growth and expansion.
- Modern Pioneers: Identifying the individuals with a high degree of

self-sufficiency who will contribute to Canada's future economic success.

Based on submissions they received, they summarized the key qualities considered necessary for such a Self-supporting Class to succeed and contribute to the economic prosperity of Canada:

- a high level of education;
- skills likely to be recognized in Canada;
- competence in at least one official language;
- varied work experience;
- relative youth;
- business/entrepreneurial skills;
- economic ties to Canada (schooling, work experience);
- knowledge of Canada (including employment conditions); and
- self-sufficiency (funds for settlement in Canada).

These objectives and desirable qualities are certainly all appropriate to a standard of excellence. So too are the basic minimum core standards they proposed for admission to Canada:

- Education: An academic, technical or trade qualification equivalent to at least two years' full-time post-secondary study in Canada.
- Official Languages: Sufficient proficiency to enter the Canadian labour force in at least one of the two official languages to be demonstrated through formal standardized testing.
- Work Experience: This must relate to the area of work for which the applicant is being considered. For Skilled Workers, this should be two years' experience in a successful business; and that experience should have been obtained during the three years preceding their applications.
- Age: Candidates should be not less than twenty-one years of age and not more than forty-five years of age.
- Self-sufficiency: Maximum levels of settlement funds must be established for economic immigrants to ensure that they are able to support themselves and their families during their first six months in

Canada, including self-funding for language training should this prove necessary, and be without recourse to social welfare. In addition, the Advisory Committee emphasized that the selection criteria for economic immigrants should stress attributes and assets which evidence a high degree of self-sufficiency beyond the financial.

All of this sets a potentially new and desirable course, should there ever be a government in Canada determined to manage the immigration/refugee program in the interests of the nation.

One of the key messages received by the authors of *Not Just Numbers* during their consultations on the qualities required to succeed in the Canadian environment was the overwhelming importance of official-language ability. They point out that the current system attaches only modest importance to this requirement. Indeed, references to language ability appear throughout the text of their report, and are included in six of their recommendations as a core requirement.[18]

There is support for this in the work of the Toronto organization "Skills for Change", which is devoted to assisting immigrants in finding employment. They offer this advice on their web site:

> In virtually every profession, English language skills are becoming critical. Employers expect all employees to be able to communicate with clients or patients, write reports, contribute to meetings, and execute marketing plans. You may find that even if you are a highly qualified professional, your ability to find a good job will be affected by your level of English.

On September 11, 1996, nearly sixteen months before the publication of *Not Just Numbers*, Minister Robillard and Senator Dan Hays, president of the Liberal Party of Canada, in their capacity as co-chairs of the Liberal Election Platform Committee, met in Vancouver with several selected groups of citizens. In the immigration session, a participant[19] informed Minister Robillard and Senator Hays that 60 per cent of the immigrants to British Columbia did not speak English; that of the immigrants to B.C. in 1994, 16,400 adults and 7,600 public-school students (filling 300 classrooms) did not speak English; and that a November 1993 study by the British Columbia Teachers' Federation revealed that 40 per cent of the English as a Second Language enrolment in the Vancouver area were born in Canada.

Five years later that figure was 50 per cent. That message was delivered to the minister by the Vancouver Area School Boards' spokesperson at the minister's February 1998 consultations meeting in Vancouver.

The federal contribution for adult ESL in 1995 was $18,600,000. This covered only 5,544 (34 per cent) of the 1994 intake for a single year. As an indication of the burden this situation placed on the B.C. taxpayer, an examination of the school-building program in the post-1996 election budget of a B.C. New Democratic government revealed the delayed construction (because of deficit budgets) of 11,535 student classroom places.

The minister and the senator learned that post-1980 immigrants to B.C. earned 60 per cent of the income of Canadian-born people in equivalent age brackets. Moreover, they were quoted the testimony of Meyer Berstein, director of research and analysis in Madame Robillard's ministry. He had told the Commons Standing Committee on Labour and Immigration that:

> Immigrants who don't have French or English are half as likely to participate in the labour market; the unemployment rate is twice as high and even after a period of eight years in the country there are still significant performance differences. . . . Language ability is correlated more strongly with settlement success and with contribution and income and taxes, etc., than almost any other measure you can think of.

In her statement to the minister and the senator, Dr. Roslyn Kunin said that her research findings revealed that "language is one of the best predictors of success" and that "suitability and having the spark are more important than any [government-designated immigration] class."

Madame Robillard was so obviously impressed with the above recital of fact that, as the session closed, she assured the representatives of the ethnic/immigration lobby present that current levels of Family Class immigration would continue.

Anticipating the *Not Just Numbers* report, a CBC Vancouver television forum was held on November 10 and 11, 1997. Replying to the moderator's question, "Are there some kinds of immigrants to whom it is reasonable to say, 'You ought to be able to speak English before you come here'?" immigration activist Susan French replied:

> Would it help immigrants if they spoke English or French when they come into Canada? I would say absolutely yes, because I deal with people every day who are highly educated and who cannot find employment because they are struggling with the issues of language or pronunciation. And I think it would help those people to be able to speak English or French better because of the barriers which exist in our country that prevent them from integrating. But to require that and make it an absolute requirement to immigrating, I think you would find yourself in trouble.

She was right.

Dr. Hedy Fry, MP, secretary of state for multiculturalism and for the status of women, was angered by the thought of any language requirement. Her retort to the same question:

> What do you mean by some kind of immigrant should be required? Are you going to discriminate? On the basis of what? I think we already have a point system. The point system looks at a lot of things. English and French rank very high on that point system. And so does the profession you have, the post-secondary levels you have. A lot of these things count. It is a very complex mix of the points you have to achieve before you become an immigrant here. So you have a myth. One that many people come in here just because we want them, and not because they come in here. Many of them having a great deal to offer this country.

There was nothing incoherent in the response of Mobina Jaffer, unsuccessful Liberal candidate, and president of the National Women's Liberal Commission. To Ms. Jaffer, language requirements under any circumstances were racist, pure and simple:

> The complex problem is English people. When they say they want English, it's a code word for wanting like-minded people who look like them. . . . They don't want people who look like me to come here. They want people from the British Isles or Europe to come here. That's where the problem arises. . . .

> What we are talking about is people coming here. What we are saying is English you can learn here. . . . Once people arrive here, if we are serious about wanting to get the skills to build our country, we should provide English so we can build a stronger Canada.[20]

It was hardly surprising, therefore, that the first day of the minister's 1998 cross-Canada consultations was defined by opposition to the official-languages recommendations of *Not Just Numbers*. Of the twenty-four organizations scheduled to appear on the opening day, eleven were ethnically based and their opposition to any English-language requirement was almost unanimous. Some of the statements from their presentations:

The Chinese Entrepreneurs Society of Canada

We need blue-collar workers in our labour force. It is unfair to shut our doors to those who are willing to contribute to the well being of our society. Our immigration policy should not discriminate those who cannot satisfy the language requirement.

The Taiwan Entrepreneurs and Investors Association

We are strongly opposed to the core requirements for Entrepreneurs of language education and age, . . . [or] for Investors language and education.

The Vancouver Chinese Benevolent Association

The language requirement clearly and unmistakenly seeks through future immigration to divide the present multiculturalistic Canadian into a preferred group of prospective English or French speaking immigration on the one hand and an unwanted group consisting of all non-English or non-French speaking peoples on the other.

Vancouver Chinese Merchants Association

The proposed language requirement must be removed.

Canadian Ethno-Cultural Council

We find the recommendation regarding the Official Language Requirement to be very unfair to new immigrants. It would alter the country of origin of future applicants. . . . The economic growth for a number of regions of Canada will be affected. . . . Those from low income countries could not afford the new language fee.

Mosaic (an immigrant service organization)

Mosaic is opposed to any requirement that immigrants must possess one of Canada's official languages.

Before the end of the first day of consultations, the minister had received the message and any interest she had in any immigrant's fluency in our languages had withered. At the opening of the afternoon session she said: "Let me assure you here today that I understand the concerns expressed. I must confess that I also have some serious concerns."

The minister was joined in her concerns by several Liberal stalwarts. Liberal MP Sophia Leung (Vancouver Kingsway) called a press conference. On the language question: "That is not appropriate. It would be exclusive." Raymond Chan, secretary of state for Asia Pacific and his Cabinet colleague Hedy Fry both emphasized the report was only a starting point, although Ms. Fry contended that its very existence would "inhibit a lot of people who have a lot to offer and who have offered a lot."[21]

But the political opposition was just starting to mount. Less than two weeks later, British Columbia's attorney general, Ujjal Dosanjh, launched his government's attack on the proposals, saying that such reform would violate Canadian tradition on law and severely curb British Columbia's influx of affluent investors.[22] It was apparent by the end of April that the ethnic lobby and their political representatives had killed the *Not Just Numbers* language proposals. Two Vancouver Cabinet ministers, Raymond Chan and Herb Dhaliwal, minister of revenue, told the *Vancouver Sun* that they considered the English-language proficiency recommendations a dead issue.[23] And MP Leung, on being presented with a 5,000-name petition protesting the English-language proposal, assured her constituency that the prime minister and Minister Robillard were against the proposal. The petition, which Leung took to Ottawa, had been organized by the Chinese Benevolent Association and was supported by forty other groups. Finally, Indo-Canadian delegates to the biannual Liberal Party Convention in Ottawa returned with the news that the proposed language requirements would not be adopted by the federal government.[24]

The prime minister, no doubt, was trapped. Three of four British Columbia Cabinet members, plus MP Leung (his personal nominee in the constituency of Vancouver Kingsway), were all opposed. It didn't matter what the Department of Immigration's research director testified; what the independent research findings of Dr. Kunin revealed; what the overwhelming majority of those involved with immigrants and employment told Minister Robillard's Legislative Review Committee and what their *Not Just Numbers* report recommended; what almost every mandarin and frontline officer in Immigration had reported; or what Sergio Marchi had been forced to recognize when, in November 1995, he increased the percentage value in the point system for both official languages.

Mr. Marchi's press release said "the program is being cancelled because it has permitted entry of highly skilled people who lack the necessary attributes to successfully find work in Canada." He put it this way: "We would be deceiving people to think it was going to be easy to become an engineer in Toronto if they don't speak English." Exactly. The effect was not to increase the immigrants who spoke English or French. They were already being accepted. It was to deny admission of the skilled who, without language points, had been admitted as landed immigrants.

It didn't matter. Since 1990 more than 700,000 immigrants had arrived in Canada without any knowledge of either English or French. The ethnic lobby would not be ignored. The ethnic vote was too important.

On September 11, 1998, the *Vancouver Sun* ran a report on a poll that Angus Reid Associates had done earlier in the year for Madame Robillard's department:

> The poll . . . indicates an overwhelming number of Canadians (76 per cent) want newcomers to be able to speak either French or English when they arrive and want immigration officials to institute tough measures to ensure that immigrants are healthy and have no criminal record.

ENDNOTES

1. The author.

2. In a subsequent media interview, Minister Marchi made it clear that these numbers were not going to be subject to debate: *Toronto Star* column by Richard Gwyn, reprinted in the *Vancouver Sun,* July 20, 1994.

3. At the time, schools were not ready to communicate with parents who spoke no English, nor to teach children suffering trauma such as that caused by the Somali civil war. In addition, the non-Somali population soon suffered a siege mentality, outnumbered and ignored in the local schools. Other services suffered the same frustrations.

4. While writing this book, the author corresponded with the Hon. Ujjal Dosanjh, the attorney general of British Columbia, who is also minister for immigration. Federal-provincial deliberations have taken the form of an exchange of letters between the two ministers responsible and discussions between senior officials. The two levels of government have established a more formal and extensive joint-consultation process, based on research and analysis of the demographic, economic, social and labour-market impact of immigration on British Columbia and Canada. So far, provincial input into determining annual immigration levels appears to have been negligible, in spite of the attorney general's assurance that "generally speaking", the British Columbia government "supports immigration levels proposed by Citizenship and Immigration Canada, provided sufficient federal and provincial resources are in place to absorb the numbers."

5. The author attended this conference, having received an invitation addressed to him and to "Canadians for Immigration Reform", a quite exclusive organization. It would appear that somebody in Ottawa felt that he should be present and invented this organization for him to represent. Five years later, mail so addressed continues to arrive.

6. A request to the Information Commissioner of Canada for a copy of this report was unsuccessful. The report could not be located and we have only the *Toronto Star* story to go on.

7. The *Vancouver Sun*, March 10, 1995.

8. Lila Sarick in the *Globe and Mail*, June 7, 1995.

9. Their December 31, 1997 report provides the following biographical data:

   Robert Trempe [chair] recently retired as Assistant Deputy Minister of the Quebec Ministère des Relations avec les citoyens et de l'Immigration. He was formerly Assistant Secretary for Budgetary Policy for the Conseil du Trésor du Quebec, and has been Deputy Minister for Linguistic Policy and Assistant Deputy Minister for the Ministère de l'Education.

   Susan Davis has been a consultant to the Department of Citizenship and Immigration since 1995 under the Interchange Canada program. Prior to that, she was the National Executive Director of Jewish Immigrant Aid Services of Canada. While there, she was a member of the Ministerial Advisory Committee on Appointments to the Immigration and Refugee Board. From 1983 to 1988, she served as a member of the Refugee Status Advisory Committee. Ms. Davis has also worked as a Program Officer and a Protection Officer with the United Nations High Commissioner for Refugees from 1979 to 1983.

   Dr. Roslyn Kunin is Executive Director of the Laurier Institution Inc. and President of Roslyn Kunin & Associates Inc., an economic consulting firm. From 1973 to 1993, she worked as a Regional Economist with the former Employment and Immigration Canada. She has been Visiting Assistant Professor at the University of British Columbia and Simon Fraser University, and has published several papers on business immigration issues.

10. Ottawa, Minister of Public Works and Government Services Canada, 1997, 168 pp.

11. James C. Hathaway and R. Alexander Neve, "Making International Law Relevant Again: A Proposal for Collectivized and Solution-Oriented Protection", *Harvard Human Rights Journal*, Vol. 10, 1997.

12. *Le Groupe de travail sur les réfugiés*, Vivre Ensemble, Vol. 6, No. 22

(Fall 1997). The reader will note the similarity of the views expressed here to those of Gerald Shannon, Canada's Permanent Representative to the UN in Geneva, at the UNHCR meetings in 1991. See Chapter III, pp.67–68.

13. The Region of Peel in Ontario keeps detailed figures on such costs. According to a "Memorandum from Regional Councillor R. Begley, Chair, Human Services Committee to Members of Budget Sub-Committee, Region of Peel", dated March 8, 1994, the welfare payments to refugees over a three-year period were approximately equal to those paid to sponsorship cases ($2,694,000 and $2,879,000, respectively), which suggests an annual national welfare bill to refugees of another $700 million in 1994.

14. Figures obtained by the author from the Vancouver office of the Federal Court of Appeal.

15. The *Globe and Mail,* January 16, 1999.

16. This position is supported by B.C. government studies. See Don McRae (Manager, Population Statistics Section), "Some Economic Issues Surrounding Population Change", *B.C. STATS* (Victoria: Government of British Columbia, 1994). Also available on the BC Government web site at: http://www.bcstats.gov.bc.ca [population/population stats/methodology and analysis].

17. Chapter III, pp. 34–35.

18. The Skills for Change Internet web site: http://www.skillsforchange.org/ontario.htm#top.

19. The author.

20. The replies of French, Fry and Jaffer were transcribed from a videotape of this CBC Vancouver forum.

21. The *Vancouver Sun,* February 28, 1998.

22. The *Globe and Mail,* March 10, 1998.

23. The *Vancouver Sun,* April 30, 1998.

24. *Sing Tao* newspaper, as excerpted in the *Vancouver Sun,* April 13, 1998.

Chapter VIII

CITIZENSHIP FIRE SALE

"Really the only thing that people need [to emigrate to Canada] is good health and a certificate of no conviction. The leading criminals don't have convictions.

"Canadian immigration is very much a laughing stock of criminals, and Canada is used by criminals such as drug traffickers as a soft spot for the entry of drugs into North America and as an exit point for the laundering of funds."

Michael Blanchflower,
Hong Kong Crown Prosecutor[1]

The Entrepreneur category was introduced into the system as part of the 1978 legislation with the following definition:

> Entrepreneur means an immigrant who intends and has the ability to establish or purchase a substantial interest in the ownership of a business in Canada whereby employment opportunities will be created and continued in Canada for more than five Canadian citizens or permanent residents and that the Entrepreneur will participate in the daily management of that business.

It began with the requirement that the Entrepreneur would create "employment opportunities" for "more than five Canadian citizens or permanent residents." When that didn't work, the requirement became two jobs and, when that didn't work, just one job in addition to members of the Entrepreneur's family. Since that single job could quite properly be taken by a landed immigrant who arrived on the same plane as the employer, the persistent publicity lauding the program as an attack on Canada's unemployment statistics left the value of the program in doubt.

In 1986, the Immigrant Investor program was initiated by the Mulroney government with the objective of providing seed money to fund Canada's economic growth. At the outset, an investment of $250,000 was required in British Columbia, Ontario and Quebec, and $150,000 in the other provinces. The investment was secured for three years in return for immigrant visas for the principal investor, the spouse and minor children. The intent was to provide risk capital, yet, in its 1991 reports on the *Economic and Social Impacts of Immigration,* the Economic Council found:

> There is good evidence of a plentiful supply of resident entrepreneurs. Thus there is no shortage that must be filled by immigration. Logic, theory and evidence all suggest that there would neither be fewer businesses nor a lower rate of business growth in the absence of immigrant entrepreneurs.

With respect to the Investor Class, the council pointed out that many immigrants bring capital with them and whether it comes in this way or in large sums by Investor immigrants, they all retain both the principal and the yield on it.

The council wrote:

> A statement of the type, 'immigrants last year brought in billions of dollars of capital to Canada' ignores the crucial distinction between hosts and newcomers. Once that distinction is made the main argument for believing that immigrant capital is beneficial to Canada falls apart.[2]

The council also found no shortage of available capital for investment in domestic and international markets, adding that there is no reason to expect Investor immigrant capital will represent a net addition to the supply of capital available to new businesses.

The argument is that to have any economic value to Canada,

those funds must provide additional funds, over and above the funding already available in the financial markets. It is acknowledged that some benefit could result if the officials were able to direct these funds to highly technical, high-risk ventures, but only if the officials can determine that a genuine market gap is being filled and a beneficial investment would not otherwise occur.

Six years later, in 1997, Madame Robillard's Advisory Group, when recommending the joining of Investors and Entrepreneurs into a Self-supporting Class, including the Independents, expressed this opinion of the Investor Class:

> It has been a controversial and politically sensitive element of Canada's immigration program. It is evident the majority of persons immigrating to Canada under the Immigrant Investor program are unable to function in either official language and are poorly educated. Further there is little control over questionable financial arrangements, money laundering, the involvement of organized crime and funds from illegitimate business activities.

Affirming the conclusions of the Economic Council, the Advisory Group wrote further:

> The historical basis of this program is to provide risk capital. However, recent estimates show that there is a current surplus of risk investment in Canada with little real demand, except for very small enterprises just starting up, and many of the submissions we received indicated that most investor immigrant money is risk adverse. As a consequence, there is a perception that instead of attracting risk capital we are merely selling, and thereby devaluing Canadian citizenship.

It is not as though shortcomings of these business programs had not been well known and understood within the Immigration Ministry. In 1987, distinguished reporter Victor Malarek had described for Canadians the failures and abuses of these policies in his book *Haven's Gate: Canada's Immigration Fiasco.*[3]

In Hong Kong, a major source of Entrepreneur immigrants, the officers were aware even then "that many Hong Kong businessmen who had received permanent residence and status in

Canada had returned to the colony to do business as usual while their families were safely ensconced in some posh Canadian suburb." Twelve years later, in increasing numbers, they are called "astronauts".

Mr. Malarek reported that immigration officers in Toronto, Montreal and Vancouver had been suspicious that many of the Entrepreneurs had no intention of ever starting a business in Canada and that their proposals were fictitious from the start. An immigration manager in Montreal told him that "The problem is that the people running the show in Ottawa don't want to hear about the problems because this is their pride and joy. We don't know where most of these Entrepreneurs are. They don't report to us and we don't do any serious follow up work. It's a big joke."

In early 1985, there was a decision in the ministry to determine the benefits of the program. There had been no monitoring, thus there were no records. They did a telephone survey of 1,056 Entrepreneur immigrants who had obtained landed status in Canada to establish a manufacturing business. They couldn't locate 395 of them. Another 308 were either absent or refused to participate. Of the 353 who participated, 40 per cent had switched to the lower investment requirements of the retail and service sectors. Only 20 per cent of that random group had even attempted to meet their commitment. There was no evidence produced that any of them had successfully completed their business commitment.[4]

Four years later, the Auditor General, in his March 31, 1990 year-end report, repeats the tragic story:

During the first nine months of 1989, 2,345 entrepreneurs became permanent residents. Our audit revealed that only 60 percent of these entrepreneurs were landed with terms and conditions imposed.

Less than half of those were required to report to Immigration Canada to provide evidence of compliance with conditions imposed.

Until the fall of 1989 there were no entrepreneurs referred to inquiry for breach of conditions.

A year later, a 1991 report, produced internally, placed a more favourable interpretation on the Entrepreneur program.[5] This was based on government statistics and a 45-per-cent response from those contacted. Yet there were these reservations:

> Economic analysis of the business Immigration Program is directed to the use of data which for the most part has been collected for administrative purposes. The data is not ideally suited to research and analysis.

> In terms of social control Canadians are willing to tolerate very little intervention. Consequently, once landed, even with terms and conditions attached, Business Immigrants are free to do as they please within the same limits as everyone else.

> The Entrepreneur Monitoring System (EMIS) used to monitor those Immigrant Entrepreneurs landed with terms and conditions are usually updated with business information only when the Entrepreneur voluntarily interacts with Employment and Immigration Canada.

> Thus EMIS is of limited value for longitudinal studies of business growth, reinvestment and the like. . . . Permanent jobs associated with major projects will appear in fund reports frequently before such employment actually begins.

The nature of Canada's welcome to the investors was best illustrated by a 1992 advertisement placed by First Canadian Capital Corporation in Dubai in the United Arab Emirates.[6]

First Canadian had only 166 opportunities left in its latest offering. The executive director of First Canadian Capital, interviewed in the Dubai paper, was selling his program and the pitch was loaded with advantage. He spoke of the misconception that an investor had to stay in Canada for a minimum period to assure he got citizenship. Under the resident-return permit scheme, an investor need not stay in Canada to get his citizenship. After an initial stay of about ten days, he could continue with his business or his job anywhere in the world. The permit, valid for two years, was renewable on an annual basis. The prospective immigrant could even mail in his renewal form and need not visit Canada.

The pamphlet advertising this investment opportunity provided a long list of benefits, a selection of which follows:

The freedom and luxury of unconditional permanent residence status in Canada for you and your family.

To maintain and operate your existing business and assets abroad while your family enjoys Canada's medical and educational benefits.

No requirement to ever start or be active in any Canadian business or employ existing Canadian nationals unless you choose to do so.

No requirement to transfer assets to Canada.

The only requirement: a net worth of $500,000 and an investment (then) of $150,000.

The stories of two 1992 Entrepreneur immigrants illustrate the serious state Canadian immigration was in at that time. The first was the landing in Canada of the "Ice Queen", Ms. Lee Chau-Ping, her estranged husband, Mr. Cheuk, and two young sons.[7]

Lee Chau-Ping, a skilful businesswoman, first drew the attention of the Hong Kong police in 1986, on suspicion of smuggling drugs from mainland China to Hong Kong. Based in Hong Kong, and later Vancouver, she rapidly developed her fledgling drug enterprise in southern China into a massive operation. She produced and distributed an extremely addictive type of crystallized methamphetamine with the appearance of a chip of ice, hence her designation the "Ice Queen".

Aware that mainland China dealt ruthlessly with drug traffickers, she planned ahead and, in August 1990, using the services of a Canadian immigration consultant with offices in Hong Kong, applied to enter Canada as an Entrepreneur. She was the principal immigrant. Her husband, for immigration purposes, was an accompanying family member and not subject to examination of his suitability as an immigrant. Together they claimed a net worth of $1.1 million, including the Wah Kong Seafood Restaurant in Canton. She prepared the way well, opening a Canadian bank account and purchasing two homes in the Vancouver area (one for her and one for Mr. Cheuk and the two boys), as well as two cars and other assets.

Canadian immigration requirements were satisfied by her declared intent to purchase a Chicken Delight franchise in La Ronge, Saskatchewan which, with her estranged husband, she visited twice as part of the immigration approval process. She would engage on site her not inconsiderable entrepreneurial skills and promise to successfully distribute Chicken Delight in all its forms among the 2,800 population of that northern community.

Following passage of necessary medical and security clearances, Lee Chau-Ping was interviewed by an immigration officer at the Canadian Consulate in Seattle in April 1992. She and her family were issued visas and entered Canada as landed immigrants in May. Subsequent investigation by the Hong Kong police found no Wah Kong Seafood Restaurant in Canton, no record of Ms. Lee ever filing an income-tax return, no record with Chicken Delight of Canada Ltd. and no evidence of either Ms. Lee or Mr. Cheuk ever purchasing a franchise.

Nigel Thomson was the senior Canadian immigration officer in Seattle where Ms. Lee's application was dealt with. His only comment was, "I'm sure the processing was normal, as it was for hundreds of other cases at the time." He thought that a business-immigration proposal for northern Saskatchewan would have been uncommon, but not "so unusual that I would think that it would be entirely out of the ordinary." The report tells us that Mr. Thomson later became an immigration consultant.

Even so, the family had landed-immigrant status and were well settled in Canada. Just in time. In January, three months before the Seattle interview, the Chinese police were arresting the Ice Queen's colleagues in China. In July 1992, anxious to get her back and believing her to be in Canada on a visitor's visa and not knowing she was a landed immigrant, they requested her detention by the Canadian authorities. This was not acted upon until September when the RCMP received a second request.

While both the Hong Kong police and the RCMP were gathering evidence and the net was closing in, Lee Chau-Ping fled with, the police surmised, a well-prepared exit plan and a new identity and passport. In time, all of her assets in Canada were seized. When last heard from, landed-immigrant Cheuk, an unemployed seam stitcher, was settled on welfare in a "squalid one room apartment in a Canadian city where the young boys attended public school." Not much need in Canada for professional seam stitchers.

The second story is that of Huang Hsieh-Liou Chou and Wen Chi Chou of Taiwan, who decided to emigrate to Canada with their two children. Though neither spoke English, they travelled to London, England to make their application at the Canadian High Commission. In the meantime, they were divorced and Mr. Chou gained custody of their two children under Taiwanese law.[8]

Mr. Chou was admitted to Canada in 1992 as an Investor immigrant after depositing $150,000 in the Prairie Security Fund in Saskatchewan. With the proceeds of the sale of assets in Taiwan he purchased a $526,000 house in the Vancouver area and brought his children to Canada. His wife followed on a visitor's visa. He bought another home for her and the two landed-immigrant children. Under Canadian law, Mr. Chou, now a landed immigrant, had family responsibilities and when court proceedings ensued over their support, the court ordered the sale of his two homes with two-thirds of the proceeds going to Mrs. Chou and one-third to a trust fund for the children.

Mr. Chou's financial situation was further complicated. He acknowledged under oath in court that when he told Canadian Immigration officials he had $2.1 million in assets, he was simply repeating what his immigration consultants had told him to say. No one checked the value of his assets; the judge dismissed his estimates as "puffery".

Mr. Chou returned to Taiwan. When the heavily mortgaged houses were sold and the legal fees paid, Mrs. Chou, on a visitor's visa, was left with two landed-immigrant children, no home, no visible means of support, no prospects of a job, not very much money and no ability to communicate in English.

To make their immigration applications, both Mrs. Lee and Mr. Chou had travelled thousands of miles, respectively from Hong Kong and Taiwan, where their records could have been easily checked and their applications denied. How many of those other hundreds of applications, normally processed in Seattle, or London, or Los Angeles or elsewhere, have been made in those distant places for similar reasons?

In the five years since the Auditor General had reported the problem officially, none of these abuses of the process had been addressed as part of the political agenda. Late in 1994, Minister Marchi mustered the courage to suspend the initiation of new, privately run Investor programs effective November 1, 1994. He established an interim policy limiting new programs to those administered by the government. He then appointed an "Immigrant Investor Advisory Panel" to study and recommend. At this stage the investment required was $350,000 in British Columbia, Ontario and Quebec and $250,000 in the other provinces.

In their August 1995 report, *Refocusing the Immigrant Investor Program,* the high-level accountants on the panel revealed that Investor immigrants were averse to risk. The accountants met this challenge with a program guaranteeing return of capital in five years, a term acceptable to "immigrant investors who would prefer to provide relatively short term low risk debt."

Under their proposal, a portion of the immigrant investment would be used to purchase strip bonds with a five-year value equivalent to the investment. The bonds would be held by the investor and those funds would find their place with other relatively short-term money available in the money-market pool. The balance would be transferred to Immigrant Investor trusts administered by independent investment managers, and directed to small- and medium-sized enterprises. Return on these investments would be divided equally among the federal government, the provincial government and the investor. Presumably lacking confidence in the whole concept, the government rejected this proposal. In the meantime, the $350,000 investment level was made applicable in all provinces.

In a March 18, 1997 news conference, Minister Robillard announced changes in the Investor program involving an increase of $100,000 in the principal investment. This was to be the first in a series of pre-election immigration announcements. There was the cancellation of the proposed increase in the financial responsibility of sponsors for sponsored family members; more flexibility for new immigrants in the payment of the Right of Landing fee (announced on April 15); the removal of the visa restriction on travel to Canada for citizens of Portugal, imposed when 5,745 Portuguese had earlier made bogus refugee claims in Canada (announced on April 20); and, finally, an April 25 news release cancelling her earlier proposals and re-establishing the long-lived interim Immigrant Investor program, to run until December 31, 1997.

Why? The minister had learned in her March 18 news conference, when an irate observer had pointed it out to her, that in Quebec a cheque for $97,000 by itself gets a family landed status.[9] With a $100,000 increase in the principal amount, this fee would simply rise to $125,000 (see details below). The facts were well known, but not to the minister of immigration.

Under that plan the investor wrote a cheque for $97,000. The investment manager arranged a loan for $253,000, then made the appropriate $350,000 entry in their investment fund. The $97,000 provided for fees and interest spread between loan costs and investment-fund returns. For a family of five it established the value of Canadian citizenship at $20,000 each. But then, including both sets of sponsorable grandparents heading for Canada's health-care system, the value of Canadian citizenship for each member of a family of nine dropped to $11,000. A bargain-basement bargain!

When challenged, Minister Robillard denied that investors were buying citizenship. Her response: "This is not the only criteria for this person to come to Canada. It is not because she has money that she can come. Our citizenship is not for sale."

All of this did not go unnoticed.

The April 1997 British Columbia Statistics Report *(BCSTATS)* disclosed that although half of all Investor Immigrants to Canada in 1996 moved to British Columbia, less than 6 per cent of the investments made it across the country. The report points out that resettlement of Investor immigrants is costly, since more than half speak neither English nor French and bring more monolingual dependents with them. Between 1986 and 1995, British Columbia received 53 per cent of all Investor immigrants, but only 10.3 per cent of the funds were invested in British Columbia on their behalf.

This issue of *BCSTATS* then alerted readers to what appears to be an internal analysis of the Investor immigrant crisis. This report, prepared by the Immigration Department and entitled *Regulatory Impact Analysis Statement,* includes the following description of the Investor program.[10]

> Although the Program has substantially met its original objectives, it has evolved into a highly technical program, requiring significant federal resources to deliver. Despite a significant interventionist role on the part of the CIC, the Program has been vulnerable to mismanagement, abuse and fraud. Several studies have identified flaws in the design and operation of the Program and concluded that the management of private investment is not a core function of CIC. Non compliance with Program rules has reduced economic benefit and eroded program objectives. Some investors have suffered substantial losses and some Canadian businesses have been harmed.

There is no doubt that there are successful Investor immigrants, not only among those arriving before the rules changed in 1978, but since. Yet beyond the limits of the 1986 telephone survey referred to above, and the 1991 *Economic Impact of Business Immigration into Canada* study, there have been no official on-site economic assessments of the results produced by these entrepreneurial ventures or of the benefits, if any, to be enjoyed by Canadians. We know little about who the successful Entrepreneur immigrants were or why they succeeded.

A 1997 study of the profiles of ten selected Chinese-Canadian entrepreneurs was commissioned by the Asia Pacific Foundation of Canada.[11] Nine of the ten had, in fact, entered in the normal immigrant stream and the single Entrepreneur immigrant among them, pleased to be a Canadian, had lost his money. The significant message of this study, though unstated, is the general relationship between degree of success with both fluency in the English language, and education in Canada. In one instance, an engineering degree from an American university was earned en route to Canada.

But that fluency with the language was not typical of the class. Latest government statistics for 1996 show that there were more immigrants in each segment of the Business Class who did not speak one of Canada's official languages than in any other group.[12]

The statistics for those who spoke neither English nor French are as follows: principal immigrant – 51 per cent; dependents over fifteen years of age – 62 per cent; children under fifteen years of age – 83 per cent. Those figures do not describe immigrant families ready and able to contribute positively to Canadian society.

Evidence was building of abuse, mismanagement, fraud and confusion. More important, the evidence proved conclusively that Canada has sufficient entrepreneurs of its own and, except for isolated situations, there is no need to reward immigrant investors and their families with all the benefits of Canadian citizenship. There is certainly no evidence of any plans to offer Canadians investing similar amounts with a parallel benefit of comparable value to the citizenship bestowed on the aliens.

Then on December 15, 1998 another news release appeared from the minister. Having failed to produce in the fall the immigration legislation promised in the spring, Madame Robillard, as 1998 was coming to a close, and four years after Mr. Marchi set the process in motion, substituted with an "Immigrant Investor Program Redesign".

The minister's Advisory Committee had listed the two basic obstacles. First, there is a surplus of risk investment available in Canada and most immigrant Investors are averse to risk. Second, under the current program most Immigrant Investors are not only poorly educated but are unable to function in either official language. The approach of the minister's Advisory Committee was emphasis on "immigrants who invest rather than investors who immigrate." They would have to meet the core standards of education, official-language ability and self-sufficiency. The committee proposed a $500,000 interest-free loan, returnable after five years. The funds would be unencumbered and represent no more than 50 per cent of the applicant's required net worth of at least $1 million. "The obvious benefit would be the improvement in the overall quality of Investor immigrants with the admission of a pool of well-educated immigrants with good language skills." The committee calculated the real cost to the investor at almost $140,000 (5 per cent interest on $500,000 compounded for five years).

In her exuberant news release promoting her Advisory Committee's proposal, the minister gives the assurance that "the new program is dynamic . . . can support the economic requirements of job creation . . . and is a concrete example of flexible federalism"; that "immigrant investors bring a wealth of international business expertise to Canada" and they "can now be assured of the financial security of their investment. . . ."

The outstanding omission is any reference to the need to meet the Advisory Committee core standards of education, official-language fluency and self-sufficiency.

Aside from expected savings in administrative costs and a guarantee to the investor of the return of his/her money, little would have been achieved beyond increasing the sale value of Canadian citizenship to $28,000 each for a family of five, or $15,500 each for a family of nine. Still a bargain-basement bargain!

Then, in February 1999, fourteen months after the release of the minister's Advisory Committee report, Dr. Roslyn Kunin, co-author of the committee proposals, spoke at a workshop sponsored by the Institute of International Relations at the University of British Columbia. Her message was again very clear. In the Canadian experience, 58 per cent of Entrepreneur immigrants from Hong Kong have fewer than twelve years of formal education; and that while 47 per cent have some knowledge of English, 50 per cent have neither English- nor French-language ability. Her studies had shown that "most of the entrepreneurs were teachers or people engaged in other professions from which they were often retired." She explained: "Analyses show that, the way current programs are run, the net contribution of immigration is $18,000 per immigrant. Investors don't want to lose too much money and look for certainty."

Of Investor immigrants, Dr. Kunin noted that favourable public perceptions of businesspeople, when applied to Business immigrants, are "quite removed from the actual reality":

> Of the investors, 61% have twelve years of education or less. . . . Self-declared evaluations of language ability tend to be over positive. 66% of those who have a self-declared ability to speak either English or French could not speak a word in either language. 32% could speak some of one or the other. . . .

> The average immigrant investors are older persons with low education and no language ability. . . . Furthermore, they tend to be passive investors who bring their savings with them but don't necessarily start a business.[13]

Following publication of the *Immigrant Investor Program Redesign,* there was a forty-five-day period for public comment responded to primarily by nineteen immigration lawyers, consultants and private-sector program fund managers. In turn, the minister responded with reductions in the required investment to $400,000, and the minimum net worth of the investor to $800,000.

The resulting legislation requires payment of the $400,000 by the investor to the Receiver General of Canada. The investor receives in return an interest-free debt obligation in the amount of $400,000, repayable after five years. The Canadian Immigration Commission will allocate immigrant investment to approved provincial funds. After five years the province will be responsible for repayment to investors.

This plan forecloses the sale of family-citizenship packages for a cash payment equivalent to five years' accumulated interest. But it doesn't eliminate bargain-basement citizenship. The net cost to the investor, before taxes, remains limited to the forgiven interest. For the $400,000 investment, presuming a 5 per cent interest rate, the $112,000 forgiven taxable income puts the value of Canadian citizenship at $22,400 each for a family of five, and at $12,400 each if the grandparents follow under sponsorship. Canadian citizenship—always a bargain.

Although the minister's news release assures us that the re-designed program is consistent with the recommendations of the minister's Legislative Review Advisory Committee, the committee's requirements that investors meet the core standards of education, official language ability and self-sufficiency are again notable by their absence. The participating stakeholders could not have been concerned about the obvious failure of Canada to recognize the importance of those core standards and so benefit from a pool of well-educated immigrants with good language skills.

*   *   *

On June 24, 1999 the *Vancouver Sun* headlined a top news story with "Poolhall operator linked to heroin ring." Thirty Asians faced dozens of charges involving conspiracy to export, import and traffic in heroin, mischief, extortion, drive-by shooting, credit-card fraud, assault, weapons and firearms.

One investigation was initiated by the RCMP in early 1997, and another by the British Columbia Coordinated Law Enforcement Unit (CLEU) in 1996. That each investigation originated on Canada's west coast can be attributed to the description by a member of the RCMP drug squad of Vancouver as "definitely one of the major areas for the distribution of heroin coming from South East Asia for the entire North American market."

The lengthy investigations extended to "Hong Kong, Bangkok, and into areas of Myanmar and China—right into the poppy fields." They involved a power struggle between the Wo On Lok Triad of Macao and the 14K Triad of Hong Kong. Crimes committed included a drive-by shooting in Vancouver of the alleged leader of the Wo On Lok Triad, allegedly by one of the four individuals identified in both investigations. He was subsequently charged with the shooting. An investigation into how he gained entry into Canada revealed that an immigration officer in Los Angeles had neglected to check his background with the embassy in Hong Kong.

Police described most of the suspects as citizens of Canada, but some as landed immigrants. Others may have been born in

Canada, but more than anything else, this exposure describes a massive failure of Canada's procedures in selecting immigrants for landed status and in determining their qualifications for the privileges of Canadian citizenship.

Did they come as Entrepreneurs? They certainly demonstrated all of the qualities that made the Ice Queen a successful entrepreneurial candidate. Did they come as Investors? As Family Class? As Independent immigrants accepted for their skills? Or did they benefit from the up to 2,000 blank visa forms that disappeared from Canada's Hong Kong office between 1986 and 1992, as alleged by an RCMP officer and an immigration control officer and published in the *Vancouver Province* on August 26, 1999?

Aside from everything else, this dismal tale of failure obliges Madame Robillard's successor, newly sworn Immigration Minister Elinor Caplan, to direct her deputies to check the records of each of those charged offenders to determine how Canada's selection procedures could fail so completely in the granting of both landed-immigrant status and citizenship. That would be followed by the necessary changes in both procedures and personnel to assure such a disaster cannot be repeated.

*   *   *

After only five weeks of carrying the responsibilities of Canadian immigration and refugee policy on her shoulders, Mrs. Caplan will have been alerted by the front-page headline in the *Globe and Mail* on September 15, 1999. It read, "Immigrant investor plan denounced as massive sham." The story confirms the messages of the multitude of studies, reports and recommendations for action available to her predecessors, but always neglected.

David Webber is a senior forensic accountant with the World Bank in Washington, D.C. Between 1994 and 1998 he was engaged by the Department of Immigration to conduct compliance reviews of forty-two immigrant investor funds. Coincident with this, three other accountants were engaged to review sixty additional funds.

In the *Globe and Mail* article, Mr. Webber described those immigrant-investor programs, designed as they were to provide foreign investment for small businesses in Canada, as being riddled with fraud. He said that claims made by Immigration Canada about the program's success were a gross exaggeration and that rules introduced by Ottawa earlier this year to combat that fraud are completely ineffective. Feeble as they may be, they only apply in what is known as "the rest of Canada". Quebec's continued insistence on operating its own immigrant-investor program allows immigration consultants to continue to circumvent the new federal laws by simply setting up shop in Quebec under the old rules. A department spokesman described this as a large and enticing loophole to potentially unscrupulous investors. One can only wonder if these investors are like the ones mentioned earlier who favour residence in British Columbia.

Mr. Webber went on to say, "I found that in many cases there was no investment at all or that the amount of that investment was grossly inflated" and that "Canadians gave up something of real value—a visa or a passport—and received very little in return."[14]

One example he cited involved a phantom theatre project in Atlantic Canada said to cost $750,000; investigators found nothing. "A lot of people made a lot money, mostly lawyers and consultants who set up these bogus investments." Mr. Webber described them as a "massive sham", and added that "the middlemen made hundreds of million of dollars." He scoffed at the defence of a senior investment analyst with Immigration Canada, who repeated the claims of $4.5 billion in investments and the creation of thousands of jobs.

The work of Mr. Webber and his colleagues was commissioned by and for the government, presumably to assist and guide in the administration of the Investor/Entrepreneur programs. Their findings must have been received continuously over the four years 1994 to 1998, and a succession of ministers, in turn, must have been aware of the running disaster. Yet it has remained for Mr. Webber to tell his story in an act of public responsibility to Canada.

The Investor/Entrepreneur immigration ball is now in Mrs. Caplan's court.

ENDNOTES

1. The *Globe and Mail,* February 27 and 28, 1996.
2. *New Faces in the Crowd,* Economic Council of Canada, 1991.
3. *Haven's Gate: Canada's Immigration Fiasco,* Victor Malarek, Macmillan of Canada, 1987.
4. Ibid.
5. *The Economic Impact of Business Immigration into Canada.* Employment and Immigration Canada, Regional Economic Services Branch BC/YT, September 1991.
6. *Khaleej Times,* March 16, 1992.
7. The *Globe and Mail,* February 27 and 28, 1996. Great reading.
8. The *Globe and Mail,* August 19, 1996.
9. As seen on CBC Television news.
10. Immigration Department, undated report referred to in *BCSTATS,* April 1997.
11. *Succeeding: Profiles of Chinese Canadian Entrepreneurs,* Asia Pacific Foundation of Canada, Vancouver, April 1997.
12. Percentages based on *Facts and Figures 1996, Immigration Overview.* Citizenship and Immigration Canada.
13. Roslyn Kunin, *Immigration Issues: Hong Kong after the Transition,* Proceedings of a Workshop. Institute of International Relations, University of British Columbia, pp. 25–29.
14. The sources of Investor immigrants accepted between 1986 and 1998:

Hong Kong	7,418
Taiwan	5,721
South Korea	673
China	550
Phillippines	309
Macao	256
Germany	161
Iran	130
Egypt	125
Saudi Arabia	84
TOTAL	15,427

Including family members, the total number granted permanent residence is estimated at up to 80,000.

Chapter **IX**

THE AUSTRALIAN SOLUTION

*"It is the government, not some sectional interest or loud intoler-
ant voices or ill defined international interests, or the courts that
determine who shall and shall not enter this country and on what
terms. That is the defining feature of Australia's Immigration
Program."*

Philip Ruddack, Australia's Minister of
Immigration and Multiculturalism, 1998

Following a period of open public discontent with Australia's immigration laws, a new coalition government, formed in
March 1996, had the political courage to make honest and open
evaluations of the consequences of their nation's Migration Program, and to develop solutions to the problems they found. That
experience provides Canada with a model to follow.

The new government had inherited a set of immigration policies that were badly in need of reform. The entry levels had
been allowed to grow with no public explanation or rationale for
that growth. Australia's Migration Program had come to be
dominated by "Family Stream" immigration, and even some of
the "Skill-supplementation" immigration categories had allowed
entry of people with relatively poor employment prospects. The
"Spouse" and "Prospective Marriage" Interdependency categories were subject to unacceptable abuse, and sham marriages
were contributing to a serious lowering of public confidence in
the program, providing fertile ground for intolerance and racism.

The Australian political establishment recognized a serious
problem and set out to correct it. In Canada, where the same
problem has been highlighted as critical by the Auditor General

in his 1982 report, the country has yet to find a minister with the political courage to follow that example.

The Australians discovered one of the fundamental truths about success that Canadian politicians, faced with their perception of the importance of the ethnic vote, are finding increasingly difficult to accept. It is that "research has consistently shown that if migrants are young, with good English language skills, and vocational skills that are recognized in Australia, they will have a highly positive impact on the economy and on government finances." So they set about rewriting the regulations for Independent, Business and Family Class immigrants consistent with that fundamental principle, always recognizing the opportunities available in the Australian economy and labour market. They introduced a far more rigorous assessment process for those categories, and instigated thorough investigations of all spouse and dependent applicants.

The results were dramatic. Non-genuine applicants were deterred from trying their luck; for those who persisted, refusal rates more than doubled. In two years, offshore applications fell by 45 per cent, and onshore applications by 23 per cent. They substantially reduced parts of the Family Stream, including parents, pending a review of regulations to effect a situation whereby these migrants and their sponsors would take on a fairer share of the costs involved with their resettlement.

INDEPENDENT SKILLED MIGRATION

Those wishing to migrate to Australia as Independent immigrants face a rigid points test "designed to ensure the principal applicants have the skills and other attributes to allow them to quickly enter the Australian workforce and support themselves and their families without relying on the Australian government." In addition, the family must be healthy and of good character.

The skill level is restricted to those occupations in Australia requiring a trade certificate, a degree, a diploma or an associate diploma, and qualifications must be obtained at least three years before the application to migrate was filed. Further, the applicant must have been working at his usual occupation three years prior to filing, and have been active in that "usual occupation" for two of the three intervening years. That the qualifications of the prospective immigrant meet Australian standards is not a simple paper check by a visa officer as it has become in Canada, but an assessment by the relevant Australian authority regulating the particular trade or profession. The "usual occupation" is the key. Without this, applications fail.

The second test is the ability to communicate effectively in a range of situations in at least three of the four skills of reading, speaking, understanding and writing the English language. However, there is a limited list of occupations where the immigrant is not required to meet the language test on entry but must meet the costs of learning English in Australia.

The third requirement under the Australian points schedule is that applicants must be under age thirty-five to be accepted as immigrants.

These criteria have proven effective. The finding of the importance of skills, age and language ability was such that effective July 1, 1999, those standards were adjusted with a view to improving on the level of success.

The Australians are building a nation. They recognize that in today's highly competitive global village, only excellence will succeed, and they intend their immigration policies to make a positive contribution to their future development.

SKILLED AUSTRALIAN-LINKED MIGRATION

This class, with a subclass "Regional linked–skilled migration", was redesigned by the coalition government to emphasize the reunification in Australia of those linked to the country by blood or marriage, and focuses predominantly on immediate family relationships such as spouses/fiancé(e)s and dependent children. The majority of applicants in this family program are Australian young people (and sometimes not-so-young people) going overseas, meeting their life partners and wishing to bring them and their families home. The immigration authorities are interested in the qualifications of both the Australian sponsor and the sponsored family members.

PARENTS

All new applicants in the Parent category must be at least 65 years of age for men, and 61, increasing annually to 65, for women. Working-age parents are no longer eligible to apply for a permanent-residence Parent visa, the government having found that those parents over 45 generally face extreme difficulty finding employment. Hence, the working-age parent will have a series of options:

1. the Employer Nomination Scheme (where a job is waiting);
2. long-term or short-term visitors' visas, provided they intend a *genuine* visit; or
3. a Retirement visa (where there is assurance of support).

For sponsored parents or other aged relatives, in addition to assuring the sponsor has the financial resources to provide necessary support, there are "assurance of support bond" requirements as well as a "non-refundable health services charge".

Then there is the "Balance of Family test". In Australia the principle of family reunification is defined as possible only if the prospective immigrant parents already have "an equal number or more of their children living lawfully and permanently in Australia, as opposed to other countries overseas." In turn their sponsor must have lived in Australia lawfully for at least two years.

The Australians are not without compassion. They recognize the need under the Preferential Family subclass with special rules for aged single dependent relatives, special-needs relatives and the last remaining relatives outside Australia.

REFUGEES

The new Australian government, seeking an explanation for an exponential increase in judicial reviews in the refugee area, discovered the reason to be not unlike the abuses leading to the monstrous refugee backlog in Canada. It was abuse of the visa system by allowing the application for protection visas simply to prolong the stay of refugee claimants in Australia. As is the case in Canada, this includes the right to work and access to medicare and the other social-assistance benefits provided asylum seekers.

In response, the government established a Refugee Review Tribunal to decide appeals against decisions made by Immigration Department officials. In four years, 10,000 immigration decisions to refuse refugee status or protection visas were upheld by the tribunal. Of these, 979 were appealed to the Federal Court, where only 21 succeeded (but at an overall cost to the Australian taxpayer of A$20 million). Those Canadians familiar with the calendar of our Federal Court of Appeal, where hundreds of appeals are filed simply to extend stay in Canada, will understand.

BUSINESS IMMIGRATION

In the area of Business Immigration, Australia has four categories:

1. Business Owner,
2. Established Business in Australia,
3. Senior Executive, and
4. Investor.

The *Business Owner* is someone who wishes to emigrate and establish a business in Australia. This program is the equivalent of, but not comparable to, the Canadian Entrepreneurial program.

To acquire the necessary visa, there must be a genuine and realistic commitment to participate, as a substantial owner, in the management of a new or existing business of benefit to Australia. In addition, the candidate must meet the requirements of a points test in an assessment of the annual turnover, labour costs, net assets of that business, plus age and language assessment.

Approved applicants receive visas valid for five years, giving them the right to travel to and from Australia. They are required to participate in surveys monitoring their business activities, twenty-four and thirty-six months following grant of visa. For the unsuccessful, the minister for immigration and multicultural affairs may, within three years, cancel permission for the immigrant family to remain in Australia.

When making the application for landed status, the prospective immigrant must be able to show net assets in an actively operating business of not less than A$300,000 in two of the last four financial years, and there must be active involvement and responsibility for the overall management and performance in a qualifying business. This business must not have been set up for passive or speculative purposes, the applicant must have held at least 10 per cent of the equity in two of the last four years and have at least five full-time-equivalent employees.

To meet Australian objectives, settlement in the regions is encouraged by requiring only A$200,000 net assets in the business in two of the past four years. Beyond that, a record of performance is essential.

This is, in reality, a business-development enterprise. In Australia, the Entrepreneur immigrant and his or her family are not given landed status on arrival as they are in Canada, but are expected to perform to the benefit of the Australian economy. The program has been developed and is managed to meet this objective. There is no opportunity for entrepreneurship to become a shortcut to citizenship, and no opportunities for enterprising immigration consultants to peddle entrepreneurial packages to candidates for immigration to Australia as they do in Canada. Would the Ice Queen have met Australian standards?

The *Established Business in Australia Class* applies to those living in Australia legally who have an established business and wish to be admitted as a landed immigrant. The requirements parallel those for the Business Owner category and, for each, fluency in the language is essential.

Investor-linked Immigrants must be in Australia, have a record of successful business/investment activity, and pass a points test similar to those applicable in the Business classes, be under fifty-four years of age and have functional English. The emphasis, as with the others, is on achievement. The minimum investment considered is A$750,000. This must be personally owned and unencumbered, and must have been legally accumulated as a result of the candidate's business or investment activities.

Provision is also made for the entry of *Senior Executives.* This option is open to those with a successful business career, who have been employed in the top three levels of management of a major business, with an annual turnover of at least A$50 million in two of the past four financial years, and have been responsible for strategic policy development in a major component of, or a wide range of, its operations. In the points test for them, their minimum aggregate assets must be A$500,000, which is only applicable if those funds are in Australia or available for transfer to Australia within two years.

Clearly the Business-Investor-Executive immigration programs in Australia, which emphasize both excellence and performance, provide a model Canada could adopt to great advantage.

In 1998, Canada's minister of citizenship and immigration, Lucienne Robillard, travelled to Australia and New Zealand to meet with immigration officials in those countries. Is it possible Canadians will witness benefits from that expedition?

CHAPTER **X**

WHAT WE MUST DO

"A critical role for government, still, is public advocacy based on complete and factual information. Governments must make the connection between what Canadians think, what Canadians value, and what is real."

Not Just Numbers
The Report of the Minister's Advisory Group
December 31, 1997

The recommendations of the *Not Just Numbers* report might have begun a long-overdue national debate. They didn't. The experience of the Australians might point the way. It hasn't. More important, of course, are the observations of the minister's senior advisors and of the frontline immigration officers, as detailed in their leaked 1994 recommendations. These career people, having worked on a daily basis with immigrants, refugee claimants and the government policies that make every abuse of our system possible, fully understand what is wrong and have a major contribution to make in fixing it. That is, if anyone in authority is prepared to listen. And they haven't been.

The objectives of Canada's admissions programs must be twofold. First, they must select immigrants, regardless of their origins, capable of meeting the needs of this nation, with the ability to succeed, integrate and contribute to the inevitable pursuit of excellence so essential in today's competitive society. Second, Canada must receive and resettle, to the best of our ability, our share or more of the genuinely persecuted of this world requiring resettlement as defined in the United Nations Convention on Refugees. As well, Canada must continue, as it has in the past, to grant asylum, either permanent or temporary, to groups of people suffering under circumstances that demand special consideration.

At this stage in our history, immigration policy based, as it has been, on political expediency and those five immigration myths must be abandoned. The information required to assure sound policy decisions is extensive and convincing. It is available in a multitude of reports from government departments, external agencies and from ministerial committees, extending over twenty years. Each, in turn, has been neglected by a succession of ministers. Fortunately, all of that wisdom continues to be available to deal with what has become a crisis.

The easy conclusion is that Canada has no need for an immigration department because it has a very limited need for immigrants, while the plethora of failed programs has become excessively costly. In today's global village this is not a realistic solution, but the days when staffing our visa offices abroad is based on the demands of the applicants and not the needs of Canada must end. There is the opportunity and responsibility for the government to re-examine immigration and refugee policy in the shadow of the wealth of information available, to develop new policies that meet the needs and obligations of our country, then to provide the leadership to sell that program to the—as yet largely uninformed and misinformed—electorate.

There are recommendations in the *Not Just Numbers* report of Minister Robillard's Advisory Committee that, together with the effective modifications to the immigration regulations undertaken in Australia, provide a practical basis for establishing new and appropriate immigration regulations for Canada.

The essential premises must be that Canadians do not benefit from an increase in population, that economic growth of a nation depends on the quality of its people and the disposition of the nation's assets, and that it is essential that immigrants be fluent in the language of the workplace, whether English or French, and be skilled to Canadian standards in trades or professions.

To assure their ability to begin their integration into Canadian society on arrival, all of those in the immigrant stream entering either the school system or the labour force must have the language and skills necessary for their education or job-entry level. Since admissions would be limited to Canada's needs and responsibilities, those requirements would impose a minimal burden on both immigrants and their Canadian-born neighbours.

For many in other parts of the world, life in Canada appears attractive. Those people, wherever they are, have a country, a culture, a heritage and a home. The perception of the advantages of life in Canada cannot, by itself, justify our demand-driven immigration policies. Beyond our responsibility to accept and assist in the settlement of genuine United Nations Convention Refugees, the only objective of those policies must be a measurable benefit to Canada.

INDEPENDENT IMMIGRANTS

Skilled workers must meet established core standards. For education, it should be an academic, technical or trade qualification with the appropriate diploma or degree to be approved by the equivalent licensing organization in Canada. For work, required experience should be two years at the usual occupation within three years immediately prior to making the application. For official-language ability, it should be sufficient fluency in at least one of the official languages at the level of entry into the Canadian labour force; and for age, it should be not less than twenty-one years of age and not more than forty-five years of age at the time of application. Youth has its advantages and any points schedule should benefit qualified applicants up to thirty-five years of age. When Canada's labour requirements are limited, admission should be restricted to the younger applicants. And all immigrants, except refugees, must have the resources necessary to establish themselves and their families in Canada.

FAMILY CLASS

Canada has always recognized the fundamental values of the family and the importance of family support. In order to assure the success of this tradition, the Family Class, providing as it does for sponsored admission without consideration for skills or literacy, would be abandoned. The immediate family of the principal applicant, including the spouse and dependent minor children, would together be accepted as a family, subject to health, literacy and good character.

The Australian regulations regarding family sponsorship state that the majority of the family members being reunified must already be citizens of Australia. This is a model for Canada to follow.

Studies in both Australia and British Columbia demonstrate that, generally, immigrants in their retirement years, benefitting as they do from social programs, become a net cost to their new society. In those families where care for the senior family members is part of their culture, it is reasonable the tradition be respected by both Canada and the younger generation of the immigrant family.

Retirement immigrants must, therefore, have sufficient resources within their family to provide for their care. In keeping with the recommendations of the immigration mandarins in 1994, they would carry their own medical insurance. With these restrictions they would enjoy special residency status, without the social cost benefits of citizenship. The age of entry in retirement years would be restricted to the established sixty-five.

The Assisted Relative class would be abandoned because of the failure that it has become.

INVESTORS AND ENTREPRENEURS

The Investor and Entrepreneur programs, given the absence of any material evidence to justify their existence, would be cancelled and replaced with an industrial-development program conducted jointly by the Departments of Immigration and Industry. Under this program, Investor/Entrepreneur immigrants capable of advancing valid and desirable wealth-producing industrial developments would be provided with industrial-development visas and rewarded with permanent residence dependent on performance. The operative word would be "wealth-producing", rather than "service-providing", with particular emphasis on areas of high unemployment.

REFUGEES

Separate and apart are the Refugees. The evidence is clear

and conclusive that Canada's refugee-determination program has been allowed to run out of control since 1980 and, particularly, since January 1, 1989. This condition demands major surgery. The surfeit of negative reports by the Auditor General, the Law Reform Commission and ministerial committees covering the operations of the Convention Refugee Determination Division of the Immigration and Refugee Board, call for a complete and thorough overhaul of that division.

It is fundamental that government be responsible for determining who comes into Canada, who can be granted landed-immigrant status, and who becomes a citizen. Whether the membership of the decision-making body concerned consists entirely of career visa officers with experience in refugee-producing countries, or includes other citizen members, the source of the guidelines on which those decisions are based must be the government and the government alone. The government has a duty to assure those guidelines are consistent with the United Nations Convention, and that they are monitored and observed by UNHCR personnel as they were from 1977 through 1988 under the former Refugee Status Advisory Committee.

In his May 1984 report to Immigration Minister John Roberts, Professor Ratushny wrote:

> Canada's basic objective is to limit direct access to Canada as a place of refuge in order to ensure that asylum is made available to the greatest possible number of those most in need of protection.

For twelve years, the government and its creation, the Immigration and Refugee Board, have failed to heed this important advice.

The Supreme Court of Canada's *Singh* decision requires that there be a refugee hearing. From the succeeding decision of Chief Justice Nathan Nemetz of the British Columbia Court of Appeal, it is reasonable that a hearing conducted at the border across a desk could suffice to weed out the frauds. Canadian ambassadors, high commissioners and consular officers serve this country all over the world. Wherever possible, refugee claimants should apply for our help and protection where they live, or in a neighbouring country, where the facts of any case can best be determined. Whatever the country, Canadian officials will be in a position to assess to what extent conditions of persecution exist, and to what degree. That should form a continuing record in Ottawa, and officers at the border would have a list of non-refugee-producing countries. Refugee claimants would not be considered to have entered the "Land of the Charter" until they had been accepted at the border.

That principle, had it been applied to the first batches of bogus claimants from Trinidad-Tobago and Portugal, instead of consigning them to the backlog would have signalled to the world that we Canadians no longer tolerated this abuse of our border. It would have prevented the out-of-control ballooning of the backlog, and the addition of hundreds of millions of Canadian taxpayers' dollars to our national debt.

More recently—in August 1999—there was an opportunity to deal successfully with unwelcome Chinese migrants dumped unceremoniously from floating rust buckets on the shores of British Columbia. Every media interview with authorities on Chinese world movements describes a thriving economy attracting those from other parts of China to Fujian Province, the source of these migrants. These interviews also reveal a long-term undercover exodus of thousands of Fujians to North America, particularly New York City. Their interest is only in economic advantage; there is never the suggestion of a reason to claim refugee status.

But unlike in Trinidad-Tobago and Portugal, human rights and the rule of law, as Canadians understand them, are not characteristics of the administration in China.

The arrival of boatloads of smuggled human cargo could not have come as a complete surprise to Canadian authorities. If not already available in the Documentation Centre of the Immigration and Refugee Board, information on the conditions in Fujian Province could have since been obtained through Canada's embassy in China. Among those hundreds of immigrants there may indeed be some, though unlikely many, who can present a legitimate claim to fear persecution at home. At least those for whom any doubt exists would have been detected by the experienced immigration and police officers who conducted the initial interviews. For those who were honest about their origins, there has been time to check out their stories and their backgrounds through Canada's officials in China.

All of the information available to the public suggests that the evidence to be presented by the immigration officers to the decision-makers, whether adjudicators or members of the Immigration and Refugee Board, provides an opportunity to send two messages. First, the refusals would be in sufficient numbers (that is the direction of the information) to send a clear signal that Canadians intended to recover control of their border. And second, should any of the migrants even suggest the need for refuge, Canada would confirm its reputation for generous exercise of fairness and compassion for those in genuine need of permanent residence.

Recovery of the control of our border demands a display of decisive decision-making. But that requires political will. In terms of immigration policy there has been little evidence of that will for twenty years. Madame Robillard's successor, newly sworn Immigration Minister Elinor Caplan, faces an important challenge and a great opportunity to serve her country.

The Auditor General confirms that 60 per cent of refugee claimants arrive without passports or other identification, even though they were necessary to board the aircraft. There must be a major concerted attack on this gross abuse of our border. Those denied entry will send a message that handing over of their documents to the smuggler shepherds, or their deposit in the aircraft plumbing, will not give them an advantage. No other country in the world would permit this nonsense, and the *Singh* decision, along with the Charter of Rights and Freedoms, is not sufficient reason to allow it to continue.

Those from countries whose governments are in disarray will find it easier and cheaper to visit a Canadian consular office at home or in a neighbouring country than to delay that effort until they arrive on the other side of an ocean in Canada. Our record of fairness has always extended to our overseas offices and their competent staffs.

Failing any of that, there is the "notwithstanding" clause of

the Charter of Rights and Freedoms. And for what greater purpose could it be used than to establish the right to control our
nation's border, to determine who shall enter our country and
who shall experience the privilege of becoming a Canadian citizen?

Altogether, the objective would be a society in which children, whether born overseas or born in Canada, would begin life
exposed to at least one of Canada's official languages. On entering school, along with the possible advantage of being bilin-
gual, they would be fluent in entry-level English or French.
They would discover that they had entered an educational world
where they were being taught the history of Canada and where
they could learn to appreciate the contributions of those who
created this nation—and learn why Canada is attractive to them
as immigrants. They would understand what being a Canadian
is all about, and would enter adulthood able and anxious to contribute and succeed in meeting the challenges that the future is
bound to present.

The extent of those challenges and their significance for the
future of Canada was signalled by headlines on December 3,
1998, in Canada's two national newspapers. The *Globe and
Mail* read, "Economy is lagging, Canada warned." The article
was subheaded, "OECD forecasts a major tumble in our relative
standard of living." The *National Post* read, "Kill all programs
that don't spur growth, MPs urge." The subhead read, "Shift in
priorities—'Productivity covenant' would test all spending for
economic impact."

The Commons Finance Committee and the Organization for
Economic Cooperation and Development had independently
reached the conclusion that, without fundamental and immediate changes in government policies, the future of the Canadian
economy and the quality of life of the Canadian people would
go into steady decline.

The OECD emphasized that compared with the other six
countries in the G7 (the United States, Germany, Japan, France,
Britain and Italy) and with five fast-growing smaller ones (Australia, the Netherlands, Ireland, New Zealand and Norway),
"Canada has not kept pace on several accounts over the 1990s."

The report warned that even with a solid improvement in Canada's showing, the country is likely to slip below the OECD average by about the year 2015. But if the country cannot even maintain its recent performance, Canada could fall to about 25 per cent below the average.

And then the clincher:

> "Because its population is growing faster than that of other leading nations," the OECD said, "Canada has to run faster just to keep its place as an above-average performer."

In the three years between 1992 and 1995, Canada's natural population growth and net growth through immigration each accounted for about 160,000 new Canadians, for an annual growth of 320,000, or about 1 per cent. Even the OECD understands that it is not in Canada's interest to attempt the absorption of such large numbers of immigrants.

And from the Commons Committee news story:

> The committee, alarmed at the speed with which Canada's productivity performance—and therefore its living standard—has fallen behind that of the U.S. this decade, argues that reversing course must be an urgent federal priority.

> The committee will ask the federal Cabinet to put in place a 'productivity covenant.' . . . The covenant is a mechanism that would automatically screen every government spending decision and program to make sure it strengthens rather than harms the nation's long-term economic growth.

The well-publicized Departmental Reviews following the 1993 election, and preceding the five-year budget-cutting exercise, avoided immigration policy. The immigration ministers also avoided immigration policy; they continued instead with unproductive consultations.

When Madame Robillard succeeded the Honourable Sergio Marchi to the Immigration and Citizenship post in 1996, she faced two tasks. The first was to share with Senator Hays the responsibility of producing a winning election platform for the Liberal Party in the upcoming June 1997 election. The second was to either assess the volume of wisdom available in the accumulated studies and reports recommending immigration-policy changes, and develop revisions consistent with the national interests of Canada, or, alternatively, to forestall the development of any progressive revisions to the legislation.

There was some immediacy to the platform job. In the meantime, the revision-of-policy task was taken care of with her appointment of a Legislative Advisory Committee to study and report back on December 31, 1997—conveniently six months after the election. The report arrived on schedule. The minister followed up with extensive trans-Canada consultations. There was to be legislation in the fall of 1998. Nothing happened.

Then, in an elaborate announcement of a White Paper on January 6, 1999 entitled "Building a Strong Foundation for the 21st Century", the Honourable Lucienne Robillard opted for more study—just like every other immigration minister since Lloyd Axworthy in 1980. There would be legislation in the fall of 1999, she said.

Believing, she said, that the public is entitled to be included in the discussion, Madame Robillard set out "the broad direction the government intends to pursue in the modernizing of immigration and refugee protection, legislation and policy." After eighteen years of consultations, and multiple reports by both internal and external agencies, the minister was still uncertain about her next move. She was "seeking views and practical advice on the specific policies and legislative proposals that will enable [her] to achieve the broad directions that have been set out."

They include "reinforcement of the family class", with an increase in the age of dependent children from under nineteen years of age to under twenty-two, and redefinition of "spouse" to include common-law and same-sex relationships. There will be a more significant requirement for education and language skills for Business and Independent immigrants but "language would not be made a rigid pass/fail criteria as this would introduce too much rigidity into immigration selection." The program for selecting skilled workers would "retain its flexibility and ensure no one is excluded because of a failure to meet a single criterion." Would that include skills or literacy?

Declaring that Canada's refugee policy needs to balance the two principles of fairness and efficiency, the White Paper describes the Immigration and Refugee Board as part of a protection system that has earned Canada respect around the world, a Board the government proposes to retain, always ensuring that it become more effective and less costly.

None of that suggests the Government of Canada has any intention of facing up to a serious national problem. Indeed, the concluding page of the White Paper is more persuasive of the proposition that delay, rather than progress, was the political objective when Madame Robillard set her project in motion three years ago. Here are three quotations from that page:

> One of the key themes to emerge from the public consultations was a desire for further consultations.

and

> A great deal of work remains to be done. Proposals are not finalized. Much detailed analysis is required. By working together differences can be bridged and solutions found. The focus of consultations will now shift to examining how these broad directions can best be implemented.

and then

> The revision of immigration and refugee policies and legislation represents both a great challenge and a unique opportunity to take full advantage of a changing global environment and to shape the future.

That is where Mrs. Caplan took over on August 3, 1999. A month later, on a visit to British Columbia to assess the Fujian Chinese arrivals, she addressed the Vancouver Canadian Club and began by "stating the obvious". She confessed to not having all of the answers, nor a quick-fix solution, and that she has a lot to learn. She intends to listen. She will meet with her regional officials; she will have a series of low-key discussions with community leaders and organizations, and "of course with my fellow caucus members here in B.C."

Only one thing is certain. Canada does not need more consultations. What it does need, desperately, is a new and courageous immigration minister who cares about the future of Canada and is prepared to accept the overwhelming evidence that our immigration and refugee policies do not by any means serve the interests of our country. With the advice and support of her deputies, who understand the problems, and the guidance of those whose work has produced all of those valuable reports, she must develop new legislation directed only to the future of Canada.

The reports of the OECD and the Commons Finance Committee are a signal to every member of Canada's political establishment. Any continuing perception they have of political advantage in accepting large numbers of both Family Class and Business immigrants into Canada, without first requiring that they meet core standards for language and skills, must be abandoned.

The failures of Canada's immigration and refugee policies have now been thoroughly exposed. Those policies are prime candidates for immediate consideration and action under the Commons Committee's "productivity covenant".

The Five Immigration Myths and that succession of critical official reports provide the necessary impetus for Canada to change course. Canadians face both a challenge and an opportunity to begin the rebuilding of a great nation. Mrs. Caplan's share of that challenge is to provide the neccssary leadership.

* * *

A POSTSCRIPT! In her November announcement of immigration levels for the year 2000, the Minister's commitment was "to the 1993 Liberal Red Book target of one percent of the population each year, over the long run." In support she invoked Canada's birthrate and aging workforce. She assured us that the goal is for "brain gain, not brain drain" with "family reunification as a key priority." Those five myths will not be abandoned.

PRINCIPAL SOURCES
AND SELECTED READINGS

TASK FORCE REPORTS TO THE MINISTER

The Refugee Status Determination Process. A Report of the Task Force on Immigration Practices and Procedures to the Honourable Lloyd Axworthy. W. G. Robinson, chairman, November 25, 1982.

A New Refugee Status Determination Process for Canada. A Report to the Honourable John Roberts by Professor Ed Ratushny, special advisor, 1983.

The Report of the Royal Commission on the Economic Union and the Development Prospects for Canada: The Macdonald Report. Donald S. Macdonald, 1985.

Refugee Determination in Canada. A Report to the Honourable Flora MacDonald, by Rabbi Gunther W. Plaut, special policy advisor, April 17, 1985.

Immigrants and Language Training. A Report to the Minister by the Canada Employment and Immigration Advisory Council, March 1991.

The Quality of Mercy. A study of the processes available to persons who are determined by the Immigration and Refugee Board not to be refugees and who seek humanitarian and compassionate treatment. To the Honourable Sergio Marchi. By Ms. Susan Davis and Mr. Lorne Waldman, March 1994.

Refocusing the Immigrant Investor Program. Report of the Immigrant Investor Program Advisory Panel, August 1995.

Not Just Numbers: A Canadian Framework for Future Immigration. Report of the Immigration Legislative Review Advisory Group to the Honourable Lucienne Robillard, December 31, 1997.

REPORTS BY PUBLIC AGENCIES

Handbook on Procedures and Criteria for Determining Refugee Status. Office of the United Nations High Commission for Refugees, September 1979.

Reports of The Auditor General of Canada for 1982, 1985, 1990 and 1997.

Reports of the Law Reform Commission of Canada, *A Preliminary Study*, February 1, 1991; *Draft Final Report,* March 5, 1992.

Review of Immigrant and Ethnic Services. Report prepared for the Vancouver Social Planning Department and Immigration Canada, December 1987.

Measuring the Costs of Literacy in Canada. Report of the Canadian Business Task Force on Literacy, February 1988.

After the Door has been Opened. Report of the Canadian Task Force on Mental Health Issues affecting immigrants and refugees, 1988.

Job Futures: An Occupational Outlook to 1995. A joint publication of the Canadian and British Columbia Governments, 1989.

Canada's New Refugee Status Determination System. Margaret Young, Research Branch, Library of Parliament, January 1989, revised July 1989.

Attitudes and Perceptions of Selected Dimensions of Refugee and Immigration Policy in Canada. Prepared by Angus Reid Associates Inc. for Employment and Immigration Canada, March 1989.

Scholastic Adaptation and Cost Effectiveness of Programs for Immigrant/Refugee Children in Canadian Schools. Report of the Canadian School Trustees' Association, May 1989.

Immigration to Canada. Aspects of Public Opinion. Prepared by Angus Reid Associates Inc., October 1989.

Immigration and Labour Adjustment. Paper presented by Ms. Shirley B. Seward of the Institute for Research and Public Policy to the House of Commons Standing Committee on Labour, Employment and Immigration, May 15, 1990.

New Faces in the Crowd and *Economic and Social Impacts of Immigration.* Reports of the Economic Council of Canada, 1991.

A Lot to Learn: Education and Training in Canada. The Economic Council of Canada, 1992.

Lower Mainland Multicultural Education Project. Report of the Social Planning and Research Council of British Columbia, December 1992.

The Dilemma of New Canadian Youth. Report of the Asian Youth Task Force for the City of Vancouver – Social Planning Department, undated.

The Immigration Dilemma. A publication of the Fraser Institute. Edited by Steven Globerman, 1992.

Children of the Inner City. A brief to the Governments of Canada and British Columbia and the Vancouver School Board, from the Vancouver Inner City Education Society, September 1993.

Rebuilding Trust. A report of the Review of Fundamental Justice in information gathering and dissemination at the Immigration and Refugee Board of Canada. By Professor James C. Hathaway, York University, December 1993.

National Consultation on Family Class Immigration. A report by Professor James C. Hathaway, Osgoode Hall Law School, June 1994.

The British Columbia Teachers' Federation ESL/ESD (English as a Second Language/English as a Second Dialect) Project. Prepared by the BCTF Research Department, June 1994.

Ethnic Conflict in Vancouver. A report of the B.C. Civil Liberties Association, 1995.

Diminishing Returns. The Economics of Canada's Recent Immigration Policy. Published by the C. D. Howe Institute and the Laurier Institution, Dr. Don J. DeVoretz, editor, January 1995.

Succeeding: Profiles of Chinese Canadian Entrepreneurs. Publication of the Asia Pacific Foundation of Canada, Vancouver, April 1997.

The Silent Debate: Asian Immigration and Racism in Canada. Edited by Eleanor Loquian, Aprodicio Loquian and Terry McGee. Institute for Asian Research, University of British Columbia, 1998.

Creating Opportunities: The Liberal Plan for Canada (The "Red Book"), September 1993.

INTERNAL GOVERNMENT REPORTS

Equality Now. Report of the Special House of Commons Committee on Minorities in Canadian Society, March 1984.

Equality for All. Report of the Parliamentary Committee on Equal Rights, October 1985.

Family Reunification. Report of the Standing Committee on Labour, Employment and Immigration, June 1986. Response of the Government, October 1986.

Current Demographic Analysis. Report on the demographic situation in Canada. Statistics Canada, 1988.

Communications Framework for the Immigration Program. Prepared by the Public Affairs Branch, Immigration Canada, June 1989.

The Role of Immigration in Changing Socio-Demographic Structures. A report prepared for the Demographic Review by Professors Roderic Beaujot and J. Peter Rappack of the Sociology Department, University of Western Ontario, October 1988.

Charting Canada's Future. A Report of the Demographic Review. Three-year study by the Department of Health and Welfare, December 1989.

The Economic Impact of Business Immigration into Canada. Report for Employment & Immigration Canada Regional Economic Services Branch BC/YT by Dr. Roslyn Kunin, September 1991.

Economic Impact of Recent Immigration: Diminishing Returns. Subcommittee of the Standing Committee on Citizenship and Immigration, November 1995.

EMPLOYMENT AND IMMIGRATION CANADA STUDIES

Family Class Immigrants to Canada, 1981-1984: Labour Force Activity Aspects, 1985.

The Revised Selection Criteria for Independent Immigrants, 1985.

Report to Parliament on the Review of Future Directions for Immigration Levels, June 1985.

The Employment Effects of Immigration: A Balance Sheet Approach, June 1986.

Population Aging and Immigration Policy in Canada: Implications and Prescriptions. David K. Foot, August 1986.

Canada's Immigration Levels and the Economic and Demographic Environment 1967–1987, March 1988.

Annual Reports of the Immigration and Refugee Board, 1989 to 1995.

Quarterly Reports of the Immigration and Refugee Board, 1989 to 1998.

Minister's Annual Immigration Plan Report to Parliament, 1983 to 1999.

INDIVIDUAL PUBLICATIONS

Handbook on Procedures and Criteria for Determining Refugee Status. New York: United Nations High Commission for Refugees, 1979.

Canada and the Immigration Problem. Stephen Leacock. National English Review, April 1911.

None is Too Many. Irving Abella and Harold Troper. Toronto: Lester & Orpen Dennys, c/o Key Porter Books, 1983.

Continuous Journey: A Social History of South Asians in Canada. Toronto: McClelland & Stewart Inc., 1985.

Ethnic Conflict in Vancouver. R. A. H. Robson and Brad Breems. Vancouver: B.C. Civil Liberties Association, 1985.

Haven's Gate: Canada's Immigration Fiasco. Victor Malarek. Toronto: Macmillan Canada, 1987.

Double Standard: The Secret History of Canadian Immigration. Reg Whitaker. Toronto: Lester & Orpen Dennys, c/o Key Porter Books, 1987.

Merchants of Misery: Inside Canada's Illegal Drug Scene. Victor Malarek. Toronto: Macmillan Canada, 1989.

Critical Years in Immigration: Canada and Australia Compared. Montreal: McGill–Queen's University Press, 1989.

A Time Bomb Ticking: Canadian Immigration in Crisis. Charles M. Campbell. Toronto: The Mackenzie Institute, 1989.

Closing the Doors: The Failure of Refugee Protection. David Matas with Ilana Simon. Toronto: University of Toronto Press, 1989.

First Generation. Nancy Knickerbocker and Stephen Bosch. Vancouver: The Asia Pacific Initiative, 1990.

The Trouble With Canada: A Citizen Speaks Out. William D. Gairdner. Toronto: Stoddart Publishing Company Ltd., 1990.

Strangers at our Gates. Valerie Knowles. Toronto and Oxford: Dundern Press, 1992.

The Immigration Dilemma. Steven Globerman, editor. Vancouver: The Fraser Institute.

Pounding at the Gates: A Study of Canada's Immigration System. Daniel Stoffman. The *Toronto Star*, September, 1992.

Underground Nation: The Secret Economy and the Future of Canada. Diane Francis. Toronto: Key Porter Books, 1994.

Nationalism Without Walls: The Unbearable Lightness of Being Canadian. Richard Gwyn. Toronto: McClelland & Stewart Inc., 1995.

Boom, Bust and Echo. David K. Foot with Daniel Stoffman. Toronto: Macfarlane, Walter & Ross, 1996.

Who Killed Canadian History? J. L. Granatstein. Toronto: HarperCollins Publishers Ltd., 1998.

MAGAZINE ARTICLES

"The Japanese in Canada", William Peter Ward. Canadian Historical Association, 1982.

"The Chinese in Canada", Jin Tan and Patricia E. Roy. Canadian Historical Association, 1985.

"Canadians Wanted! No Skills Necessary", Daniel Stoffman. *Canadian Business,* August 1993.

"Towards a More Realistic Immigration Policy for Canada", Daniel Stoffman. C. D. Howe Institute, 1993.

"How Many Immigrants Should Canada Admit?" Transcript of a CBC Morningside program. Peter Gzowski with Daniel Stoffman and Professor Morton Weinfeld. The *Globe and Mail,* February 4, 1994.

"The Bitter Poison of Multiculturalism", *The Western Report,* April 18, 1994.

"How Many and Which Ones?" Daniel Stoffman. *Canadian Living,* May 1994.

"The Facts Behind the Faces", *The Canadian Forum,* November 1994.

"Travesty: Canada's refugee system will let in just about anybody who asks", Daniel Stoffman. *Saturday Night,* November 1994.

"Dispatch from Dixon", Daniel Stoffman, *Toronto Life,* August 1995.

"People of a New Land", Angelika Sauer, *The Beaver,* Dec./Jan. 1997.

LIST OF ARTICLES BY CHARLES M. CAMPBELL PRINTED IN THE *VANCOUVER SUN*

"Don't drop the gate: Immigration amnesty only works for the guilty." August 31, 1990.

"Close to collapse." November 16, 1990.

"The real cost of handling refugees." April 14, 1992.

"Acceptance rates depend on who is making decisions." August 2, 1994.

"When you hear of well off immigrants, ask when did they arrive." August 24, 1994.

"Why Canadians must get back the keys to the refugee gate." December 27, 1994.

"Save money, close our borders." February 21, 1995.

"B.C. can't afford Canada's immigration policies." November 15, 1995.

"Immigration policies show a rate of diminishing returns." November 20, 1996.

WEB SITES

United Nations Home Page: http://www.un.org/

Australia, Department of Immigration & Multicultural Affairs Home Page: http://www.immi.gov.au/

New Zealand Immigration Service Home Page: http://www.immigration.gov.nz/

Citizenship & Immigration Canada Home Page: http://cicnet.ci.gc.ca/

INDEX

Boldface indicates table.

A

adaptation, of immigrants to Canadian society, 6, 10, 19–20, 37, 44, 45, 46, 47–48, 204–5

adjournments, 131, 132, 133, 135

Administrative Review, 61, 78, 86, 87, 92–93, 100, 102, 107, 108

admission, guidelines for, 98

admission standards, 5–6, 20, 22, 28, 29, 33, 40, 108, 167–68, 177, 191, 205, 214

ADRs, 87, 108

Advisory Committee, 188–89, 204

Akbari, Ather, 22

aliens, 10, 88

amnesty, 29–30, 50, 61, 70, 78, 87, 99, 101, 107, 108, 118

Anderson, David, 2

Angus Reid Associates Inc., 63, 144–47, 174

appeals, 29, 69, 77, 86, 162, 164

Asia Pacific Foundation of Canada, 187

Assisted Relatives, 35, 49, 56, 148, 206

"astronauts," 180

asylum: shopping, 101; temporary, 101, 127

Australian solution, 195–201, 203, 204, 206

Average Earnings of Foreign-Born Individuals, **55**

Average Income Comparison Between Immigrants and Canadians 1984, **21**

Axworthy, Lloyd, 11, 36, 40–41, 65, 70

B

background checks, 29, 30, 33, 191, 192

Backlog Breakdown of Refugee Claims by Region and Nationality, **90, 91,** 111

backlog clearance process, 104–7, 109, 115, 117–20. *See also* Refugee Backlog Clearance Program; Refugee Backlog Subdivision; refugees: backlog of

Balance of Family test, 198

Bauer, William, 66–67

Best, J.C., 3, 120–21

Bill C44, 156–57

Bill C55, 87

birth rate, 14–16, 25, 31, 161

boat people, v, 208

British Columbia Coordinated Law Enforcement Unit (CLEU), 191

Bruk, John, 5

"Building a Strong Foundation for the 21st Century", 212–13

business immigration program, 157

C

Canada, as economic haven, 156
Canada, as major destination for refugees, 93, 101, 106
Canada, population needs of, 10, 11, 14–20, 25, 31–32, 52, 143, 161, 204, 211
Canada Employment and Immigration Advisory Council, 62
Canada's Immigration Levels and the Economic and Demographic Environment 1967–87, 30–31
Canadian Attitudes Towards Immigration Levels 1975–1987, **144**
Canadian Public Opinion on Immigration and Refugees: A Review of Public Opinion Research, 144
Canadian Public Opinion on Population, Immigration and Refugees, 145
Canadians for Immigration Reform, 175*n*
capital punishment, 4
Caplan, Elinor, 12, 127, 192, 213–14
case scheduling, 131–32, 133, 135. *See also* refugee hearings: adjournments of
Chan, Raymond, 173
Charter of Rights and Freedoms: abuse of, 97; and Honduran refugees, 128; as key legislation, 3, 121; legislative change to, 164; "notwithstanding" clause, 76, 209–10; and right to refugee status, 163; and *Singh* decision, 74

Charting Canada's Future, 16–17
Chau-Ping, Lee, 182–84
Cheuk, Mr., 182–84
Chilean Refugee Claimants 1995–1997, **160**
Chinese-Canadian entrepreneurs, 187
Chou, Huang Hsieh-Liou, 184–85
Chou, Wen Chi, 184–85
Chrétien government, 138, 149, 156–57
citizenship: bargain basement, 186, 189, 190; buying of, 186; devaluing of, 179; discussion of, 177–94; family packages, 190; and landed immigrants, 51–52, 58; and permanent residents, 64*n;* privileges of, 163; and refugees, 101; sale value of, 189; and selection, 192, 210; sold on black market, 78; and sponsor's commitment, 53; and stay in Canada period, 181–82; suspension of processing, 157
Citizenship Act, 35, 50, 64*n,* 154
Collacott, Martin, v
Commons Standing Committee on Labour and Immigration, 169
Communications Framework for the Immigration Program, 24–25, 144, 146–47
Convention Refugee Determination Division (CRDD), 68, 83, 88, 93, 125, 127, 128, 139, 140, 207

Convention refugees, 33, 38, 40, 66, 67, 73, 89, 93, 205
"Courier Parent," 42–43
Credible Basis test, 102, 103, 106, 107
criminal activity, 2, 3–4, 40, 97, 126, 128, 154, 162, 177, 179, 191–92. *See also* drug trade; money laundering

D

Davis, Susan, 160, 175*n*
Deferred Removal Order, 126
Demographic Review (Department of Health and Welfare), 17, 18, 20, 32
Demographic Situation in Canada, 15
denial of application, 61
Department of Manpower and Immigration, 27
dependency ratio, 31
deportation, 4, 40, 67, 105, 112, 115, 123, 126, 127, 154, 157. *See also* Deferred Removal Order
Desautels, Denis, 134
DeVoretz, Don, 22–24
Dhaliwal, Herb, 173
Dosanjh, Ujjal, 172, 174*n*
drive-by shooting, 191
drug trade, 3, 128, 177, 182, 191
Dublin Convention, 101
Dye, Kenneth, 43–46, 65, 133

E

earnings of immigrants, 7, 20–24, **21, 23,** 30, 53, **55,** 55–56, 63, 148, 166, 169

Economic Council of Canada, 1, 17–19, 32, 44, 152, 178
Economic Impact of Business Immigration into Canada, 187
Economic Impact of Recent Immigration, 7
economic impact of refugees, 176*n*
economic migrants, 160
Economic and Social Impacts of Immigration, 17, 44, 178
education, 19, 24, 62, 155, 166, 167, 179, 182, 189, 191
education funding, cuts to, 163
employment, 28, 37–38, 44, 52–54, 59–60, 61, 63, 71, 77, 159, 168, 177, 198
Employment and Immigration Canada, 48, 181
Employment Insurance, 54
English as a Second Language (ESL), 10, 68, 78, 162–63, 169
Entrepreneur category, 28, 35, 155, 158, 166, 177–78, 180, 206
Entrepreneur Monitoring System (EMIS), 181
Equality for All, 51, 58
Equality Now, 47
ethnic vote, 9, 36, 43, 46, 76, 105, 196
European immigration, 99
"Examination under Oath," 69, 86
Expedited Process, 115

F

Fairweather, Gordon: on adjournments, 134; annual report 1989, 110–11; defends IRB record, 108–9; and deputy chairpersons, 102; determined not to be "gatekeeper," 99, 103–4; heads IRB member selection Advisory Committee, 141; "immigration czar," 97; obligations of, 136; public relations tour of, 113–14
family, definition of, 34–35, 165
Family Class: Australian solution as model for, 205–6; and backlog clearance process, 105; change in regulations proposed, 153; criteria, 24, 28; defined, 33–34; earnings of, 56, 148; economic implications of, 52–54; emphasis on, 56–58; enter Canada by right, 40; freedom of entry of, 51; increasing numbers, 46; India as principal source, 159; and *Not Just Numbers* findings, 165; regulations modified to favour, 46; reinforcement of, 212; and Report of the Auditor General 1982, 44–45; restrictions recommended, 155; statistics, 158; and statutory entitlement, 54; three-tier recommended, 165; and welfare, 78, 156
Family Class Immigrants to Canada, 1981–1984: Labour Force Activity Aspects, 52

family members, sponsoring of, 6, 29–31, 39, 49, 51–52, 59, 82, 118, 153–54, 186, 190. *See also* Family Class
family members, sponsorship of, 197–98
family reunification, 34, 39, 51, 54–58, 106–7, 148, 157, 197–98
Family Reunification Report, 54
Farrow, Moira, 80
fertility rate, 15–16, 31
Financial Post, 19–20
First Canadian Capital Corporation, 181–82
"first opportunity" principle, 101
five-year plan, 148
foreign-policy considerations, 159–60
frontlog, 103
Fry, Hedy, 170, 172

G

Gander situation, 113
Gerlitz memorandum, 112–13
Girard, Raphael, 159
Globe and Mail, 9, 67, 81, 89, 103, 109, 122, 192–93, 210
Green, Mendel, 106
Green Paper, 31–32
growth, projected, 163

H

Harder, Peter, 98, 104, 108–9, 139
Hathaway, James C., 137–38, 142*n*, 175*n*

Haven's Gate: Canada's Immigration Fiasco, 179
Honduran Refugee Claims Processed in Vancouver 1996–1999 (First Quarter), **129**
honest information, need for, 146
Hong Kong, as source of immigrants, 179–80, 189, 192
How Canadians Govern Themselves: A Federal State, 76

I

identity documents, 89, 105, 120, 157, 163–64, 209
illegal entry, 65
illegal immigrants, 50, 108
immigrant capital, 178–79
Immigrant Investor Advisory Panel, 185
Immigrant Investor Program Redesign, 188–89
Immigrant Investor Program Redesign, 190
Immigrant Investor programs: changes to, 185–86; and fraud, 193; initiation of, 178–80; privately run, 185; problems described, 187–88; and Québec, 186, 193; redesign of, 190; reservations about, 181; "sham," 192; source countries for, **194**
immigrants, illegal, 2, 4, 5
immigration: black marketeering of, 78–79, 81, 87; and Canada's needs, 151, 157; consultants, 79, 81; costs of, 163; economic impact of, 1, 7, 13, 17–19, 20–24, 25, 27–28, 62–63, 144, 146, 149, 151, 155, 166–67, 178–81, 196; as economic tool, 148; figures, 47, 87, 88; lobby, 78, 100–101, 152, 170; myths, 13–26, 149, 161, 214; need for, 1, 11, 14–16; promoted, 158–59; rate, 13–14, 18, 25; reform, 163; statistical breakdown, 157–58
Immigration Act, 6, 22, 32–33, 43, 66, 69, 100, 116, 138, 157
Immigration Appeal Board (IAB), 2, 3, 29–30, 39, 45, 61, 87
Immigration Appeal Division (IAD), 40, 87–88
Immigration Commission, 24–25, 46, 53
immigration industry, 25, 50, 93, 97, 124, 154
Immigration Legislative Review Team, 58
immigration policies: abuse of, 63; behind closed doors, 149; and Canada's needs, 6, 16; and Canadian economy, 210–12; condemnation of, 43; decrease of immigrants, 148; errors accepted, 11; failures of, 214; failure to address real issues, 152–53, 157; and federal election 1984, 46, 71; and federal election 1988, 81; and federal election 1993, 37, 124; and federal election 1997, 186; and immigration industry, 50; and immigration

myths, 13, 161; increase of immigrants, 147–48; and labour market, 61; laxness of, 2–3; loss of control of, 114; make abuse possible, 203; "modernizing of," 212–13; under Mulroney government, 100–101; narrowness of directives, 111; open door, 83, 97–130, 144, 155; overhaul of, 66; politically motivated, 146, 204; polls on, 144–146, 147; and population needs, 143; as priority of government, 33–35; promotion of, 36–37; and racial tension, 46–48, 50; rationale for, 151; rejected by immigration service, 156; review of, 51; 1960s, 27–29; selective, 145; selling to public, 25; studies by Daniel Stoffman, 93; and UNHCR, 68

Immigration Policy Perspectives: A Report of the Canadian Immigration and Population Study, 31

immigration programs, monitoring and modifying of, 166

Immigration and Refugee Board Decisions — Record of Refugee Claims, **85**

Immigration and Refugee Board (IRB): annual report 1989, 104; appointments to, 136–37, 138, 154; budget, 68, 78, 162; close to collapse, 10; creation of, 6, 65–67; divisions of, 87–88; forced resignations from, 125–26; history of, 97–130; image of, 122; independence of, 98, 139, 141; judicial inquiry into, 125; mandate of, 116; member selection advisory committee, 141; members unfit, 137; negative assessment of, 119–20; negative reports of, 207; new appointments to, 124–25; reasons for inefficiencies, 135–37; removal of members requested, 117; responsibility to render quick decisions, 132–33; rules, regulations and procedures, 99; staffing of, 102–3; statistics, 103, 164; studied, 131–32. *See also* Convention Refugee Determination Division (CRDD); Immigration Appeal Division (IAD)

immigration system: abuse of, 3, 5, 10, 38–39, 44–45, 79, 88, 97, 163–64; compared to other countries, 2, 6; criticized by immigration officers, 43; failures of, 41–42; mismanagement of, 2

Independent Class: and arranged employment, 51, 52; compared to Family Class, 24; described, 36–38; earnings of, 56, 148; increase in, 30; restricted, 41–42, 46, 49, 54–55, 62; selection, 28, 154, 158; selection of, 148; as "Self-supporting Class," 166, 179; and solutions, 205

infrastructure costs, 163

Institute for Research on Public Policy, 19, 32

Investors, 166, 178–79, 206

J

Jaffer, Mobina, 170–71
job creation, 24–25, 28, 35, 144, 149, 177–78, 193
Job Futures—An Occupational Outlook to 1995, 61

K

Kharas, Firdaus J., 106–7, 115
Kunin, Roslyn, 160, 169, 173, 175*n,* 189

L

language ability, 10, 19, 28, 35, 47, 155, 162–63, 165, 166, 167, 168–74, 179, 187–88, 189, 190, 191, 196, 197, 204–5, 205, 210, 212
Law Reform Commission of Canada, 131–32, 133, 135, 136–37, 137–38, 207
Legislative Review Committee, 160–62, 164, 165, 173, 191
Liberal Party policy convention (1992), 7, 8–9
literacy, 19, 28, 37, 213

M

MacDonald, Flora, 51, 73, 75, 76, 95*n*
Macdonald Royal Commission (1985), 18, 60–61
Maclean's, 2
Malarek, Victor, 179

Marchi, Sergio: becomes Minister of Citizenship and Immigration, 12*n;* and language ability, 173; obligations of, 156; and Occupations lists, 37; problems faced by, 149; and "Red Book" figures, 174*n;* and removal of IRB members, 117; and selection of IRB members, 141; strategy of, 157; Summer of Consultations, 150–54; on visa restrictions, 80
marriage, 39, 42
marriage of convenience, 38–39, 42
Mawani, Nurjehan, 138, 140
Maxwell, Judith, 152
McDougall, Barbara: on amnesty, 107; on backlog, 89; becomes Minister of Immigration, 143; and budget, 104; and Caribbean vote, 81; and Family Class, 58; and Occupations lists, 62; presentation to Standing Committee on Labour, Employment and Immigration, 147–48; on reduction of refugee claims, 109–10; term as Minister of Employment and Immigration, 64*n*
medical care, 10, 68, 154, 162, 182
money laundering, 177, 179
mortality rate, 31
Mulroney, Brian (Prime Minister), 97, 143
Mulroney government, 7, 14, 78, 83, 100–101, 138
multiculturalism, 5, 155

N

nannies, 154
Nansen Medal awarded to Canada, 92
National Consultation on Family Class Immigration, 165
National Post, 210
National Women's Liberal Commission, 170
Nemetz, Nathan, 207
"never married" children, 57–58, 148
New Faces in the Crowd, 17
Nielsen, Eric, 49
Nielsen Task Force, 49–50, 77–78, 139
Nominated Relatives, 28
North American Free Trade Agreement, 18
Not Just Numbers: A Canadian Framework for Future Immigration, 10, 11, 143, 161–62, 164, 165–68, 170, 171, 172–73, 203, 204

O

obligation of Canada to refugees, 5, 33, 103, 114, 116, 127, 203–4, 205, 207, 208
Occupations lists: Designated, 36, 37, 42; General, 36, 37, 38, 62, 148
O'Donahue, Padraig, 116–17
Old Age Pension, 54
Ottawa Citizen, 9

P

Pearson government, 20
Percentage Comparisons of Earnings, **23**
Personal Information Form, 135, 136
"personal suitability," 155
Plaut, Gunther, 72–73, 74, 75
points system, 28, 35, 42, 154, 170, 173, 196, 197, 205
political betrayal by governments, 6
political expediency, 7–12, 14
political fiascoes, 108
Post Determination Refugee Claimants in Canada (PDRCC), 126–27
Progressive Conservative Party policy convention (1991), 7–8
Protection Act, 164
public misinformed about immigration, 63
public opinion, 1–2, 72, 101, 114, 124, **144,** 144–146, 156, 164

Q

queue jumpers, 2, 145, 151

R

racism, 46–48, 50, 171
Ratushny, Ed, 71–72, 74, 75, 207
RCMP, 4, 191, 192
Rebuilding Trust, 137
"Red Book," 9, 13, 150

Refocusing the Immigrant Investor Program, 185
refugee-assistance programs, 71–72
Refugee Backlog Clearance Program, 61
Refugee Backlog Subdivision (of IRB), 104–6
refugee claims: abandoned, 83, 108, 126–27, 136, 160; acceptance rate, 6, 92–93, 100, 103, 106, 107, 110, 116, 118, 122, **123,** 124, 136, 149–50; appeals, 69, 77, 86; backlog of, 86, 92–93, 99, 100, 140–41; bogus, 1, 3, 12*n,* 43, 61, 69–70, 72, 75, 76, 78–79, 80–81, 82–86, 100, 105, 140, 155, 164, 208; "cooking the books," 113; dismissal of strong cases, 122–24; failed, 162; negative decisions, 116–17; pending, 140; processing time, 132, 140; "psychological damage," 82
refugee determination process: abuse of, 79, 82, 88, 157; assessment of, 72–73; and backlog, 77; Canada's prerogative in, 75–76; changes to, 70–71; close to collapse, 110; cost of, 102, 107, 139, 151; debate, 10; desire to expedite, 145; failure of, 120–21; "flagging badly," 164; generous nature of, 68; government responsibility for, 97–98; humanitarian standards of, 104; integrity of, 100, 161; under IRB, 114–15; judging of, 6–7; as model system, 109; 1978 Act, 69; in trouble, 65. *See also* Expedited Process; refugee redetermination
refugee hearings: adjournments of, 131–32, 133–34, 135 (*See also* case scheduling); figures on, 103; importance of early hearings, 72; initiated, 69; under new IRB, 103; not decided, 111; as principle of justice, 75; "psychological damage" claim, 82; and refugee backlog, 70; as right, 74; and *Singh* decision, 207; single-member panels, 138–39; transcripts of, 69, 111, 132
refugee policies. *See* immigration policies
refugee redetermination, 86, 157
refugees: admission to Canada, 40–41; Australian solution, 198–99; backlog of, 70–71, 73, 77, 78, 79, 80, 81, 87, 88, 89–92, **90, 91,** 102 (*See also* backlog clearance process; Refugee Backlog Clearance Program; Refugee Backlog Subdivision); bogus, 141; Chilean, 159–60, **160;** Chinese, v, 122, 208–9; Convention refugees defined, 38; cost of, 4, 127, 162; definition of, 67–68; desirable changes to refugee class, 206–14; employment of, 71, 77; figures on, 89–92, 111; Honduran, 128, **129,** 164; impact of, 77–78; Iranian, 3; Kosovanian, 101; "landing" of, 86; Portuguese, 79–80,

110, 208; postwar, 5–6; re-settlement of, 101, 151; se-lecting, 155; Somali, 151, 174*n;* source countries of, 89; statistics, 158; Trinidadian, 81, 82, 110, 120–21, 208; Turkish, 80–81; and welfare, 86; welfare costs, 78. *See also* Conven-tion refugees
Refugee Status Advisory Com-mittee Record of Refugee Claims, **84**
Refugee Status Advisory Com-mittee (RSAC), 32, 70, 72, 74, 83, 87, 92, 106, 110, 149–50
Regulatory Impact Analysis Statement, 187
Reimer, John, 80
Removal Orders, 112
Report of the Auditor General: 1982, 43–46, 48, 49, 50, 54, 65; 1985, 52; 1990, 44, 65, 110, 133, 180; 1997, 131, 134, 136
reviews, humanitarian and com-passionate, 111–12
Roberts, John, 71, 72, 73, 207
Robillard, Lucienne: and Advi-sory Group, 179; and Aus-tralian solution, 201; and consultations, 160; and De-ferred Removal Order, 126; and direction of policy, 212; and language ability of im-migrants, 168–69; public consultations of, 11; replaces Marchi, 12*n*

Role of Immigration in Chang-ing Socio-Demographic Structures, 20
Ruddack, Philip, 195

S

Schelew, Michael, 125
selection, 28, 40, 44, 45, 47, 48, 49, 60, 75–76, 98, 153, 155, 167–68, 192, 203
self-sufficiency, 189, 191
"Self-supporting Class," 166–67, 179
Seward, Shirley, 19–20, 32
Shannon, Gerald, 67–68, 101–2, 176*n*
Singh Bal, Inderjit, 125
Singh decision (Supreme Court of Canada), 72–75, 76, 94–95*n,* 101, 128, 163, 164, 207, 209
skills, 37, 44, 157, 204–5, 213
"Skills for Change," 168
smuggling of immigrants, 4, 88, 128, 156, 208, 209
social-security net, 5, 14, 45, 50, 54, 101, 143, 156, 165
solutions to Canadian immigra-tion problems, 203–14
Special Committee on Visible Minorities in Canadian Soci-ety, 46–48
special-interest groups, v
Sponsored Dependents, 28
sponsorship breakdown, cost of, 162, 176*n*
Statistics Canada, 15
Stoffman, Daniel, 93
strip bonds, 185

Success Rate for Refugee Claims, 1983–1992, 122, **123**
Summer of Consultations, 98, 150–55, 157–58, 175*n*

T

Task Force on Immigration Practices and Procedures, 70, 74
Taylor, Chris, 145
The Determination of Refugee Status in Canada: A Review of the Procedure, 132
The Economist, 97
The Refugee Status Determination Process, 70
Tiananmen Square, 122
Tienharra, Nancy, 145, 147
Toronto Star, 93, 152–53
travel documents, counterfeit, 156
Trempe, Robert, 160, 175*n*
Trudeau government, 7, 43, 46, 83

U

United Nations Convention criteria, 149
United Nations Convention on Refugees, 203
United Nations High Commission for Refugees (UNHCR), 67–68, 70, 101, 150, 151
United States Commission on Population and the American Future, 17
universal access, 3, 121

V

Valcourt, Bernard, 36, 37, 148–49, 156, 157
Vancouver Province, 192
Vancouver Sun, 2, 4, 9, 11, 13–14, 59, 109, 116, 155, 173, 174, 191
visa requirements, 72, 159, 160
visa restrictions, 79–81, 86, 110
visible minorities, 47, 48

W

welfare, 10, 46, 54, 68, 71, 77, 78, 86, 156, 165, 176*n*
White Paper, 27, 31, 212–13
work permits, 61